More than Neighbors

More than Neighbors

Catholic Settlements
and Day Nurseries in
Chicago, 1893–1930

Deborah A. Skok

NORTHERN

ILLINOIS

UNIVERSITY

PRESS

DeKalb

Published by the Northern Illinois University Press, DeKalb, Illinois 60115
Manufactured in the United States using acid-free paper

Library of Congress Cataloging-in-Publication Data

Skok, Deborah A.
More than neighbors: Catholic settlements and day nurseries in Chicago, 1893–1930/
Deborah A. Skok.
   p.   cm.
Includes bibliographical references and index.
ISBN 978-0-87580-374-6 (clothbound : alk. paper)
1. Social settlements—Illinois—Chicago—History. 2. Catholic Church—Charities—
Case studies. I. Title.
HV4196.C4S56 2007
362.83'83—dc22
2007004629

This book is dedicated to James Edward Skok and Phyllis St. John Skok. Without their support and encouragement, it would never have been written. Their integrity, decency, brains, and wit inspire me every day. It is also dedicated to Charles and Georgette St. John, who are sorely missed.

Table of Contents

Acknowledgments

So many colleagues, mentors, archivists, and others have provided assistance over the years that I find it difficult to know where to start. Among the mentors who nurtured this project, I cannot forget my dissertation advisors, Catherine Brekus and George Chauncey. My dissertation director in particular, Kathleen Neils Conzen, has continued to encourage and advise me through the arduous process of transforming the dissertation into a book. Her skill and integrity as a scholar and teacher continue to inspire me profoundly in my own career. I am indebted to Robert Johnston for reading the manuscript and providing thoughtful comments, and to Maureen Flanagan for her advice and assistance. I would like to thank Rima Lunin Schultz, who read and commented upon parts of the project, for her invaluable expertise in the history of Chicago settlements, and Hull House in particular. I owe a debt of gratitude to the members of the Newberry Library Settlement House Project for providing inspiration, especially Jen Koslow, Rachel Bohlmann, Robin Muncy, Joe Bigott, and Peg Stroebel.

Through the Cushwa Center for the Study of American Catholicism, Notre Dame University afforded me the opportunity to be a fellow in a project to study Catholicism in twentieth-century America. Thanks go to the director of the Cushwa Center, Scott Appleby, and to the participants of the working group on Catholic women in the twentieth century, including steering committee members Mary J. Oates, CSJ, Suellen Hoy, Jane Hunter, Kathleen Joyce, Sandra Yocum Mize, and Kathryn Kish Sklar and fellows Patricia Byrne, CSJ, Ana Maria Díaz-Stevens, Claire Wolfteich, Amy Koehlinger, Darra Mulderry, Laura Murphy, and Gina Marie Pitti. Further thanks go to Ellen Skerrett, expert on the history of all things Catholic in Chicago, and to Margaret McGuinness, pioneer in the research of Catholic settlement houses.

Every historian knows just how much our profession owes to the invaluable work of archivists and other guardians of primary source material. Special thanks go to Sister Catherine Mary Norris, formerly the executive director of the St. Vincent de Paul Day Care Center, for allowing me access to the center's historical records. Many thanks are also due to Lois Martin of the Daughters of Charity Archives, housed at Mater Dei Provincialate in Evansville,

Indiana. The chapters on St. Vincent's Church and the De Paul Center would not have been possible without the assistance of the late Father Patrick Mullins, CM, of De Paul University, who graciously allowed me to use materials in his possession. Catherine DeGraff and Morgan McIntosh of the De Paul University Archives provided good advice and pleasant conversation. I also wish to thank Father Lou Derbes, CM, archivist of the Priests of the Congregation of the Mission (popularly known as the Vincentians). His knowledge of the order, his sense of humor, and his help many years ago in repairing my car all made my trip to Perryville, Missouri, much easier.

For assistance with the records of Madonna Center, I wish to thank Philip Runkel and the staff of the Department of Special Collections and University Archives of Marquette University. Thanks also to Father George Lane, SJ, of Loyola University Press in Chicago for helping me find Mrs. Agnes Amberg Fiedler. Of course, I also owe a debt of gratitude to Mrs. Fiedler herself, an inspiring person who recently passed away at the age of ninety-eight. She kindly allowed me to interview her about her aunt Mary Amberg and her grandmother Agnes Ward Amberg, and their work.

I would like to thank Archie Motley of the Chicago Historical Society for his advice early in the project, and the rest of the CHS staff for their years of unfailing helpfulness. Julie Satzik of the Joseph Cardinal Bernardin Archives and Records Center of the Archdiocese of Chicago provided invaluable assistance at many stages of the project. Michael Connolly of the Office of Paulist History and Archives in Washington, D.C., helped me with my research into the Paulist Settlement.

Generous financial support for this project was provided by the University of Chicago through the Phoenix Prize Fellowship, as well as by the Mellon Foundation, and Notre Dame University through a fellowship in the Catholicism in Twentieth-Century America Project of the Cushwa Center for the Study of American Catholicism. I am grateful to Hendrix College for several Faculty Project Grants that enabled me to turn my dissertation into a book, and to the Newberry Library for a Great Lakes Fellowship that also furthered this goal. Thanks are due to Evelyn Taylor of the *Journal of Illinois History* for allowing me to reproduce parts of my article "Negotiating Chicago's Public Culture: Guardian Angel Mission and Settlement House, 1898–1920," which appeared in the summer 2004 issue.

I would also like to thank my students at Hendrix College, especially the participants in my Progressive Era seminar, for continually bringing fresh ideas, opinions, and challenges to the historiography of the period. For research assistance, I am grateful to Avi Rubin of the University of Chicago and Peggy Tuck Sinko of the Newberry Library. While inspiration and assistance for this project came from many sources, any mistakes remaining in this work are mine alone.

More than Neighbors

A Hull House and a Church

Interpreting Catholic Settlements

Madonna Center moved into a spacious building in Chicago's West Side Italian district in 1922. A Catholic settlement house founded in 1898, the center was originally located just around the corner from the far better known Hull House. Hull House had spacious and imposing facilities, but Madonna Center began in a succession of storefronts and rented rooms. It moved when a neighborhood priest objected to the center's recreation program for girls and then became furious that laywomen had challenged his authority. Madonna Center's director, Mary Amberg, found a new location to the north and west of the old neighborhood, outside his jurisdiction. In their new neighborhood, the women of Madonna Center found an elegant old house that had fallen into disrepair. As they busied themselves with the move, washing windows, arranging furniture, and dealing with contractors, their new neighbors wondered who they were. Seeing well-dressed ladies working in the large brick building, most of the neighborhood children believed a new school was opening. Yet some knew better. While taking a walk one day, the settlement's director overheard one child inform another: "This ain't no school. This is a Hull House and a Church."[1]

While the story of Hull House has been told many times, the work of Catholic women's settlement houses has until fairly recently been largely invisible. Yet between 1892 and 1930, laywomen in Chicago founded nine settlements and day nurseries and assisted with eleven

other institutions in the city doing this work. How can we understand institutions that functioned as both "Hull Houses" and "churches"? How can
we interpret these institutions when leaders such as Jane Addams, the famous director of Hull House, portrayed settlement houses as inherently secular and Catholics as primarily struggling immigrants, corrupt political
bosses, or quarrelsome priests? Catholic settlements reflected the unique
position of the church and the faithful in America at the turn of the century. Settlements emerged at a crucial moment for the church, when substantial numbers of "new immigrants" from southern and eastern Europe
were pouring into the city, just as many "old immigrant" ethnics from Ireland and Germany were taking their first tentative steps into the middle
and lower-middle classes. Hence, while the leaders of Catholic settlements
tended to be middle-class or even affluent, the settlement volunteers were
often relatively close in class background to the "neighbors" they sought to
help. In fact, Catholic settlements could not have existed without the labor,
both paid and volunteer, of lower-middle-class, working-class, and even
poor women. The settlements enabled Chicago's laywomen to create a significant cross-class effort for the economic improvement of the city's
Catholic community. In the process the struggling, emerging Catholic middle classes benefited as much from their settlement work as did the people
they sought to help. Helping others enabled these women to negotiate
some of the tensions inherent in middle-class formation and changing gender roles, to shape new opportunities for laywomen, and to claim for
Catholics a larger role in the political and cultural leadership of the city.[2]

Settlements and Catholic Literature

The Progressive-Era settlement house movement has often been understood through the writings of its most prominent theorists and activists,
particularly Jane Addams and the Hull House group. Addams posited that
the function of a settlement house was to bring middle-class people into
the slums in order to establish neighborly relations with the slum dwellers.
Yet this model did not entirely fit Catholic settlements, whose volunteers
were often residents already of the parishes in which settlements were established. Because the volunteers and those who used the services of the
Catholic settlements belonged to the same church, they had a common set
of rituals that helped to bind them together in ways that secular settlements could not replicate. Indeed, secular settlements generally wanted
people of various faith traditions to use their services, which would not
have been possible if they had promoted a sectarian agenda. Further,
Catholic settlements relied not just upon middle-class volunteers; instead,
they received crucial assistance from the upper, middle, and working
classes, and even the poor. Addams argued that despite the great social rifts

caused by industrialization, the classes were in fact mutually dependent upon each other. As members of a poor community that was struggling for economic advancement, Catholic settlement leaders understood this instinctively. Despite conflicts over ethnicity and labor issues, the people who ran Catholic settlements and the people who used them needed each other: they were more than neighbors.

Because Catholic settlement workers tended to be more preoccupied with the daily difficulties of their work than with theorizing, these settlements lacked a single spokesperson of the stature of Jane Addams. In addition, when social theorizing was done by Catholics, it was usually the male clergy and hierarchy who dominated such formal discussions: priests had control of the pulpit and formal authority within parishes. It was Pope Leo XIII's important encyclical on social issues, *Rerum Novarum*, that first encouraged laypeople to help the less fortunate. In effect, the encyclical gave Catholic women permission to do charity work outside the home, which they had done very little of before.[3] Yet the voices of laywomen themselves are harder to find. A few elite laywomen wrote about their settlement activities, but none of them claimed to establish a single, overarching theory of Catholic settlement work. They all spoke about serving God, but the focus of their writings was on practical works rather than on theological or social scientific analysis. The voices of less prominent women are even harder to hear.

In spite of these difficulties, some of the ideas behind Catholic settlements can be found in unexpected places. Catholic newspapers, for example, and especially Chicago's archdiocesan newspaper the *New World* can provide some help in understanding these settlements. Traditionally, most Catholic charity work had been performed by religious sisters and laymen. Laywomen gradually became more involved during the 1890s, and soon after, fictional stories about their work began to appear in the *New World*. A popular genre of the era, "rescue" stories showed pious women saving the needy and helping new immigrants, especially Italians, adjust to life in an American city. Often the rescuers were portrayed as Irish, German, or English American women, while the characters being rescued were Italian. The writers of the rescue stories had to contend with a newspaper controlled by male clergy, but the stories, if read carefully, can reveal some of the tensions faced by the laywomen within the Catholic community as they established their settlements: especially ambivalence about class mobility and interethnic relations, class conflict over labor issues, and anxiety over the dramatic changes taking place in the role of women. These stories also suggest a crucial fact of Catholic settlements: they sometimes portray working-class and even poor people as rescuers in their own right.

When rescue stories featured working-class and poor people helping others, they reflected an important reality: the wage labor and even the voluntarism of day nursery mothers were central to the settlements' efforts to bolster the economic standing of Chicago Catholics. Most

Catholic settlements started as day-care centers, and many never grew beyond that stage. While the leadership for the settlements usually came from the upper levels of the city's Catholic community (middle-class professionals and a handful of wealthy women), these leaders depended upon women of all classes to carry out their plans. Mothers who used the nurseries, driven by economic need, were expected to earn enough money to take care of their own families. In addition, these mothers were gathered into charity clubs to help people even less fortunate than themselves. The settlements were meant to provide educational and employment opportunities for laywomen studying social work—thus, poor women were literally giving women above them a boost from below, serving as "clients" so that those better off could enter white-collar careers.

The settlements also relied upon the volunteer labor of young working women, including typists, stenographers, clerks, and (most important) schoolteachers. Many of these young women had both white-collar jobs and blue-collar roots; they were taking their first tentative steps into the lower-middle class. Often, such "working girls" were viewed by Protestant and nonsectarian social work agencies as people in need of charity themselves. In contrast, the Catholic settlements viewed them as indispensable and educated volunteers, essential for teaching catechism, running sewing classes, and staffing other vital programs. "Working girls" made substantial contributions to the well-being of the entire Catholic community. Because these women were moving from their working-class roots to white-collar work, the story of laywomen's settlements will increase our understanding of the role of women in social mobility and middle-class formation, especially in an era during which the boundaries between classes were relatively fluid.[4]

Even though the settlements relied upon the labor of poor women and working girls, their voices are less well preserved in the historical record than those of the more affluent women who ran the institutions. Even the rescue stories usually featured middle-class or even affluent women as heroines. Although these poor women and working girls have a largely silent presence in Catholic settlements, we have a bit more evidence of what they did than of what they thought or said. Their wage labor gave an economic boost to their own families, while their voluntarism gave a boost to the community as a whole, providing religious instruction, recreation, and social services to many people in need. Further, by making the Catholic settlements possible, they enabled more prominent laywomen to have careers in social work and government, which helped to create and shape Chicago's emerging social services bureaucracy. Ultimately, the prominent women also gained positions of authority (albeit subordinate to clergy) within a professionalizing system of Catholic charities.[5]

Settlement work enabled upwardly mobile laywomen to negotiate a new status for themselves as they began to attain a modest level of material comfort. For Catholics, class mobility was a process fraught with ambiguity.

The rescue stories reflect class conflict, including fears that upwardly mobile women might look down on the poor or abandon the cause of organized labor. Rescue stories promoted benevolent work as a model of genteel behavior for an upwardly mobile population. Helping the poor could be a way for these women to embody a new status without losing their ties to the larger working-class Catholic community. Even the handful of wealthy laywomen who ran settlements used their settlement work to negotiate their status. Mary Amberg's family had money, for example, but her father was a self-made man who had made his fortune selling office supplies. Playing the lady of the manor enabled Amberg to create a new class status for herself while also putting her faith into practice. Yet even would-be aristocrats like Amberg realized how much they depended upon Catholics of other classes: she once bragged that "certain politicians with powerful labor connections" attended Madonna Center's fund-raising events.[6] Even though there was certainly class conflict among Catholics at this time, much of the Catholic elite owed its existence to its ability to represent the working class.

The settlements also helped a number of prominent laywomen achieve a new relationship with the state. Their experience running settlement houses made them useful to politicians, especially Democrats, who wished to claim for themselves the mantle of reform. Once laywomen attained positions in city government, they contributed to the remarkable expansion of the state social welfare apparatus that was taking place during the Progressive Era. Like non-Catholic women, a number of women used their experience in Catholic settlements and women's clubs as a springboard to higher positions. These women included several school board members and the first director of Chicago's Department of Public Welfare, Leonora Z. Meder. Appointed by Mayor Carter Harrison IV when the department was first established in 1914, Meder helped develop a new branch of city government. When laywomen entered city government, they brought with them the labor orientation of the larger Catholic community. Ironically, these women tended to promote labor causes through their club work and government service, rather than using their settlements for organizing as non-Catholic women did. And while they may have used "maternalist" rhetoric about the need to mother Italian children in their settlements, like many labor priests and male union leaders they tended to favor "paternalist" government social insurance programs that would deliver benefits through male breadwinners. The settlement women included not just public officeholders but also union leaders and numerous wives and family members of important male politicians. These women lobbied to promote favored legislation, and several of them ran for political office. Even though our models of women's political activism during the Progressive Era have centered largely on Protestants, Catholic women also transformed "benevolence into reform and reform into political activism."[7]

The relationship between Catholic settlement leaders and non-Catholic reformers was complex. Sometimes they cooperated to achieve common goals. Mary Amberg of Madonna Center said that Jane Addams's example inspired her, yet Madonna Center was created to compete directly with Hull House for leadership over the West Side Italians. Madonna Center also competed with Protestant missionaries and ethnic Italian leaders to win influence over these new immigrants, who were filling the slums that the Irish and Germans had begun to vacate. Settlement leaders hoped to instruct the Italians in their faith and incorporate them into Chicago's existing Catholic community. Gaining influence over the Italians could also give laywomen access to positions in Chicago's emerging social welfare bureaucracy. For example, in the newly established Juvenile Court, the settlements would play a mediating role between their neighbors and the state—sometimes using the coercive power of the state to control their neighbors' behavior and sometimes intervening to protect their neighbors from the harsher aspects of the legal system.[8]

Settlements also enabled laywomen to challenge gender conventions, grapple with changing ideas of leisure, and perhaps even explore their own sexuality. Settlements introduced new forms of recreation for women and girls into conservative communities that normally frowned on female amusements outside the home. Hence by the 1910s, Catholic settlement women helped usher in an emerging heterosocial culture of leisure by providing facilities, resources, and chaperones. Settlement work also gave positions of respect to unmarried women, who would otherwise have been looked down upon because of their single status. Settlement housing arrangements provided some laywomen with opportunities to form same-sex partnerships, or "Boston marriages." While the nature of these relationships was ambiguous, living in a settlement could provide these women with freedom from family scrutiny and perhaps the opportunity to explore their sexuality.[9]

Even as these tremendous changes in gender roles, class status, and ethnic makeup were taking place within the community, rescue stories could reassure readers about the nature of Catholic settlement work—perhaps, most important among those readers, the many priests who exhorted Catholic women not to abandon domesticity as they took up new roles outside the home. Because the fictional rescuers were portrayed as pious, domestic, and nonthreatening, rescue stories helped reassure such conservative Catholics about laywomen's settlement work and provide women with the justification needed to build a network of social service organizations that vastly expanded their options in the public sphere. Even though the stories portrayed the rescuers as pious and obedient, and even though priests needed these laywomen to help minister to a growing population of newcomers, settlements still posed a threat, albeit limited, to the authority of the clergy. As long as they were relatively autonomous institutions run by laywomen, settlements could draw promising youth away from other parish activities and even teach them things unauthorized by the pastors. Priests and members of the hierarchy recognized the need for settlements to serve the vast social and recreational needs of Chicago's faithful, and they also promoted charity work among women of all classes, hoping to keep them away from socialism and feminism. In order to minimize the challenge that laywomen could pose to their authority, however, they found ways to bring settlement work under close supervision by male church leaders.[10]

The phrase *a boost from below* was inspired in part by the experiences of African American club women and their motto *Lifting as We Climb*. The phrase suggests an image of black club women, while struggling to attain middle-class status themselves, reaching back to provide economic assistance, education, and moral uplift to those lower down on the ladder. While white Catholic women never faced the extreme racial discrimination and violence experienced by black women, both black and Catholic women struggled to define themselves as they rose in class status and labored to help less fortunate community members. Both groups of women also became politicized, although Catholic women gained opportunities because of their men's political influence whereas black women protested their men's disfranchisement. Like black women, upwardly mobile Catholic women helped those below, but the phrase *a boost from below* reminds us that their efforts could not have succeeded without the labor—both volunteer and paid—of poor, working-class, and lower-middle-class members of the Catholic community.[11]

Catholic settlements and day nurseries helped many people during the Progressive Era; several of these institutions survive today and continue to provide services for their neighbors. They delivered child care, recreation and social services, and religious education to people in need. They also enabled settlement leaders to achieve positions of authority within the Catholic community and in government, helping forge new options for laywomen. Yet without the labor of poor women and "working girls," mostly anonymous, the settlements never could have accomplished what they set out to do. Volunteers taught catechism, led play groups, put on plays, taught sewing classes, and showed wholesome films to their neighbors. Day nursery mothers earned money to sustain their families and even found the time to help others needier than themselves. Although laywomen in the middle and upper classes benefited from the volunteer work and labor of women with humbler economic status than themselves, the phrase *a boost from below* is not meant to suggest exploitation. Rather, it posits that all groups enjoyed benefits from settlement work, albeit in the context of an unequal distribution of power. Day nursery mothers exerted no influence on the policy decisions of settlement leaders, and white-collar volunteers exerted very little influence, at least until they started to acquire training in social work. In any case, we must recognize the contributions of working girls and day nursery mothers to the successes achieved by more affluent laywomen in attaining positions of authority in church and state.

Varieties of Catholic Settlement House

Catholic settlements have been underrepresented in the settlement and reform literature in part because they do not always fit the classic settlement pattern. They were generally smaller, had fewer residents, and were less well-known than institutions like Hull House or Chicago Commons, primarily because they had far less money. Catholics built a number of day nurseries that were supposed to grow into full-fledged settlements with substantial numbers of residents and varied programming, but many of them lacked the resources to do so. In starting with day care, Catholic settlements actually were following a pattern similar to Protestant and nonsectarian institutions: settlements like Hull House found themselves offering day care and kindergartens almost as soon as they opened because the need for child care was so urgent. Catholics merely lacked the funds to expand. To focus on institutions that fit the classic settlement pattern in fact privileges Protestants, who formed the majority of residents in nonsectarian settlements. Including institutions that aspired to be settlements gives a far more accurate picture of the scope of interest in settlement work during the Progressive Era.[12]

Instead of following one pattern, Catholic settlements were built according to three different types, or models, termed here the club model, the proprietary model, and the parish model. Club-model settlements were built by Catholic women's clubs, which emerged just as other women's clubs were also becoming popular in the late nineteenth century; proprietary settlements were funded and run by wealthy families; parish-model settlements were founded within parishes. Club and proprietary settlements enjoyed the most independence from oversight by male clergy; they afforded a degree of autonomy for laywomen and occasionally even presented a challenge to the authority of the clergy. Parish-model settlements often came under more direct supervision by parish priests, yet even they provided opportunities for laywomen to enlarge their role outside the home. Over time, club and proprietary settlements diminished in number as more settlement work was done in parishes and as the church built a more centralized charities infrastructure in Chicago and the nation at large. Settlements would provide laywomen with access to a place within that infrastructure, a professional role within the church that they had never had before.

If we look beyond the classic settlement pattern, we find that between 1892 and 1930 twenty-one Catholic institutions in the city of Chicago were engaged in settlement and day nursery work. Of these twenty-one institutions, at least twelve were founded by Irish and German Americans. The majority of these twelve were run by laywomen, and most of them fit either the club or the proprietary model. Five institutions (All Saints/St. Mary's, St. Anne's, St. Elizabeth's, St. Juliana, and the West End Catholic Woman's Club Settlement) were founded by women's clubs. Two (St. Mary and St. Agnes, Casa Maria) were founded by private individuals. One (Guardian Angel/Madonna Center) was founded by a club but then became proprietary when a single family took it over. Note that the models themselves are not strict or mutually exclusive but are intended merely to provide a rough idea of the different forms possible for Catholic settlement work. Often laywomen founded institutions within parishes that technically came under the jurisdiction of parish priests (St. Peter's is an example). Only three were actually established by clergy or religious. One (Paulist Settlement) was founded ostensibly by priests, who consolidated the lay charities in their parish into one institution. One (De Paul Settlement and Day Nursery) was founded by a priest and run by nuns, with the assistance of laywomen. Finally, one (Catholic Social Center) was both established and run by nuns.

Catholic settlements have largely been considered a laywomen's enterprise, yet the relationship between settlements and religious sisterhoods was complex. Nuns founded some settlements; in other cases, laywomen raised the money while sisters ran the institutions, resided in them, and performed much of the work. Settlements housing nuns took on some of the features of convents, including chapels and dormitory space. Yet this is perhaps not surprising; even the residents of Hull House referred to each other as "Sister Lathrop" or "Sister Kelley." Settlement work itself strongly resembles parish ministry, which is one reason why priests may have felt threatened by nonsectarian settlements.[13]

The settlement women were largely of Irish and German extraction, groups that first came to Chicago in the 1840s. The Irish came mostly to perform manual labor, and the more prosperous Germans opened stores and other businesses. By 1860 the city had 22,230 inhabitants who had been born in Germany, and 19,889 from Ireland. Between 1870 and 1900 members of these old immigrant groups continued to enter the city, but they were joined by large numbers of new immigrants. In 1900 the city had 170,238 Germans, 73,912 Irish, and 16,008 Italians, out of a total population of 1,698,574. By 1910 first- and second-generation immigrants made up a total of 77 percent of the city's population; 33 percent of these were foreign-born.[14]

Laywomen's settlements emerged at a time when lay Catholics began to demonstrate a heightened awareness of social issues, and the church started to allow greater lay participation in some church matters. The papal encyclical on social questions, *Rerum Novarum,* was issued by Leo XIII in 1892, and a flurry of lay activity ensued. Lay congresses, although they were a short-lived phenomenon, helped spur interest in benevolent work at a time when national and international networks of Catholic benevolent and reform organizations were serving millions of poor Catholics and influencing the formation of the American welfare state. Held in 1893 in conjunction with the Chicago World's Fair, the Columbian Catholic Congress provides an example of lay activism: a number of the same people who were active in the congress helped establish the settlements. They included several members of the Catholic Woman's League, which ran four settlements in Chicago.[15]

For a number of reasons, Chicago provides a useful location to study Catholic settlements. First, the city was prominent at the center of the larger settlement movement. Second, settlement women in Chicago took advantage of their location at the center of liberal Midwestern Catholicism. In contrast, Boston's archbishop was successful in creating a more isolated community, in part because of the city's long history of animosity between Catholics and Protestants. Third, Chicago had a number of prominent labor priests and bishops who supported Catholic settlements. Fourth, consolidating the power of the hierarchy took longer in Chicago than in Boston. Chicago's strongest centralizing archbishop, George Mundelein, was not appointed until 1916.[16] Although Catholic settlements existed in other cities, nationwide these institutions do not appear to have coordinated their efforts to any significant degree.[17]

While the heroines in the rescue stories were primarily Irish or German, a significant amount of benevolent work was also done by new immigrants themselves, especially some Italian religious orders and Polish Catholics. The Poles resented the Irish domination of Chicago's hierarchy and preferred to build their own institutions that would nurture their sense of Polish identity. The Italian religious orders tended to regard the United States as an uncivilized mission field and viewed their work as caring for Italian immigrants who had been maltreated or neglected by American Catholics. These institutions were substantial enough to command a history of their own, but that task is beyond the scope of this work, which concentrates instead on institutions established by Irish Americans and some German Americans. To further focus my research, I do not deal with Catholic Worker Houses of Hospitality; these resembled settlement houses but were not created until the 1930s, a later time period than the one investigated here.[18]

Our story begins with a focus on the Catholic Woman's League (CWL), a women's club that ran a number of settlements and day nurseries in various locations across the city. An analysis of the *New World* rescue stories and of the cultural and social activities of the league reveals some of the major concerns of laywomen and some of the tensions within the Catholic community during the late nineteenth and early twentieth centuries. The league's members were diverse, including wealthy and prominent women as well as schoolteachers and clerks who were rising from their blue-collar roots into white-collar jobs. The rescue stories admonished upwardly mobile Catholics not to forget their working-class origins and even suggested that poor women could be "rescuers" of the rich. The stories thus contained a grain of truth: when the league opened its settlements, it came to rely upon the paid and volunteer labor of poor women and white-collar "working girls" to run them. The labor of these women was to form the basis for a comprehensive effort toward the economic uplift of Chicago's Catholic community. Settlement leaders gained a reputation as reformers from their settlement work, and they used this reputation to obtain important positions in city government, especially in the expanding welfare state. Once in government, the CWL women would use their positions to advocate the church's teachings about organized labor and the rights of the poor.

Guardian Angel Mission, which later became Madonna Center, provides an example of the proprietary model of settlements. At first glance, the leaders of the proprietary settlements resemble some of the idealized woman rescuers: pious, domestic, well-to-do women spending their time, energy, and money laboring on behalf of the poor and the immigrants. Yet Guardian Angel also served the essentially political purpose of enabling Catholics to compete with Protestant and ethnic leaders for the allegiance of neighborhood Italians. Winning influence over them could prevent Italians from leaving the church and could give settlement leaders greater legitimacy in mediating between their neighbors and the expanding welfare state. Further, proprietary settlements gave laywomen authority over their neighbors and greater autonomy in their own lives. After Guardian Angel became Madonna Center, its leaders formed unconventional relationships with each other, ushered in a new and controversial heterosocial leisure culture in the neighborhood, and challenged the authority of neighborhood clergy.

In response to the autonomy gained by laywomen in proprietary settlements, parish-model settlements sought to reassert the control of the clergy. At the De Paul Center in St. Vincent's Parish, the pastor would attempt to use settlement work to steer his female parishioners away from politics. However, the parish women continued their political interest even as they enthusiastically joined the settlement club. They also used settlement work to redefine themselves as modern and up-to-date, without rejecting domesticity. The "unexpected rescuers"—mothers who used the day nursery and nuns—also asserted themselves through the settlement. While the pastor of St. Vincent's sought to control their behavior by trying to professionalize the parish's social work, nuns and day nursery mothers quietly maintained their own priorities. The mothers resisted the pastor's attempts to manage their actions, and the nuns, Daughters of Charity of St. Vincent de Paul, maintained a different ideal of professionalization than the one he had in mind.

The Paulist Settlement, located in Old St. Mary's parish, provides a case study in how professionalization involved the clergy's creation of structures to coordinate and oversee existing lay charities. In the city as a whole, autonomous laywomen's institutions were brought under the umbrella of the Associated Catholic Charities of Chicago, while other settlement work was absorbed into parish structures. Nevertheless, settlements continued to provide laywomen with meaningful volunteer opportunities outside their homes, as well as with professional careers in social work. The process followed at Old St. Mary's replicated processes going on in Catholic charities in Chicago and nationwide.

While they helped shape Chicago's welfare state, Catholic women never achieved a "dominion" in city government, an agency in which they could claim a certain amount of autonomy, separate from male politicians even if subordinate to them. They were brought in when Catholic male politicians, especially Democrats, wished to claim for themselves the mantle of reform, and they were marginalized when they were no longer needed. Similarly, the church allowed laywomen a certain amount of autonomy as long as it faced massive immigration and did not yet have enough structures to care for the newcomers without laywomen's help. Over time, however, the church hierarchy worked to bring laywomen's organizations under the control of a centralized Catholic charities apparatus run by laymen and priests. Lacking in power relative to the male politicians and clergy, the laywomen moved back and forth between worlds—sometimes cooperating with the city's non-Catholic women reformers, sometimes competing with non-Catholics and others to win the allegiance of immigrants for the church. They mediated between their neighbors and an increasingly sexualized leisure culture. They even moved back and forth between their own competing impulses, caught between their allegiance to domesticity and their desire for a more active role in the world, their aspirations for gentility and their loyalty to the primarily working-class Catholic community. Yet because they were needed, laywomen were able to establish a foothold for professional careers in church and state.[19]

CHAPTER ONE

Laywomen to the Rescue

Literature, Charity, and the
Catholic Woman's League

In March 1893, Chicago was engaged in hosting a spectacular World's Fair on its South Side. Hoping to contribute to the fair before the whole event was over, Catholic artist Harriet Hosmer was hurriedly trying to finish a large bronze statue of Queen Isabella. The official newspaper of the Archdiocese of Chicago, the *New World,* explained that Hosmer's statue of Columbus's patron was meant to highlight the role of Catholic womanhood in the discovery of America. Even though the fair's Board of Lady Managers enthusiastically showcased queens as images of women in powerful public roles, they rejected the Isabella project, largely because of anti-Catholic prejudice. Mary Newbury Adams, official historian of the Board of Lady Managers, wrote that it was necessary to "foil the Isabellas" in order "to prevent a rally under a Spanish Catholic Queen." It is also telling that the conference organizers placed the Irish and German attractions near exhibits from places considered exotic and racially inferior, rather than locating them in the more "respectable" part of the fair, the "White City," where Hosmer sought to place her statue of Isabella. As a result of prejudice, the statue was never displayed in Chicago. Catholic women also failed to rally around Isabella, perhaps because the Catholic community already had a reigning queen: Mary, the Queen of Heaven. Yet where Hosmer failed to establish a public presence for laywomen in the city, others would succeed.[1]

Catholic women's participation in the fair was inspired in part by the papal encyclical *Rerum Novarum,* which encouraged greater lay involvement in charities and in spreading the faith. A number of the same women who participated in the fair were also founding members of Chicago's Catholic Woman's League (CWL).[2] Like other women's clubs of the era, the CWL sponsored adult education, social events, and benevolent work. It constructed a network of settlement houses and day nurseries in various locations across the city, which harnessed the labor of poor, working-class, and middle-class women to enhance the economic status of the city's Catholic community. How can the league's activities be interpreted? Fictional stories about Catholic women's benevolent work began to appear in the archdiocesan newspaper the *New World,* at about the same time that the league and its settlements were established. Rather than exactly mirroring the actual work of the league settlements (see Chapter Two), these "rescue stories" reveal the tensions over class, ethnicity, and gender existing within the Catholic community, which had to be negotiated in the establishment of settlements. The stories tended to reassure readers that these tensions could be overcome, but some of the league's social and educational activities actually produced more tension among Catholics, as the CWL sponsored controversial activities that gave members a boost by preparing them to assume positions of leadership in the city.

The Women of the League

Examining the membership of the Catholic Woman's League will give us a glimpse of Chicago's lay leadership, during the late nineteenth and early twentieth centuries, and enable us to analyze some areas of tension. The league stood out from other lay organizations because it had a relatively high percentage of prosperous, socially connected (or at least socially pretentious) members. Yet the majority of members could be classified as middle- or lower-middle-class. Some members with modest white-collar jobs even had blue-collar family members. Conflict existed among members of different classes and different views, especially on labor questions. However, CWL members of all classes also needed each other to acquire and maintain their status and to achieve their goals. Union leaders mingled with government officials and politicians' wives, each group dependent for their leadership upon the good graces of constituents, many of whom were also CWL members. Schoolteachers socialized with a handful of wealthy women who needed educated volunteers to staff the settlement houses. The humbler members in turn received opportunities for education and voluntarism. It seemed sometimes as if differences among members might tear the CWL apart, but differences could also strengthen the organization, as each group provided something the others needed.

The Irish were politically powerful in the city, and many CWL women became influential in politics, government, and the professions. Appointed by Democratic mayor Carter Harrison IV, Leonora Z. Meder served as the first director of Chicago's newly created Department of Public Welfare, and she later ran for judge. Four CWL members (Isabella O'Keefe, Tena MacMahon, Helen Gallagher, and Florence Vosbrink) served on the Chicago school board. The league had two members (Catherine Goggin and Margaret Haley) who were leaders in the Chicago Teachers' Federation (CTF), and a substantial block of CWL members were schoolteachers. The unionization of teachers would become one of the most controversial issues faced by CWL members, revealing class tensions within the league. Other members were involved in lobbying on behalf of parks and education projects. Although the CWL often emphasized domesticity in its publications, a few members had prominent professional careers. Two league members were lawyers, another was a physician, and two members were in the literary field—one worked as an editor and the other, Margaret Sullivan, was a prominent editorial writer for the *Chicago Tribune* and other newspapers.[3]

League members had connections to three Democratic mayors of the city. Edith Ogden Harrison was the wife of Carter Harrison IV. Julia and Kate Hopkins were sisters of Mayor John P. Hopkins. The league's annual charity ball was often graced by the presence of Edmund F. Dunne, one-term mayor of the city and later governor of Illinois. Anna Fitzpatrick was the wife of John Fitzpatrick, a leader in the Chicago Federation of Labor who also ran for mayor in 1919 as the Chicago Farmer Labor Party candidate.[4] Although Catholics were more prominent among the city's Democrats, a few CWL members were also married to Republican politicians such as Patrick T. Barry (a member of the Illinois state legislature), Ninth Ward Republican alderman Joseph E. Bidwill, and county commissioner John M. Carroll.

Despite the political success of some CWL members, even the most prominent among them often had immigrant and working-class origins. Kate and Julia Hopkins, as noted above, were the sisters of Democratic mayor John P. Hopkins, whom journalist William Stead hailed as a reformer when he was elected in 1893. Yet Kate, Julia, and John grew up poor in Buffalo, New York, in a family of twelve children. The two young women took up dressmaking to support the family. Hopkins later repaid his sisters for their hard work by supporting them in comfort for the rest of their days. It is possible that he had their financial comfort in mind when he later became embroiled in a controversy that evolved into the Ogden Gas franchise scandal.[5]

Understanding the ethnic makeup of the CWL is crucial to understanding the stigmas laywomen were trying to overcome as they entered the middle and lower-middle classes. League members were largely Irish and German Americans, and even though many of them were several generations removed from the migration experience, they still faced anti-Catholic and especially anti-Irish prejudice, although this was not as severe as the prejudice faced in older East Coast cities. During the nineteenth century, few of Chicago's Irish lived in ghettos. Rather, they tended to live in neighborhoods alongside other ethnic groups, particularly Germans. By the late 1870s, an Irish middle class had emerged consisting of people involved in politics and government, education, brewing and distilling, meatpacking, undertaking, theater, and sports. By the 1880s the upwardly mobile Irish had started moving away from their old neighborhoods in search of better housing. They would sometimes return to build settlement houses for new immigrants in the neighborhoods they had left behind.[6]

The 1900 manuscript census reveals the immigrant background of some of the CWL officeholders. Of the fourteen officeholders who can be traced, eleven had at least one parent born overseas: nine had parents from Ireland, one from Germany, and one from Scotland. The census also reveals that eight of the fourteen CWL leaders had a servant or two living in their households with them, which would seem to indicate a securely middle-class status. The heads of these households had diverse jobs including salesman, grocer, manager of a brewery, contractor, lawyer, and even fire-alarm operator. Yet because of collective wage-earning strategies, even members with relatively modest employment could sometimes afford to hire a servant. Two such CWL members (Alice and May Keary) were schoolteachers who lived at home with another sister and four brothers. Their sister was also a schoolteacher, and three of the brothers were sign painters. Together, the siblings supported their widowed mother and were able to employ a domestic, Hannah Murphy, a twenty-five-year-old woman from Ireland. The Irish middle classes tended to hire their own for domestic work; seven of the servants who worked for the CWL officers were born in Ireland.[7]

Although conflict could have arisen between the Irish and the Germans in the CWL, the league helped prevent rivalries by fostering a primarily Catholic identity rather than promoting ethnicity. Even though Germans in Chicago outnumbered the Irish, over the course of the nineteenth century the Irish came to dominate the Central Committee of the Democratic Party, the hierarchy of the church, and the leadership of the CWL. Despite the resurgence in Nativist hostility toward Catholics and immigrants during the 1890s, there were signs that the Irish in particular were making a play for greater visibility in the city. By the end of the nineteenth century, the Catholic Church had become the city's largest single denomination, and Irish Americans were competing to build churches of greater size and beauty than the Protestants.[8]

Certain prominent CWL members, especially several converts to Catholicism, had close ties to Chicago's other civic leaders. Such ties would prove useful as the CWL women sought positions of greater leadership in the city by cooperating with other women's organizations on civic projects. One example of a prominent CWL convert to Catholicism is Eliza Allen Starr, the aunt of Hull House cofounder Ellen Gates Starr. Eliza Allen Starr was a key factor in her niece's late-life conversion to Catholicism. A charter member and honorary president of the CWL, an art educator and an author, she was also the president of the Queen Isabella Association, which commissioned Harriet Hosmer's statue for the Columbian Exposition.[9] Other converts included Dr. Sarah Hackett Stevenson, an ardent advocate of women's suffrage who had served several terms as president of the nondenominational Chicago Woman's Club. League member Edith Harrison was not a convert, but she was married to a Protestant, five-term Chicago mayor Carter Harrison IV. She hobnobbed with Chicago's most important families, including the Palmers, the Pullmans, and the McCormicks, thus enhancing her husband's appeal among elite voters as well as Catholic ones.[10]

A significant number of members had social pretensions and may have been using their CWL membership to acquire more elite status. In 1903, 30 percent of league members belonged to families listed in the *Chicago Blue Book*. Participation was voluntary; the individuals chosen had to supply the information listed in the book. Hence a listing provides a measure of how many families wished to be seen by others as fashionable. Having your name in the *Blue Book* also provided certain social advantages, such as being invited to participate in a large, non-Catholic charity ball every year.[11]

Many league members belonged to families headed by successful businesspeople and professionals. A handful of league families owned or held important positions in large profitable companies, while many owned small businesses. Out of a total sample of 346 CWL members, 223 families had household heads whose occupations could be traced in the 1903 city directory; 27 percent of league household heads either owned their own businesses or held high positions in other people's companies. Important business owners included biscuit manufacturer D. F. Bremner, whose National Biscuit Company later became known as Nabisco. The heads of CWL families also owned small businesses such as retail grocery stores, construction businesses, and saloons, and 16 percent of league members came from families whose household head was a professional, a category that included doctors, lawyers, journalists, and political officeholders.[12]

While some of the heads of the CWL members' families were fairly high on the occupational ladder, a majority of the membership was probably middle- or lower-middle-class. Their household heads had modest managerial-level positions, or relatively humble white-collar work. Even many of the business owners probably owned fairly modest businesses. Managers headed 23 percent of league families, and relatively low-status white-collar workers headed 27 percent. "Managers" is a broad category, including salespeople, insurance agents, real estate agents, engineers, and even school administrators. This category also contains a few people with higher-level government jobs such as collectors for the Internal Revenue Service. White-collar workers included teachers, clerks, and bookkeepers.

The smallest category of league members was "Blue Collar Workers"; 7 percent of CWL families had blue-collar household heads. These household heads were among the upper levels of blue-collar workers: none was listed as a common laborer. One, a waiter, was listed in the 1903 *Blue Book*. Several others were skilled workers, including an electrician and two dressmakers. A few may have owned their own businesses or been well paid, including a butcher and a bartender. Others held government positions such as those of policemen, firemen, and letter carriers. The blue-collar household heads included several building superintendents and one teamster.

The majority of CWL members who were themselves employed worked at low-paid white-collar occupations. As a rule these members were single and much less affluent than married members. A number of them had family members with blue-collar jobs. Forming a substantial block of thirty-seven members, the league's schoolteachers provide the most important example. Because they had education and white-collar occupations, teachers can be considered among the upwardly mobile CWL members, yet they also had important ties to organized labor. Margaret Haley and Catherine Goggin, two prominent leaders of the Chicago Teachers' Federation (CTF), were both CWL members. They were considered two of the most militant unionists in the city, and they fought for the CTF to join the city's AFL-affiliated Chicago Federation of Labor. At least some of the other schoolteachers in the league were involved in the CTF—hence they would have been supporting unionization even while joining the white-collar world and participating in the league. Many of these women received their training from nuns in Catholic schools and then went on to teach in the public school system; by 1920, Cardinal Mundelein estimated that the percentage of Catholic schoolteachers in the public schools stood at 70 percent.[13]

Clashes occurred within the league, especially over the issue of unionization for teachers, and class differences among CWL members probably exacerbated the tensions. However, other factors encouraged league women to overcome their differences. Among the issues dividing members was the fact that some elite laywomen may have considered teachers to be too close to the working class to be appropriate company.[14] Yet, CTF leaders Margaret Haley and Catherine Goggin were themselves prominent members of the CWL, and many other league women supported the union. The politicians' wives in the CWL, especially those married to Democrats, could ill afford to offend a group that was so important to city politics. Even the wealthy women who ran many of the settlement houses depended upon schoolteachers and other white-collar working women as a source of reliable and skilled volunteers.

From labor leaders to wealthy women, schoolteachers to politicians' wives, the Catholic Woman's League constituted both a cross-class organization and one that grouped together women with varying levels of career ambition and domesticity. The fictional rescue stories in the *New World* reveal some of the tensions inherent in an institution with such disparate members. They also offer ways to soothe such differences—celebrating domesticity while providing opportunities for both careers and volunteer work outside the home. The settlement houses provided material support that enabled more members of the Catholic community to become self-sufficient, while the league itself provided cultural uplift to its members. The CWL sponsored activities appropriate to both the highest- and the lowest-income levels of its members. It could fit the wealthiest for elite Protestant social circles and prepare the more modest to defend the faith while traveling among the Protestant middle class. Promoting a certain level of conspicuous consumption enabled CWL members to embody a new class status. The rescue stories helped laywomen to grapple with the ambiguities of upward mobility, the problem of integrating "new" immigrants into the community, and the general ambivalence about the expanding roles of women.

Catholic Literature

Rescue Stories and Catholic Womanhood

Between 1892 and the early 1920s the *New World* published a number of fictional stories that featured laywomen rescuing the poor. These fictional rescuers sewed for needy children, nursed the sick, and volunteered in Catholic settlement houses. The stories appeared at the same time that real laywomen began performing social work through organizations such as the CWL, a task heretofore undertaken primarily by nuns and laymen. The fictional rescuers were usually represented as middle-class and genteel. Poor women appeared as rescuers in a few stories, however, which hinted at the reality behind the settlements: that they harnessed the labor of poor and working-class women in order to provide for the financial and spiritual uplift of the whole community. The stories encouraged readers to sympathize with organized labor, and a few even provided a voice for the city's Italians. The rescue stories helped knit together, at least in the minds of readers, the various parts of a community divided by class and ethnicity. They touted the spiritual benefits gained by performing benevolent work, and they showcased charity as a genteel pastime that would enable upwardly mobile women to remain loyal to the Catholic community even as they rose in class status. What the stories did not highlight was the degree to which settlement work would boost laywomen into positions of authority in Chicago social circles, and even city government; instead, they used domestic and religious imagery that could reassure any readers who were anxious about women's new roles outside the home.

I define rescue stories as stories whose plots involve the rescue of needy Catholics by better-off Catholics, stories that focus on settlement work or other forms of charity, or stories that focus on Italians (usually being rescued by Americans). Some of the *New World* rescue stories are un-attributed and a few were written by men, but the majority of them were written by women. Notable writers included Mary F. Nixon-Roulet, a resident of Chicago and a writer of national reputation. She authored several popular romances, travel stories, and a work on Christian art. Another of the writers, Mrs. S. M. O'Malley, was originally from the South but was resident in Chicago by the time she wrote stories for the newspaper. She was the author of three novels, a number of short stories, and a considerable amount of poetry for young people; she had published in a number of other Catholic periodicals. Mary J. Lupton was editor of a regular *New World* column, the "Woman's Quiet Hour," as well as writing for the *New World* and other periodicals. Maria Da Venezia was an Italian woman who wrote a number of stories for the *New World* about life in Chicago's Little Italy.[15]

It is not clear that any of these rescue story writers actually belonged to the CWL, but it is possible. The only extant league membership list is from 1903. It is highly probable that league members were aware of the rescue stories: as practicing, committed Catholics, these women were among the *New World*'s target audience. Indeed, the settlement leader Mary Amberg herself wrote a rescue story, which can be found among her papers, demonstrating that the settlement women were aware of the genre. Her mother was a CWL member, and Mary may well have belonged to the league herself at some point. Further, Catholic novelists living outside Chicago penned rescue tales, suggesting a more general awareness of such issues among laywomen. The *New World* also encouraged readers to read books by Catholic authors, and the CWL women may have supported this effort. The league sponsored a traveling library to bring books to those who did not otherwise have access to them; it is likely that at least some of these library books were written by Catholic writers.[16]

Although women wrote most of the rescue stories, the relative conservatism of the stories—including their heavy use of domestic and religious imagery—was undoubtedly influenced by the fact that the newspaper that printed them was edited by male clergy. Yet laywomen could also use the stories for their own ends, to negotiate class mobility, for example, and to win greater acceptance for their political and reform work by portraying Catholic settlements and female benevolent activities in nonthreatening ways. The stories feature a respect for the realities of women's lives and labor, as in "The Boy Who Went to Sewing School," where a boy named John learns that sewing is "much harder work than he had supposed." In fact, two of the stories whose authors cannot be identified by gender involve some specific knowledge of sewing, suggesting that the authors may have been women.[17]

Laywomen often claimed to support the church's conservative gender ideology, but they also found ways to create new roles for themselves in spite of the church's encouragement of domesticity. The rescue stories provide one example, and scholars have identified others. Many scholars have emphasized the ideal of the pious and domestic "True Woman" as the dominant model of Catholic womanhood during the nineteenth and early twentieth centuries. Colleen McDannell argues that the church promoted domesticity for laywomen during the late nineteenth century because of inherent conservatism with regard to gender issues, and also as a marker of middle-class status for those who had succeeded economically. Yet Penny Edgell Becker says that unintentional variations, even in writings that promoted the True Woman, opened up "cultural spaces" for critiques of the True Woman model. In a similar way, Kathleen Sprows Cummings adds that laywomen often insisted they were not "New Women," yet they went on to create new roles for themselves outside the home that greatly resembled the "New Woman" ideal. Further, because of financial necessity, single Catholic women had a long history of working outside the home.[18]

When the rescue stories began to appear in the *New World* in the late 1890s, a literary tradition of writing about benevolent women and women's cross-class interaction already existed. Prominent female novelists from Harriet Beecher Stowe to Edith Wharton and male authors such as Theodore Dreiser and O. Henry all included women characters in rescuer-type roles. Just as the *New World* was beginning to print rescue stories, several prominent non-Catholic women, including journalists and settlement house workers, went undercover to investigate the conditions of working women and then wrote about their experiences. Other authors wrote novels of working-class life, often including benevolent middle-class characters. Women writers tended to be somewhat sympathetic to such characters, whereas male novelists tended to condemn women reformers generally as ineffectual meddlers. Some reform organizations also used purportedly true stories to publicize their work and to present their views of the causes of poverty.[19]

The *New World* rescue stories had certain themes in common with the works of these non-Catholic writers, especially the theme of better-off women rescuing those in need. However, works by Catholic writers also had significant differences. Non-Catholic novelists tended to create benevolent female characters who descended into worlds to which they (and their readers) did not belong, whereas Catholic writers sketched the rescuer as interacting freely with the people she helped, portraying her as a member of a community that was still largely working-class. She supposedly met needy people in her daily life, without having to descend into a strange milieu. While non-Catholic women like Jane Addams hoped to become neighbors to the people who used Hull House, the Catholic rescue stories featured women who seemed like neighbors already.

The rescue stories used religious symbolism to create a sense of shared community and religious identity among the poor and their helpers. In one of the earliest stories, "A Client of 'Good St. Anne,'" a needy young boy sees a pious lady and her beautiful twelve-year-old daughter praying at an altar to the aforementioned saint. Because mother and daughter resemble the image of St. Anne and her child, the Virgin Mary, the boy mistakes the two females for the holy pair. With complete faith that "Saint Anne" will help his family, the boy takes the woman by the hand and brings her home to meet his mother. The benevolent woman is too modest not to reveal her own mortal status, but of course she rescues the desperate family exactly as if she really were St. Anne. In real life, of course, benevolence was undoubtedly more complicated than this. In some parishes, a middle-class woman might well have met a needy person in church. Especially in parish-model settlement houses, most volunteers were parish residents. Yet many parishes were reserved primarily for one ethnic group or another; Italians complained frequently about being forced to worship in the basements of Irish churches.[20]

Stories show Catholic settlement houses and religious rituals as crucial to establishing ties between the affluent and the poor, the immigrants and the native-born. In "Old White Dresses," Mrs. Green sorts her children's outgrown clothing for donation to charity. Yet she asks her maid to cut up their old white dresses to be used as dust rags, thinking them silly and inappropriate for slum children. Later that day she receives a visit from a worker at a settlement house for Italians, who is desperate to find white First Communion dresses for forty-two children. Embarrassed by her own thoughtlessness Mrs. Green agrees to outfit one child herself and promises to urge all of her friends to do the same.[21] Women's voluntarism could both help the poor and maintain the religious rituals, such as First Communion, that would help bind together a diverse and changing community. Female saints, like St. Anne, were thought to provide appropriate models for gentility and womanly generosity.

In the rescue stories, charity work was portrayed as generating spiritual benefits for both rich and poor while using religion to establish ties among different classes. Similarly, Jane Addams argued that settlement work would help alleviate the sense of uselessness suffered by many middle-class young people, especially young women. Instead of uselessness, however, settlement work was meant to save affluent Catholics from the dangers of upward mobility and the emerging secularism of modernity. The woman rescuer of the St. Anne story prays for some good work to do to earn the saint's intercession on behalf of a friend, "a woman of high social position and enormous wealth, who is in a sanitarium through mental trouble over religious doubts." The rescuer thus participates in a spiritual exchange (good works in return for a saint's intercession), which would link rich and poor closer to one another and benefit both.[22]

The rescue stories not only provided models of increased public roles for laywomen; they also gave readers a blueprint of how to become middle-class—how to acquire gentility, piety, and generosity. In this the *New World* stories diverged from the works of non-Catholic writers, whose main audience may have been already comfortably middle-class. Scholars who have examined fictional portrayals of working women by non-Catholics have demonstrated that male writers tended to fixate on the issue of whether women could work outside the home and still be chaste. Women writers, on the other hand, concentrated more on the social inferiority of "working girls," many of them immigrants, even as they portrayed interaction and alliances between women of different classes. The stories focus on the rough manners and "unrestrained" behavior of working women. During the 1890s Protestant-run working-girls' clubs were attempting to train working-class women to have more genteel manners. Yet in fiction, non-Catholic writers were skeptical, sometimes even mocking working-class characters who referred to themselves and their friends as "ladies."[23]

In contrast, the *New World* stories warned laywomen not to forget their working-class and ethnic backgrounds as they strove to achieve comfortable respectability. While many CWL members were of Irish descent, rescue stories sometimes featured Irish people as the beneficiaries of largesse. Given the numbers of Irish immigrants who continued to arrive in Chicago even into the 1920s, these issues reflected not only the recent past but also contemporary reality. In 1929 immigrants from Ireland made up 7 percent of the city's foreign-born population, 56,786 people out of a total of 805,482. If one included their American-born children in this total, the number increased to 145,919. Thus in one story, the children in a sewing school make a quilt for "old Grandma Dillinger, who had been sick so long with rheumatism," and clothing for "the O'Donovan family, whose home had been burned in the middle of the night."[24]

Authors in the *New World* featured poor characters as rescuers in their own right, inherently pious and generous. Humble characters would shame the affluent by being kinder and more charitable than they. Thus in "The Community Club," a poor girl embarrasses a group of wealthy ladies by her easygoing generosity. While they refuse to send Christmas turkeys to children with "unworthy" parents, her humble family uses their own money to buy Christmas gifts for the impoverished "Dagoes" in her building. In "The Boy Who Went to Sewing School," a boy named John decides to learn how to sew so that he can make clothing for the infant of an impoverished family living next door. His mother cannot help, because she is busy doing laundry in order to support the family. The sewing class volunteers to help him, and soon the baby is clothed in soft warm garments from head to toe. In another story, a number of young factory workers raise money to support European war orphans during World War I.[25]

Working-class women could even appear as rescuers to middle-class do-gooders. In "Rose Castelmond's Career," a young student at Hollybush Seminary for Young Ladies takes a job in an aluminum factory, determined to help the factory workers. There she is startled to find that the factory girls end up helping her instead. One lends her an apron to protect her clothes, others give her food when she forgets her lunch, and they all tend carefully to her when she is injured by one of the machines. Rose learns respect for working girls, and at the same time her ego is deflated by her mistakes.[26]

Stories like this had a ring of truth about them because middle-class reformers and journalists did sometimes take jobs in factories in order to research working conditions. Several of the rescue stories openly supported labor causes. The fictional rescuers, unlike real laywomen, did not involve themselves with party politics. However, the characters in rescue stories were portrayed as taking part in organized labor activities and even supporting strikes. Several stories portray such cross-class interaction, suggesting that even upwardly mobile laypeople should remain sympathetic to the community's working-class majority. In "The Christmas King," a schoolteacher joins a picket line during a garment-workers' strike. This story is particularly noteworthy because it was written in 1915, several months after a major strike by the Amalgamated Clothing Workers took place in Chicago. The rescue stories in the *New World* had an element of truth about them, because they came out at about the same time that a number of charismatic female strikers had captured the attention of journalists and novelists.[27]

To put the *New World* stories in context, Catholic authors outside Chicago were also grappling with issues of female voluntarism and class mobility. In *The Story of Julia Page,* Kathleen Norris creates a character who learns at a settlement house to overcome dirty habits, which the author attributes to her working-class background. Julia was raised in a house where "The dust lay thick on the polished wood and glass of the sideboard. . . . ashes and the ends of cigarettes filled half a dozen little receptacles here and there . . . and . . . the kitchen was hideous with a confusion of souring bottles of milk, dirty dishes, hardened ends of loaves, and a sticky jam jar or two."[28] Although the family has sufficient income, Julia's mother grew up terribly poor. She refuses to clean the house or cook, in the belief that the family is too poor to do these things. Norris thus suggests that poverty is more than just a matter of income; it is also a rejection of middle-class standards of cleanliness and order.

While the *New World* stories tended to view working-class life positively and actively promote support for organized labor, Norris was more critical, suggesting tension over upward mobility within the broader Catholic community. After Julia becomes a resident at the Alexander Toland Neighborhood House, she learns that she can become a lady while still remaining true to her religion. Norris hints subtly that both Julia and the director of the settlement, Miss Toland, are Catholic, thus Julia's class transition does not bring her apostasy. However, it does create awkwardness between Julia and her former peers. Norris gives the impression that she approves of Julia's growing sense of superiority over the girls in the settlement's clubs and classes.[29]

In an attempt to dampen such potential class tensions. the *New World* rescue stories warned middle-class women to treat the poor with dignity and respect. In one story, a woman named Ethel thinks of herself as a born social worker, but instead she is a meddlesome busybody. The author comments: "Perhaps an eastern judge had Ethel in mind when he said to a group of would-be social workers, 'treat people as your equals or for God's sake stay out of their homes.'" Another story posited that Catholic settlements were more effective than Protestant or nonsectarian ones, because "we try to understand them, put ourselves in their place as it were, don't try to force our ideas upon them, as some 'uplifters' do."[30]

The *New World* stories also focused considerable attention on Italians, a phenomenon that was paralleled in the Catholic settlement movement by a tendency to publicize work among the Italians even though many settlements also catered to the Irish and Germans. Stories portrayed Italians in conflicting ways, as exotic heathens and natural Catholics, racialized others and fictive kin. These varied portrayals indicate mixed feelings on the part of old immigrants toward the newcomers. Yet more established groups had reasons to try to incorporate Italians into the city's Catholic community. Most important, Protestant and Italian ethnic leaders were competing for influence over this client group, in order to enhance their own prestige in the city. To the church, Italians were symbolically important because they came from the homeland of the pope.[31]

In both fictional stories and in newspaper accounts of the CWL's settlement work, domestic imagery and family metaphors were used to imagine the incorporation of Italians into Chicago's Catholic community. Most noticeably, Irish Catholics and members of other old immigrant groups tended to portray themselves as substitute mothers for Italian children. This is particularly ironic given the fact that, during the nineteenth century, American Protestant reformers tended to stigmatize impoverished Irish women as bad mothers. Equating settlement work with mothering, rhetoric that could be described as "maternalist," could make more palatable to conservative readers the idea of laywomen gaining new roles outside the home. Unfortunately, in many stories this meant implying that Italian homes did not really exist but needed to be created with the help of sympathetic mission teachers. For example, in "The Mission," a writer describes the life of a neglected little girl whose mother works outside the home: "[Miss Penfield] could see the little figure . . . alone in a close cold room. No mother in reality to help her. Her school filled other wants. How could a child learn to take care of itself with no one to teach it?" This viewpoint was sometimes shared by non-Catholic reformers, who argued that children whose mothers worked outside the home were essentially motherless.[32]

The *New World* stories also used adoption as a metaphor for the inclusion of Italians into Chicago's great Catholic family: they were to be taken in, but with the status of inferiors, as beloved but dependent children. Story writers also made the case that religion could trump ethnicity, as old immigrants removed Italian children from violent or impious Italian homes. Thus Mrs. Garaghty finds "Little Bartolo," an angelic orphan, piously saying his prayers in church. After learning that he has been taken in by an Italian Protestant family, she resolves to adopt the boy herself and call him "Bart," after her brother in the "old country." The theme of adopting maltreated or abandoned children was so common that it was also used in stories where the children in question were not even Italian.[33]

Stories could also promote the idea that the Italians were really not so different from American Catholics. In "The Rosaries," a young Sunday school teacher named Helen buys a number of inexpensive rosaries to reward her young Italian pupils for learning the prayers "Our Father" and "Hail Mary." Filled with dreams of inspiring her students to greater piety, the teacher is appalled when the students pretend the rosaries are makeshift horses' reins and stage a "Ben Hur"–style chariot race around the classroom. Helen's mother only laughs at the story, however, saying: "I know of a most estimable young woman, who actually turned out to be a Sunday school teacher . . . whose favorite infant trick was to escape to kindergarten wearing her mother's amethyst rosary hanging about her neck."[34] The story suggests that the behavior of the Italian children had more to do with their age and the influence of popular culture than their ethnic background.

The *New World* stories racialized Italians at the same time that they projected optimism about the power of faith to bring these "others" into the community. Because many Italians had olive complexions and dark hair, contemporaries were often unsure how to classify them under America's strict black and white racial codes. The rescue stories noted that Italians often had olive skin and dark hair and eyes but attributed to them a simple piety that would enable sympathetic Americans to bring them into the fold. The piety of "Little Bartolo" leads Mrs. Garaghty to adopt him, for example. Religion could also help resolve the uncomfortable issue of intermarriage between Italians and other ethnic groups. In "Queer Friends," a poor Italian child named Guido is helped by an American playmate named Lucy. The story concludes: "And perhaps Guido will be a priest and perhaps Lucy will be a nun. Who can tell?" Guido and Lucy would blossom into a celibate adulthood, never realizing the implied heterosexual pairing of their youth.[35]

An important contrast to the majority of the rescue stories is provided by a number of stories written by a young Italian woman, Maria Da Venezia. Of this author, the *New World* noted only that she was an Italian American with an intimate knowledge of Chicago. If the Irish women imagined themselves as substitute mothers, Da Venezia portrayed Italian mothers as being very much present in their homes and communities. In her stories angry mothers protest when the woman rescuer makes off with their children, at least until they learn that their children are being helped rather than stolen.[36] Further, her child characters are not neglected by their parents. In one story, for example, little Conceto attends Sunday school at the Italian mission, but he is not a neglected waif. Rather, he gives evidence of a mother's care: "Were not his hands and face as clean as soap and a patient 'madre' could make them?" Da Venezia also contradicted Irish stories about filthy homes in Little Italy, contending that Italian homes were physically and morally clean because, "To the Italian the home is a sacred spot."[37] She challenged the other rescue story authors who attempted to use cleanliness as a marker of middle-class status and Americanism.[38]

Where the Irish saw mostly poverty, Da Venezia portrayed a more complex vision of community life in "Little Italy." Both Da Venezia and the Irish women wrote rescue stories: stories in which middle-class women saved destitute families from starvation. But Da Venezia's stories described something more than squalor and deprivation. She described, for example, a religious festival or *festa* in one story, and a rummage sale in another. She noted the ethnic diversity in the neighborhood. To a certain extent, Da Venezia may have normalized Italians by portraying other groups who could be considered even more exotic. At a religious festa, she notes the presence of "blacks and whites, Italians and Chinese." In her rummage-sale story, a Swedish girl quarrels with an Italian girl, because they both wish to purchase the same beautiful red hat.[39]

Da Venezia contested the racializing in the Irish American stories by challenging American stereotypes about the supposed racial characteristics of Italians. She noted variations in the physical features of Italians, characterizing a beautiful woman as a "dainty, dark-eyed signora" but also describing a young boy, "whose shock of yellow curls proclaimed him a son of Sicily."[40] Da Venezia also tweaked the meaning of cultural characteristics, portraying a love of colorful clothing as a sign of ambition and a desire for self-betterment.[41] She thus borrowed a cultural myth that Americans told about themselves, that they were by nature ambitious and upwardly mobile, and attributed it to a group that they found strange and foreign.

Even though poor and working-class women could appear as rescuers in the *New World* stories, many of the stories appear to have been aimed at keeping upwardly mobile women engaged within the Catholic community, even as they rose in class status. Poor and working-class women could serve as models of generosity and piety, encouraging those with more resources to engage in benevolent work, which in turn gave these women a boost by providing them with a genteel pastime and important work to do outside the home. While helping to keep upwardly mobile women involved in the church, the rescue stories also imagined a new set of fictive kin relationships, bolstered by religious ritual, which could help incorporate new immigrants into the community and bind the faithful of all classes closer together. Even the stories by Maria Da Venezia could help bridge ethnic differences within the church by presenting readers with a less stereotyped vision of Chicago's Italians. As a relatively conservative image of saintly and maternal benevolence, the woman rescuer would also help make acceptable an expanded role for laywomen. Thus, although many *New World* articles condemned women's clubs in general, the newspaper could also accept the CWL and its educational, cultural, and reform activities. The saintliness and generosity of the rescuer image could help insulate the CWL against criticism of its other potentially controversial activities, such as its lavish social events and conspicuous consumption.

Class Mobility, Cultural Leadership, and the CWL

The rescue stories revealed tensions within the Catholic community over issues of class mobility, immigration, and gender, and a number of the CWL's cultural activities heightened such tensions. The CWL created a Catholic version of Chicago's high culture or "high society," in part by sponsoring a lavish charity ball that mimicked the one held every year by Chicago's Protestant elite. The ball and the league's other cultural activities could prepare laywomen to move in non-Catholic circles. The most affluent laywomen could practice dancing at the CWL ball before attending the Protestant one; less wealthy CWL members could take classes in French or improve their grammar and punctuation, which would enable them to interact more comfortably with a higher class of people. While CWL members embraced these opportunities to demonstrate their new class status, some Catholics objected to lavish entertainment in the name of charity. Others feared that upwardly mobile women would leave the church in search of churches with greater social prestige. To prevent such losses, the CWL taught members to retain a sense of religious identity by defending their faith against Protestant prejudice and by upholding church teachings when faced with an increasingly sexualized dominant culture. In the process, the league hoped that its members would gain some influence as cultural leaders in the city, promoting moral values and disseminating Catholic literature as they moved beyond the boundaries of the community.

Defending the community seemed increasingly urgent at the end of the nineteenth century; the CWL was founded at about the same time that the anti-Catholic American Protective Association (APA) experienced an upsurge in popularity. During the depression of 1893, the sheer number of unemployed workers gave credence to the organization's claim that hordes of immigrants had stolen jobs from Protestant Americans. The APA was particularly interested in scaling back Catholic success in politics, and even though the organization had declined by the end of the decade, Chicago Roman Catholic Church members continued to face discrimination. In 1906 one league member, Mary E. Vaughan, was demoted from the position of assistant superintendent of the public schools as part of an attempt to lessen the influence of Catholics within the school system.[42]

A number of wealthy and influential laymen decided to join together to fight back by promoting high culture among people like themselves. Periodically, the *New World* wondered in print whether "our men are doomed to become mere 'hewers of wood and drawers of water.'"[43] The Columbus Club aimed to dispel this image. Named the Union Catholic Library Association when it was founded in 1869, the Columbus Club was renamed in 1893 in honor of the Columbian Exposition. It was modeled after the posh non-Catholic men's clubs that dotted Chicago's central business district. The husbands of CWL members belonged to organizations such as the Union League, the Illinois Club, and the Chicago Club. A few belonged to the powerful Iroquois Club, associated with the national Democratic Party. In 1893 the Columbus Club purchased an imposing clubhouse across the street from the lavish Palmer House Hotel. Unfortunately, the clubhouse was soon lost in a recession, and the club itself disbanded.[44]

While non-Catholic men and women were competing with each other for leadership in the city's cultural institutions, after the demise of the Columbus Club, Catholic men by and large left such work to their wives. Modeled on prominent women's organizations like the Chicago Woman's Club, the league offered a number of educational opportunities designed to equip its members for intelligent and refined contact with non-Catholics. The regular meetings of the league often featured discussions concerning art or literature, and one could also learn singing and French.[45] In a veiled reference to the Chicago Women's Club, the league claimed that, "No woman's club is offering to its members more opportunities for culture than the Catholic Woman's League." The Reverend Thomas E. Judge, editor of the *New World,* taught a course on the Bible, which laywomen would need in order to hold their own in a Bible-steeped Protestant culture. Such opportunities outside the home were new for these women, especially married ones. To those who might object to educational and social activities outside the home for women, the CWL could note that it had the backing of the church.[46]

The *New World* encouraged women to defend their faith out in the world just as the CWL was equipping its members to do. In one story a teenaged girl named Eileen goes to a dinner party on a Friday evening at the home of a Protestant girl. Fearful that the guests will snub her because of her religion, she eats the meat that is served rather than abstaining as she is supposed to do. After consuming the forbidden squab, Eileen sits riddled with guilt while the Protestant girls criticize the pope and the church. Finally Eileen is unable to listen in silence any longer. She bursts into the conversation, crying: "You may be sure the Holy Father knows what he's doing. He does not need a crowd of American girls to tell him [what to do]." The Protestant girls, stunned and chastened by the outburst, apologize to Eileen and admit that she is right.[47]

The CWL cooperated with non-Catholics in a variety of cultural endeavors, in a bid for greater influence in the city. The league worked to spread literature by Catholic authors, and in 1902 members took part in a traveling library program of the Illinois Federation of Women's Clubs, sponsoring a library of seventy-five volumes that went to small towns and rural areas throughout the state. The *New World* also utilized organizations like the CWL to promote Catholic literature, in a bid for greater influence in the city. The paper promoted Chicago's Catholic authors, encouraging its readers to borrow their books from the public library, hoping that the library would then acquire more such books.[48]

Through the influence of Eliza Allen Starr, the CWL also offered its members art education and cooperated with non-Catholics on city arts projects. The league's art department held receptions for Chicago artists at the Art Institute and became involved in the Municipal Art Association. The CWL also sponsored the Perboyre Art and Culture Club, a club to teach children about art. First organized at St. Elizabeth's Day Nursery, one of the CWL nurseries, the Perboyre Club subsequently became a national organization.[49]

The league's educational opportunities were probably aimed at middle-class women, but its main fund-raising event was geared primarily toward the more elite members. The advent of the league's annual charity ball in the early 1890s represents a transition from older forms of fund-raising. Nineteenth-century Catholics favored huge fund-raising bazaars with attractions for all classes. As substantial numbers of Chicago's Irish and Germans became upwardly mobile, they sought more genteel forms of recreation. A fair required tremendous effort and could net very small profits; in contrast the CWL charity ball could raise between two thousand and eight thousand dollars and did not require hours of painstaking work decorating and making items to sell.[50]

Despite the ball's financial success, some Catholics expressed a profound unease with conspicuous consumption in the name of charity. The papal encyclical *Rerum Novarum* had given the faithful permission to enjoy such material goods as would reflect their station in life, as long as they also gave to the poor.[51] However, in 1900 the *New World* noted that "some of our subscribers" had criticized the ball, saying that one ought not to wear silks in order to raise money for people dressed in rags. The *New World* defended the CWL, arguing that "practically, the question is not what people might do . . . but what they can be induced to do." The paper noted that the CWL badly needed money for its network of settlement houses, and that the ladies had to raise it however they could. The CWL did hold other kinds of fund-raising events, such as card parties, opera concerts, minstrel shows, and charity baseball games. Yet the ball continued to provide a source of substantial income.[52]

Like the rescue stories, the ball also represented part of the effort by Irish women to construct a new class, ethnic, and gender identity. The Irish in

particular faced a number of recurring racialized stereotypes over the course
of the nineteenth century and the early part of the twentieth. On St.
Patrick's Day, the *New World* repeatedly protested souvenirs, such as the
"simian-faced" image of an Irishman smoking a clay pipe and riding on a
hog.[53] The *Chicago Tribune* described the Irish "pug nose" as a cross between
the "Celtic and African," attempting to deprive the Irish of their white
racial identity, a social commodity they had struggled to achieve over the
course of the nineteenth century. To the Irish their whiteness mattered, because being recognized as white enabled them to be naturalized as citizens,
to gain the right to vote, and to build powerful urban political machines.
Challenging Irish whiteness thus challenged their political success. Even as
the rescue stories racialized Italians, Irish Catholics suffered a similar fate at
the hands of the non-Catholic press.[54]

While the stereotype of the Irish male emphasized his "simian-faced" ignorance and drunkenness, the stereotype of an Irish woman could center
on her body. In 1906 the Hyde Park public high school put on a play that
featured "Mrs. Mulcahy . . . the typical Irish woman" as one of the characters. Advertisements for the show were plastered all over the neighborhood,
featuring a drawing of Mrs. Mulcahy as a large woman with meaty arms,
stereotyped features, and heavy ugly shoes. The drawing resembles the
stereotypical characters often found in caricatures and cartoons drawn by
nativists during the nineteenth century. The *New World* reprinted the
drawing, asking: "Are you content that your mothers, daughters and sisters, the ornament and glory of their sex, should be misrepresented in
this gross, sensual, bestial manner?" This stereotype of Irish women's bodies associated excess flesh and visible muscle with hard work, and hence
working-class status. The *New World* writers implied that this image con-
noted sexuality as well—particularly insulting for a religious group that
was attempting to define itself in opposition to the sensuality of the
general culture.[55]

The conspicuous consumption of the charity ball would enable well-to-
do laywomen to redefine themselves as very different from Mrs. Mulcahy.
The *New World* described the charity ball of 1911: "Mrs. Bennett appeared
in orchid satin veiled with white chiffon. . . . Mrs. David O'Shea . . . wore
white crepe meteor with white chiffon overdress embroidered in gold. Mrs.
T. J. Webb . . . was in blue crepe meteor with blue and gold crystal trim-
ming and baby Irish lace." The reference to Irish lace helped to reinforce
the idea that high status and the consumption of luxury goods were compatible with having an Irish heritage.[56]

The evidence suggests that, having polished their dance steps at the
CWL ball, laywomen were participating in non-Catholic social events also.
Some clergy deplored this trend, while others sought to make the best of it.
In 1904 the Paulist father P. J. O'Callaghan said in a speech at the Catholic
Woman's National League Convention:

> There is a mad rush to get into society. . . . It is surprising that persons of intel-
> ligence are not devoting themselves more to following Catholic ideas. Don't
> they know that in following these ideas they attain social dignity? Don't they
> know that in this faith they find no divorced women, no women with doubt-
> ful character, and no women guilty of that which makes them ashamed?

Other clergymen attempted to prepare laywomen to withstand the snubs of
Protestants if they did venture forth. One *New World* article recounted a
speech given at Trinity College in Washington, D.C., in which the speaker
advised the young women in the audience that the grandeur of the church
should overcome any feelings of social inferiority they might have.[57]

The *New World* also revealed anxieties that women who moved beyond
the Catholic community might wind up marrying Protestants. In contrast
to actual mixed-faith marriages like that of Edith Ogden Harrison to Mayor
Carter Harrison IV, the *New World* treated intermarriage as a prelude to
loneliness and misery. The newspaper recounted the fictional tale of a
young woman named Nellie McShane, who marries a Protestant and subsequently leaves the church. Haunted with guilt over her apostasy, Nellie
confesses to an old friend her suspicion that the whole parish now looks
down on her, and her friend replies: "They do look down on you Nellie . . .
the poorest girl in the parish thinks herself above you. And so she is, for
she can go to Holy Communion and Mass of a Sunday." Nellie, of course,
meets an unhappy fate. Her Protestant husband dies a premature death,
leaving her all alone with a new baby and an uncongenial mother-in-law.[58]

Defending the church out in the world could enable laywomen to move
in non-Catholic circles while avoiding being corrupted by them. In 1904
Edmund F. Dunne, one of the founders of the Guardian Angel Settlement,
noted that Catholics would be attending a large non-Catholic charity ball
held around Christmas. He noted that "Every Catholic gentleman whose
name and address have found their way into the Blue Book will [have] an
opportunity to forward his ten simoleons for a ball ticket."[59] Dunne challenged *New World* readers to boycott the ball unless some of the proceeds
went to a Catholic institution. Even as it enabled laywomen to move into
new social circles, however, the CWL cautioned them that they must not
copy elite Protestants, who were becoming more tolerant of a certain relaxation in social and sexual standards. The church continued to insist upon
the maintenance of Victorian taboos against divorce and contraception, using such standards to delineate the boundaries of Catholic identity.[60]

Catholic settlement houses also played a role in promoting other high
culture events that enabled middle-class and elite church members to
amuse themselves and still fulfill their religious requirements. Because the
faithful were supposed to stay away from frivolous amusements during
Lent, St. Mary's Settlement on the South Side developed its annual lenten
lecture. The settlement had been assessed for street paving and was desper-

ate to raise additional funds. The settlement's treasurer, Sallie Grieves Gaynor, had also served as president of the Catholic Writers' Guild and was active with the literary Benson Club of the Paulist Settlement, so she was the ideal person to secure prominent speakers for the lecture. The lectures were very popular, but they were more staid than other forms of recreation, and hence more appropriate to the season of Lent.[61]

The league's social and educational activities gave elite and rising laywomen a boost, helping them act out a reformulated Catholic identity in line with their emerging class status. The ball could help women embody this status by dressing the part, while the CWL literary and educational activities offered programs that would cultivate their knowledge and tastes, training them to serve as ambassadors among the city's Protestants. Out in the world laywomen could demonstrate their new literary knowledge and polished manners, in addition to embracing a role as defenders of the faith against religious prejudice, changing sexual mores, secularism, and other aspects of modernism. Defending the faith presupposed activities not envisioned in the rescue stories, such as wearing lavish clothing and cooperating with Protestants. While the rescue stories envisioned a way to bind Catholics to the community, the CWL also created opportunities for women to move beyond its boundaries.

Rescue Stories

Image and Reality

While the rescue stories reflected tensions within the Catholic community related to class, ethnicity, and gender, they also suggested solutions that might be useful to the CWL. The stories gave the appearance of rejecting the ideal of the "New Woman," but they did much more than simply uphold domesticity. The stories suggested the active role poor women and working girls were playing in Catholic settlements, portraying them as rescuers in their own right. The stories provided upwardly mobile Catholics with a model of genteel behavior while admonishing them to remain loyal to their own working-class roots and to organized labor. Family and religious imagery could perhaps help tame the stereotypes of Italians as dangerous and prone to crime, enabling more American Catholics to accept them, although only in a subordinate status. Religious and family imagery could be used to link women's new benevolent work to the past, giving it the appearance of piety and making it seem less threatening to conservative Catholics in a rapidly changing world.

By reassuring conservative Catholics such as the priests who exhorted Catholic women to remain faithful to the community, the rescue stories could help the league justify the network of institutions that laywomen were building across the city. The league's benevolent projects ultimately enabled members to claim a greater leadership role in both the city and the church. Its cultural activities, while controversial, equipped its members to move beyond the community in order to promote morality and publicize Catholic accomplishments in art and literature out in the city as a whole. The league's settlements would prepare Catholic women to achieve influence in the city through citywide politics and government. There, they would continue to promote the cause of organized labor, as well as professionalization in social work and other social reforms designed to improve the lot of the poor. Ironically, even though settlements were intended to increase the loyalty of Catholics of all classes to the church, the settlements would enable some laywomen to challenge the authority of the clergy.

CHAPTER TWO

Settlements and the State

CWL Women in City Government

In 1908 the Catholic Woman's League sponsored a gala fund-raising lecture for its four settlements, featuring as lecturer the prominent Democrat William Jennings Bryan. Searching for some common ground with his audience, this most Protestant of statesmen spoke about the life of Christ.[1] Bryan had been making the rounds of important Chicago organizations in a bid for the Democratic presidential nomination, and CWL members included the female relatives of some of the city's most prominent Democrats. It was undoubtedly Edith Ogden Harrison who had arranged the Bryan lecture, because her husband was a major political ally of the Great Commoner. The Bryan lecture was the first time Mayor Harrison had so openly used his connections with the CWL, although he had derived much political mileage from his wife's religion. Stiff competition in several elections with self-styled "reformers" both Republican and Democratic would lead Harrison to try to achieve this label himself, in part by harnessing himself to the league's reputation for doing good works.

Harrison had a difficult task ahead of him, to portray himself as a reformer; although not personally corrupt, he was the political ally of some of the most notorious politicians in the city, aldermen associated with drinking, gambling, and prostitution. These men were nominally also Catholic, which frustrated the archdiocese. In 1910 a *New World* article suggested: "Sometimes the church has had to suffer because of its men, because of their lack of . . . civic

[and] personal virtue." However, "while the Church has often had to be ashamed of its men, it could always turn to its women with joy. They were always good and pure . . . noble and intelligent."[2]

In contrast to these male politicians, CWL women had a reputation for doing good works. Between 1893 and 1911 they built a network of four settlement houses and day nurseries in various locations across the city. Starting with a plan to put poor women to work and to help needy families, they also began to professionalize Catholic charities and to cooperate with non-Catholic women reformers to pursue common goals. Although the women of the CWL cooperated with a variety of political parties to achieve their ends, most were Democrats. Harrison could turn to them to help burnish his image because they were his supporters at a time when many non-Catholic reformers were allied with the Republicans. Harrison would greatly expand city services to the poor, choosing Catholic women to implement the changes; these women welcomed the chance to play a role in the political leadership of the city. Once in city government, most CWL women championed the rights of workers and an expanded role for government in social services. Competition among political parties thus helped to expand and shape Chicago's growing social-welfare bureaucracy, while the existence of Catholic women reformers played a key role in the expansion.

Settlements and Day Nurseries
The Origins of CWL Reform

The CWL settlements aimed at the economic uplift of Chicago Catholics, and the institutions were built upon the labor of poor women—it is no coincidence that the league settlements started as day nurseries. Nurseries enabled the mothers of young children to go out to earn wages, thus earning money to feed their children. Eventually, the nurseries acquired other programs including mothers' clubs, which gathered nursery mothers together to do charity work for people even less fortunate than themselves. In keeping with the rescue stories, the settlements also provided middle-class volunteers with opportunities to embody the roles of benefactors to people in need. In addition to encouraging laywomen of different classes to work together, the nurseries used religious rituals to pull Catholics closer together as a community. Yet while working to make the community more close-knit and more faithful, the settlements also enabled the CWL women to cultivate ties with non-Catholic reformers, to promote increasingly professional standards in Catholic social work, and even to become involved in politics. Thus the labor, paid and unpaid, of poor and middle-class women gave CWL leaders a boost into the larger public arena.

The origins of Catholic settlement work in Chicago reveal cooperation among women of different faiths in order to address the needs of the city's most vulnerable citizens. When the CWL women founded their own day nurseries in 1893, they were inspired in part by a successful nursery opened previously by laywomen in St. Peter's parish. Originally founded by the Women's Christian Temperance Union (WCTU), the nursery was taken over by a group of women from St. Peter's in 1892 when the WCTU ran out of money to maintain it. Originally housed in several apartments on South Clark Street, the Catholic women moved the nursery into two cottages at 174 Pacific Avenue. St. Peter's established a pattern that was later copied in Catholic nurseries across the city: it added so many different services that it soon came to resemble a full-fledged settlement house. It began with day care and then added visiting nurse services and a kindergarten. Volunteers collected clothing and blankets for poor nursery families, and a Sunday school was opened as well.[3]

Even though the rescue stories often featured settlement work among Italians, the CWL institutions were open to all with no discrimination on the basis of race or religion.[4] In 1893, the CWL founded three day nurseries: St. Elizabeth's Day Nursery on the city's North Side, St. Anne's Day Nursery on the West Side, and All Saints Day Nursery (later St. Mary's Settlement and Day Nursery) on the South Side. St. Juliana's was founded later as a spin-off from St. Elizabeth's. They were located in multiethnic neighborhoods across the city, so a wide variety of people would indeed have used them. St. Elizabeth's on the North Side, located on the northeast corner of Orleans and Wendell streets, was near the German parish of St. Joseph's, the territorial parish of St. Dominic's, and the Italian parish of St. Philip Benizi. St. Anne's Settlement on the West Side was located at 333 Loomis Street, squarely in the middle of the West Side Italian district, not far from Hull House and Guardian Angel Center. All Saints Settlement on the South Side, in a building at 4314 Wentworth Avenue, was situated in Canaryville near the Back of the Yards neighborhood. Nearby were two territorial parishes, St. Cecelia's and St. Elizabeth's, and one German parish, St. George's. The Back of the Yards housed a wide variety of ethnic groups including Irish, Polish, and Lithuanians.[5]

Modern child care has a variety of origins. It can be traced to colonial dame schools, orphanages, workhouses, and indentured servitude—even child labor functioned both to provide money for families and to supervise children. Day-care centers, also known as day nurseries or crèches, began as a way to harness the labor power of women with young children. While today women of all classes utilize day care, day nurseries were originally associated with working-class and poor women who had to work out of financial necessity. In the 1890s nurseries were still a relatively new phenomenon in the United States, having originated in Paris in the 1840s. Because of a high demand for women's labor at the time, many French factories opened crèches so that mothers could breast-feed their babies and still be available for work. The idea soon spread: before 1880 three nurseries were founded in the United States to help poor women. Between 1880 and 1898 the number of nurseries skyrocketed to 175, enough to unite and form the National Federation of Day Nurseries. Catholic nurseries tended to shy away from such federations, however, being wary of supervision by Protestants. In 1893 a model day nursery was established at the World's Columbian Exposition, demonstrating the most up-to-date methods in child care.[6]

Nonsectarian settlement reformers began to lose their enthusiasm for day care in the early twentieth century, in favor of "mothers' pensions" that would pay poor mothers to stay at home with their children. Yet day care was one of the first programs that emerged at Hull House; neighborhood children left unattended during the day would simply wander into the building. Catholics also believed that a day nursery made a good foundation for a settlement house; as the *New World* explained in 1906, a nursery could form a "true nucleus for the real social settlement."[7] Ironically, even as white Protestant and nonsectarian reformers were losing their enthusiasm for day care, Catholics and African Americans, whose communities were more dependent upon the wage labor of mothers, kept building nurseries. Catholic charity workers sometimes helped women apply for mothers' pensions from city or state governments, yet in general they preferred employment programs and benefits that delivered benefits to women and children through male breadwinners.[8]

A major depression taking place in 1893 probably helped inspire the CWL to form its day nurseries in that year; mothers could be called into the workforce as marginal labor when fathers suffered unemployment. Although nurseries could potentially undermine the ideal that mothers should remain in the home with their children, they were popular because they claimed to make families "self-sufficient," even though they were essentially charities. As one *New World* article noted in 1906: "Some there are who cavil at giving to the poor, thinking that this only makes them the more dependent. . . . But surely none can offer an objection to the idea of a Day Nursery." The league nurseries charged a small fee, claiming that this would reassure the mothers that they were not asking for charity. To make payment easier, larger families got discounted rates, while very poor families were helped for free. In addition the nurseries formed clubs of day nursery mothers, who would sew for the poor and even go out into the neighborhoods to help others.[9]

Like non-Catholic day nursery advocates, the CWL women promoted nurseries as a way to save families, a view that nicely aligned itself with the domesticity of the rescue stories. Charity workers came to see the nurseries as an alternative to orphanages, which proliferated during the nineteenth century and served both true orphans and children with living but impoverished parents. Some orphanage advocates applauded the removal of children from the supposed bad influence of their parents, while needy Catholics sometimes used church orphanages as temporary care for their children during hard times. Between 1900 and 1920 the new goal of child advocates was to keep children in their homes whenever possible. Within the Catholic community, day nurseries never achieved the clout of orphanages, which were generally run by religious orders. Nevertheless, these nurseries did spring up in cities across the country during the Progressive Era.[10]

The league settlements also harnessed the labor power of young people, as well as providing educational and employment assistance for people of different ages. Several of the CWL nurseries established schools, called "kitchengartens," to teach cooking and housekeeping to teenaged girls. These young girls were viewed as potential workers who would help their busy mothers at home. Kitchengartens were also intended to train girls for employment in domestic service and ultimately marriage. Kindergartens, not yet a part of the public school system, were another addition to the nurseries. Libraries provided educational advantages in an era when the city's public library branches were not yet established across the city. The nurseries soon added sewing schools, penny-savings banks, and mothers' clubs. Most had employment bureaus. Each nursery had volunteer physicians and nurses, who examined nursery children regularly for signs of illness and visited sick neighbors in their homes. Such medical services could help keep neighbors healthy and minimize workdays and income lost to illness. Relief bureaus could aid families stricken with sickness or unemployment.

In keeping with the piety of the rescue stories, many programs in the CWL nurseries used religious education to create greater cohesion in the community and to promote Catholic views on sexuality among older children. Dancing classes, gymnasiums, and clubs for boys and girls could help keep young people away from the sexualized entertainment to be found in the city. Sunday schools brought the church's moral teachings to children while training them for the communal rituals of first Holy Communion and confirmation. These elaborate public rituals were used to bind children to the church, but also to provide a spectacle that would keep their parents and other observers involved. Providing meeting space for neighborhood events could also help the neighbors construct themselves as a community.[11]

Teaching thrift to the nursery children was intended to promote self-sufficiency among the poor, and it also squared with church doctrine: the papal encyclical *Rerum Novarum* spoke of self-help and frugal living as one duty of the poor. Nursery workers taught the children that saving was the key to "personal independence," saying that the children "show[ed] great zeal and enthusiasm in saving their money." Nursery children would bring their pennies to the nursery penny-savings bank and would receive stamps in exchange through the postal savings system. Once they had saved three dollars' worth of pennies, they were encouraged to open an account at a downtown bank. Like other settlements, the CWL's institutions also aimed to prevent vice and crime, in part by keeping children off the streets.[12]

St. Elizabeth's day nursery on the North Side provides an example of day-to-day nursery activities. This was the first CWL nursery, and Chicago's hierarchy quickly recognized the benefits of the new institution: its rooms were blessed by the chancellor of the archdiocese. Shortly after the nursery opened, St. Elizabeth's workers cared for an infant with tuberculosis while its mother went out to work in a laundry. When the child died, nursery workers helped arrange for its burial. In an era of high infant mortality, this child was the nursery's only loss for the year. The nursery cared for a total of 2,625 children over the course of the year, with an average daily kindergarten attendance of 20. The nursery ran a Sunday school, a sewing school, and St. Agnes' Club for Working Girls. It sponsored benevolent work in the neighborhood, providing food for needy families, for example. Nursery workers procured hospital rooms for sick children and arranged for others to be baptized. A dispensary enabled workers to treat the simple ailments of children on the premises, while three volunteer doctors performed daily health inspections in the nursery.[13]

Echoing the rescue stories, real Catholic settlements relied upon volunteers for much of their programming. One example of a settlement volunteer was Mrs. Alice Mooney, a charter member of the Catholic Woman's League who "devoted all her spare time teaching the children [of St. Mary's Settlement and Day Nursery] to sew." In 1913 the children of St. Mary's planted a plum tree in her honor at the settlement's annual Arbor Day celebration. Some of the physicians and teachers who volunteered at the settlements could well have been CWL members. Many volunteers were needed, because the league's settlements were growing quickly. In the early years of the twentieth century, All Saints Settlement changed its name to St. Mary's Settlement and moved into a larger building in the Stockyards district. With their rapid growth the CWL programs may in fact have become too ambitious. In 1904 an article in the *New World* complained that "Hull House and kindred non-Catholic institutions put us to shame. The number of non-resident workers at Hull House is seventy-five, at St. Elizabeth's the matron has no personal assistance whatever." St. Elizabeth's was forced to close its sewing school, its mothers' club, its kitchengarten program, and its circulating library.[14]

While in some ways the league settlements resembled the rescue stories, promoting piety, domesticity, and voluntarism, the settlements also created professional opportunities for laywomen. Teaching kindergarten was promoted in the *New World* as a professional career for women. St. Anne's nursery on the West Side had a paid matron, who oversaw the work of volunteers. The presence of live-in matrons was more common in club-model and parish-model settlements than in proprietary ones, which were more likely to be run by wealthy women themselves. At St. Anne's, which occupied a nine-room house at 333 Loomis Street, the matron had her own apartment on the premises. She and her two assistants ran the nursery, and two experienced teachers came six days a week to work with the kindergarten and kitchengarten children while other teachers helped the older girls learn needlework. Some of these teachers may have been paid, while others were probably volunteers.[15]

The league settlements also established clubs for neighborhood mothers that mirrored its own programs, providing refreshments, educational lectures and discussions, and even opportunities to do volunteer work. Nursery advocates first hoped that they would be able to get to know poor mothers by demonstrating sympathy for their children. The idea was that this would enable nursery workers to help poor families better. The nurseries could then encourage mothers to participate in other activities. The CWL recruited "rescuers" from among the day nursery mothers, as it did among its own members—the mothers' club of St. Elizabeth's Nursery had a sewing circle, which made clothes for needy people in the neighborhood. The club's visiting committee would go out into the neighborhood looking for destitute families for the nursery to help. St. Anne's sponsored mothers' meetings twice a month, offering lectures, musical programs, and refreshments, while a visiting committee composed of mothers' club members provided donations of food and clothing to those in need. As one league member noted: "These mothers show good common sense, and a lively interest in questions of the day."[16]

Laywomen's organizations were often formed to raise money that was then spent by religious orders to run their charities. The league's settlements were novel in that they gave the laywomen the authority to disperse the funds they raised. Records show that St. Elizabeth's Social Settlement raised $482 by subscription in 1902–1903, a dramatic performance raised $386, and a rummage sale netted another $184. St. Elizabeth's Club, possibly of day nursery mothers, collected almost $10 that year, and a small amount was also raised in fees from the kindergarten sewing school. The largest expenditures at St. Elizabeth's were for rent and salaries. House rent in 1902–1903 was $286. The matron earned $311, the cook earned $167, and the director of the kindergarten earned $120. The next largest expenses were for food for the children, which came to $143, and coal and gas, which totaled $83. Other league settlements had similar expenditures and used additional methods to raise money, including card parties and balls.[17]

The league's settlement program combined church doctrine with an increased professionalization of language and methods While the CWL women do not mention that any of their nurseries belonged to the National Federation of Day Nurseries, the fact that this organization was actively promoting higher standards in child care probably influenced the laywomen's desire to professionalize their work. Like Chicago's non-Catholic kindergartens, the CWL kindergartens used the Froebel teaching method, a system of directed play originally developed in mid-nineteenth-century Germany as a system to train intelligent citizens for the liberal state. The kindergarten itself was meant to represent a small liberal state, with the children governed by consent rather than coercion. In Froebel's ideal kindergarten, the children of rich and poor would play together, breaking down traditional class barriers. Froebel even designed a set of toys in order to teach children about their relationship to the community: a set of blocks that fit together, showing the relationship of individuals to the greater whole.[18]

Kindergarten exercises were meant to develop muscles and hand-eye co-ordination, as well as the discipline and cooperation that could help mold good citizenship. Promoting discipline in a kindergarten is obviously chal-lenging under the best of circumstances, but in the CWL kindergartens the children ranged in age from eighteen months to six years, and attendance was very irregular. Mothers who were not working on any given day might not bring their children. At St. Anne's Kindergarten, these factors made the days chaotic, yet the teachers maintained some order by keeping the chil-dren busy. Activities such as threading beads or playing with clay typically lasted no more than five or ten minutes. Many of the activities—such as singing, marching together in a circle, and following the instructions of the teacher—could help teach the children to work as a group.[19]

The CWL nurseries also adopted Froebel's emphasis on nonviolent disci-pline. St. Anne's Kindergarten teachers used "A kind reproof, a gentle look of reproach, [and] a guiding hand" in order to keep the children in line. When this did not work, they resorted to persuasion and shame, singing a song to keep the children calm in between activities:

> Oh we will be patient
> Oh we will be patient
> Oh we will be patient
> While work is being prepared.

If any particular child needed additional correction, the teacher would insert the child's name into the song, in order to embarrass him or her into behaving. St. Anne's workers noted in the *New World* that "Mothers who are accustomed to give a box on the ear here, a cuff there and a 'corner' at intervals would be surprised at the influence of this magic little song."[20]

In keeping with both Froebel's ideals and the CWL's own vision of com-munal upward mobility, the league's kindergartens mingled financially se-cure and poor children. This practice also reflected church teachings: *Rerum Novarum* condemned socialism and class conflict but envisioned a system in which rich and poor would be tied together through their shared faith. The CWL kindergartens literally helped create such ties. Unlike day care, which was widely viewed as a resource for the poor, kindergarten training was supposed to be a great advantage to all children. However, it was not yet available in the public schools, so the league arranged for middle-class parents to send their children to its kindergartens. Following the idea of communal upward mobility, the fee paid by the better-off parents would enable the CWL to care for more poor children. While non-Catholics also recognized the value of kindergartens to both affluent and poor children, the practice of combining different classes of children in a single institution seems to have been particular to Catholics.[21]

Although it did not use its settlements for labor organizing, the CWL did enhance the labor connections among Catholic women. Labor issues were controversial among CWL members, but the number of members who were labor leaders and wives of labor leaders meant that labor had an advantage in the league. The CWL also took steps to inform its own members on labor issues. For example, in 1907 the Department of Philanthropy invited Agnes Nestor, president of the Women's Trade Union League, to speak to members. Nestor was not a member of the CWL, but she belonged to St. Vincent's parish and played a role in establishing the De Paul Settlement and Day Nursery. She was also an ally of Margaret Haley and Catherine Goggin, CWL members and CTF leaders.[22]

While the CWL settlements fostered ties of religion and mutual assistance among Catholics, the league was also quietly establishing relationships with non-Catholic reformers. In an era before male politicians came to view the league as an asset, the CWL chose to cooperate with non-Catholic women's networks in order to advance its favorite causes. Even though the *New World* routinely criticized non-Catholic reformers, the CWL regularly invited them, even Jane Addams herself, to come and speak about reform issues. The league belonged to the National Federation of Women's Clubs, and one president of the league also served a term as the president of the first district of the Illinois Federation of Women's Clubs.[23]

CWL women cooperated with non-Catholics in political lobbying for cherished causes. Some league women called upon members to become involved in the fight for women's suffrage. Children's issues were also important to members. In 1899, for example, the CWL joined fifty-four other Chicago women's clubs in establishing a vacation school for public school children. A CWL member, Sadie American, served with members of other women's clubs on the committee on legislation, which lobbied for the summer program in Springfield. By keeping children off the streets during the summer, the school was intended to prevent crime as well as to awaken the children's curiosity, resourcefulness, and creativity. The vacation schools used no books and focused instead on art projects, manual training, and field trips. Once a week the children would travel to a park or the countryside, gather specimens of plants, flowers, insects, and rocks, and bring them back for study in the classroom. Each school had "a kindergarten, and two manual training outfits, eight aquariums, forty window boxes, twelve ants nests . . . , six insect holders, colored chalk and water colors." The children reportedly loved it, especially compared to the regular schoolwork they had to do during the year.[24]

Building settlements enabled the women of the CWL to professionalize their social work, to expand their connections to non-Catholic reformers, and to become involved in politics. As they cooperated with these reformers, they built their own program, which they would eventually take with them into city government. In this program of communal upward mobility, the poor and the financially secure each had responsibilities. The poor were responsible for hard work and thrift; once they were helped onto their feet they were encouraged to help those even worse off than themselves. Better-off Catholics were expected to serve as stewards of their wealth for others; they were responsible for helping the poor improve their economic position. Just as the CWL would use the labor of laywomen to accomplish this vision, so too would these women play a role in the creation of a modern welfare state in Chicago.

The Rise of Leonora Meder
The CWL Embraces Reform

The CWL had been cooperating with non-Catholic women since its settlements were first opened in 1893, and the professionalization of the settlements made its work resemble that of Chicago's non-Catholic reformers. Yet throughout the league's first decade and a half, it tried to clothe its work with an aura of separateness and distinctiveness, in part by using the term *charity* rather than *reform*. Emphasizing the league's distinctiveness could help shield it from the heavy, often vitriolic, criticism heaped by the *New World* upon non-Catholic reformers. Emphasizing distinctiveness could also reassure *New World* readers that all these new activities for laywomen, like the efforts of the women in the fictional rescue stories, posed no threat to domesticity or the cohesiveness of the city's Catholic community, even as their work increasingly resembled that of non-Catholic reformers. By 1908, however, the CWL had openly embraced the term *reform*, creating a Reform Department that would cooperate with non-Catholic women on a much larger scale than the league had ever done before. Their involvement in politics, with the Bryan lecture of 1908, appears to have emboldened the CWL women to reduce their emphasis on setting themselves apart and to increase their participation in the public culture of the city. One of the main authors of this change was Leonora Z. Meder, a CWL leader who later became director of Chicago's Department of Public Welfare. Within the CWL she continued to professionalize the league's social service work and began to develop the ideas she would later promote during her career in city government, including support for the rights of labor and the need to "protect" the sexuality of the city's young women.

While the *New World* was quite supportive of the Catholic Woman's League and its activities, the paper's criticism of non-Catholic reformers was harsh. One can understand why the league might have shied away from using the term *reform*. Editor Charles J. O'Malley once called settlement workers "immoral freaks." One *New World* writer argued that many reforms they promoted were "the wildest, wickedest, cruelest and most heartless theories [ever seen]." Some writers referred to club women as ugly old maids, or "socialistic Amazons"; others damned them for neglecting their homes and children. Still others claimed that settlement workers harbored socialists and tried to convert Catholic children to Protestantism. While not always hostile to actual reform proposals, the newspaper repeatedly heaped scorn on non-Catholic reformers, apparently out of fear of proselytizing, a concern that settlement houses might be taking over the role of the church, and anxieties about the changing roles of women.[25]

Catholics and non-Catholics alike used the terms *charity* and *reform* as markers of identity during the Progressive Era rather than as mere descriptors of social work. Especially in the early years, the CWL used the idea of charity rather than reform in order to insist upon the distinctiveness of the church's own social work. As one league spokeswoman stated in 1900: "in contrast with non-Catholic denominations, [the Catholic Church] has placed at the forefront of her creed the doctrine that faith . . . must be accompanied by good works. The faith which does not bloom into charity is dead." Emotional descriptions of the day nurseries, focusing on adorable and helpless little children, could also help portray the league's work as primarily charitable.[26]

While the settlement women defined their work as charity, non-Catholic politicians and others sometimes claimed the status of "reformers" by contrasting themselves to Catholics, whom they constructed as a source of civic and political corruption. Yet both Catholics and ethnics were active in certain types of reform, and a substantial amount of Progressive legislation could not have passed without their support at the polls. A number of Catholic politicians in Chicago chose to portray themselves as reformers. The CWL women themselves would follow in this tradition, taking up a reform agenda and becoming more involved in party politics after 1908, even though they chose in the early years to portray their work as charity.[27]

Ironically, the CWL women chose to characterize their work as charity rather than reform in an era when many Americans were conflicted about the value of charity. During the late nineteenth and early twentieth centuries "scientific" or "organized" charity, considered by historians to be the first step in the professionalization of social work, was an influential theory of relief. Its proponents argued that overly generous almsgiving was the cause of poverty, claiming that charity could cause more suffering than it ameliorated because relief would make poor people lazy and unwilling to work. Charity Organization Societies (COSs) were established in many major cities in the hopes that poverty could be eliminated by waging war on "unnecessary" almsgiving. In addition these societies sponsored "friendly visitors," usually middle-class women, who would meet with poor families in their homes to offer them advice and encouragement.[28] Catholics expressed ambivalence about COS ideas: some thought them sensible precautions against fraud; others thought them heartless and distrusted COSs because of their close connections to Protestant churches. For the CWL, day care was one answer to this dilemma, allowing the league's members to adopt contemporary professional standards of social work without offending Catholic sensibilities.

Leonora Meder was a woman well equipped to negotiate these complexities. She was ambitious enough to want a leadership role in the Catholic community and the city, and she had years of experience in social work, which enabled her to promote professional standards in her work within the league. Born in Wayside, Kentucky, on May 22, 1870, she studied at a law office in Louisville before she was admitted to the bar. In 1897 she began to combine her legal work with social work. Moving to Chicago in 1904, she chose to specialize in juvenile justice, particularly for girls, and was a member of the court of domestic relations and of the juvenile and moral courts committee. She was involved in creating a children's playroom at the juvenile court and in defining the duties of policewomen when they were first added to Chicago's police force. As the *New World* described her: "Mrs. Meder has splendid executive ability and a clear insight of social conditions in Chicago. Her college training and her clear mind have caused her to be known by her close associates as 'the woman with the index memory.'"[29]

Meder was instrumental in professionalizing Catholic charities, a move that was indispensable to preparing laypeople for work in church-related and government social services. She promoted the centralization of Catholic charities and was involved with the School of Sociology at Loyola, which the school's founder and director, the Reverend Frederic Siedenburg, had turned into a leading center for social justice teaching and had probably influenced Meder's thought. In Chicago she participated in a number of other organizations, including the Chicago Educational Committee and the Catholic Travelers' Aid Society of Chicago. She served for a time as vice president of the National Conference of Catholic Charities, and she was also active in the Needy Families, State of Illinois, and the Ladies Catholic Benevolent Association.[30]

The Reform Department of the CWL, in which Leonora Meder would later play a significant role, was founded about a year and a half after Bryan's 1908 lecture. Even though the CWL women had been cooperating with non-Catholic women for years and promoting professionalization through their settlements, adopting the term *reform* was a challenging step for the CWL. As one league member said in the *New World*: "The word [']Reform['] did not appeal to us at first thought. It had such an ominous sound. The word had been . . . used to designate all sorts of things, foolish, trivial, and sensible in turn." The CWL women may have wished to promote reforms, but they still needed to reassure other Catholics that they were not the same as the "immoral freaks" and socialists so often condemned in the pages of the *New World*.[31]

In 1911 the Protectorate was opened under the offices of the league's new Reform Department. The Protectorate was a travelers' aid organization dedicated to protecting (and regulating) the sexuality of young women and girls. Meder was involved from the start, and by 1913 she was the Protectorate's chair. Inspired by the 1910 National Conference of Catholic Charities, the Protectorate also took direction from the papal encyclical *Rerum Novarum,* which advocated better wages and working conditions for laborers, in part to prevent prostitution and other threats to women's chastity. Armed with statistics about "white slavery," the Protectorate claimed that procurers would loiter in train stations, waiting to prey upon young women who seemed lost or confused. Protectorate workers would thus wait in train stations to help guide these women to respectable lodgings and employment. A central office at Madison and State served as a clearinghouse for information about job opportunities and safe lodging. A few paid staff members were acquired, and volunteer social workers were recruited from Loyola School of Social Work.[32]

The archdiocesan newspaper spoke in glowing terms of the gratitude of young girls and their parents for the work of the Protectorate. In one story, for example, a worker for the Protectorate rescued three girls aged eighteen, sixteen, and fourteen who arrived in Chicago from South Bend, Indiana, without any luggage or money. Apparently the oldest girl had wanted to see the sights of Chicago and had dragged her younger sisters along with her. The two younger girls begged the Protectorate agent to send them back home. In other stories agents rescued naive young women from the clutches of seedy young men. Even older women were not to be trusted: an article about the Protectorate noted that brothels often employed motherly older women as decoys to trap unsuspecting young girls. While these stories were undoubtedly biased toward the good being done by the Protectorate, many young women may indeed have been glad for its help.[33]

The Protectorate's work involved both the genuine protection of some young women in danger of sexual exploitation and the incarceration of others deemed to be "fallen." About four months after the new CWL department was established, its workers noted that they had helped about 350 young women and claimed to have saved fifty of these from "white slavery." From May 1, 1915, through April 30, 1916, the Protectorate found employment for 925 young women and lodging for 159. It found adoptive or foster homes for thirty-three very young girls and returned sixty-three young women to their homes. Since tales of white slavery were common during this era, it is possible that some young women were grateful for such help. While the Protectorate saved 893 young women from "evil influences," nine were unlucky enough to be placed in the House of the Good Shepherd, an institution for "fallen" women and girls. Good Shepherd Houses have been characterized as offering compassionate care for some and unwelcome incarceration for others. While the Good Shepherd inmates were institutionalized without court intervention, the Protectorate also participated in 123 court cases. In addition the Protectorate provided forty-two girls with First Communion clothing, and one with a graduation outfit.[34] With so many young women arriving from abroad during the early twentieth century, the international connections of the church proved useful to the Protectorate. Hundreds of letters were written to priests in the United States and Europe and notices were placed in religious newspapers to notify young Catholic girls and their guardians of the Protectorate's services. The organization eventually had agents in Antwerp, Bremen, Hamburg, Rotterdam, and The Hague. After a year of operation, its work became so well-known that it received a blessing from the pope.[35]

For the CWL, establishing the Protectorate involved more public cooperation with non-Catholics, more political work, and particularly more contact with city benevolent and social control officials. These non-Catholics included volunteers, social workers, police matrons, and probation officers across the city. The Protectorate coordinated its agents' hours with the non-Catholic Travelers' Aid Society, so that the Travelers' Aid supervised the stations during the day, and the Protectorate supervised them after 6 p.m. The station work was expensive; station guides were paid, as were an office clerk and a court attendant. In order to save money the Protectorate merged in 1915 with the travelers' aid departments of the YWCA and the Jewish societies and founded the Travelers' Aid Society of Chicago and Illinois. Even after the merger, the CWL continued to play an active role in the organization.[36]

While head of the Protectorate, Meder began developing several of the ideas she would later pursue in city government. She strongly supported expanding the role of government in social service provision, and she fostered Catholic involvement with the new government agencies. The Protectorate cooperated with non-Catholics in lobbying for a bill in the state legislature to establish an immigrant station in Chicago equivalent to the one at Ellis Island. In 1912 a *New World* article about the Protectorate promoted the idea that the faithful were responsible for taking care of those in need or in trouble, especially young women: "Now the time has come when the entire Catholic population of Chicago should realize that this protection of girls is a matter that vitally concerns every one of them, and that each one is responsible for the welfare of the young girls in our midst."[37] The responsibility to care for others drew Catholics into involvement with government. Under Meder's tenure at the Protectorate, the institution provided legal advice for every Catholic case that came before the juvenile court. As a lawyer specializing in juvenile justice, Meder herself probably gave a great deal of this legal advice.

The Protectorate also addressed another issue that Meder later stressed in her government work: a concern for labor conditions. At the Protectorate she made a connection between labor issues and the religious concern for controlling the sexuality of young women. In 1911 a *New World* article noted that "the poor girl trying to live on starvation wages, often deliberately chooses [prostitution] as a rest and finds it is death." The Protectorate itself did not become involved with labor organizing, which would probably have been the best way to address the issue of starvation wages. However, women from the organization did sponsor a meeting with the women managers of department stores to let them know about the services available to their employees.[38]

During her career in the Protectorate, Meder continued several trends started by the CWL in its settlement work, including professionalization, increasing cooperation with non-Catholic women, and even political involvement. Like the settlements the Protectorate helped enhance the professional standards of CWL social work and provided jobs in social work. Meder expanded this idea by helping promote the School of Social Work at Loyola University. Meder expanded the league's labor orientation and its support for greater government involvement in the public welfare. Once in government, she promoted economic justice for the poor and the protection and regulation of female sexuality. Just as she had told *New World* readers that they were all responsible for protecting young girls, once in government Meder made the case that providing for the disadvantaged and the exploited was the responsibility of everyone in the city. She made her arguments on the basis of Catholic social teaching, although many of her proposals were controversial even within the Catholic community.

Politicians, Reformers, and Schoolmarms
CWL Women on the Board of Education

The women of the CWL received the majority of their appointments to serve in government between 1908 and 1917. Although they had already cooperated with other women reformers on a nonpartisan basis, it was during these years that they realized how competition among male politicians might also help them accomplish some of their goals. As political scientist and reformer Charles Merriam wrote in 1929, Catholics could be found "in all parties, all factions and in the countless combinations across party lines" that characterized Chicago's political landscape.[39] However, it was through the Democratic Party that CWL women achieved their greatest influence. They continued to cooperate with non-Catholic women reformers, but hitching their wagon to the Democratic Party enabled the CWL women to play a much more significant role in city government. Such partisan differences led, however, to a significant degree of conflict among club members.

Chicago School Board politics were notoriously contentious, and league women found themselves caught up in the controversy. The disputes often centered on the CTF, two leaders of which belonged to the CWL. While the fictional rescue stories in the *New World* tended to support labor unions, the school board controversies revealed bitter splits among league members on this issue.

The first CWL woman to serve on the school board, Isabelle O'Keeffe, played a key part in introducing several reforms into the public school system. She was respected enough to serve under both Republican and Democratic mayors; Republican Fred Busse first appointed her in 1903, and she would return in 1912 to serve under the Democrat Carter Harrison II. O'Keeffe's reform credentials were established by long service to the CWL. She was a charter member and vice president of the league during its first year of operation, 1893–1894, and she served as president for the next two years. The innovations she pioneered in the league were reflected later in her work on the school board; most notably, she headed the league when its settlements were founded and also fostered the settlement kindergartens. Once on the school board, she supported the introduction of kindergartens into the public school system. Catholic settlement women, like non-Catholic ones, were thus instrumental in bringing pioneering reforms into city government.[40]

As a backer and close personal friend of education reformer Ella Flagg Young, O'Keeffe was also instrumental in Young's appointment as Chicago's first female superintendent of schools in 1909. Young was backed strongly by the CWL, by other women reformers, and by teachers, although she faced prejudice from male members of the school board. O'Keefe's support helped keep Young on the list of candidates for the job, even though the other board members wanted to hire a man. When Young's quick wit and impressive intellect convinced the board to hire her, O'Keeffe persuaded them to pay her the same salary as the previous (male) superintendent. In 1910 O'Keefe even accompanied Young on a trip to San Francisco when Young was elected the first woman president of the National Education Association.[41]

While O'Keeffe served mayors of both parties, it was actually competition between various factions within the Democratic Party that enabled the CWL to gain the most positions in city government. Two of the leading Democratic contenders for mayor during the early twentieth century were Edward F. Dunne and Carter Harrison IV. Elected in 1905, Dunne was a genuine reformer who attracted enthusiastic support from certain prominent CWL members, particularly those concerned with education. A Catholic himself, Dunne also had the firm support of most of the city's priests, who were tired of seeing Catholic politicians connected with scandal. As one priest noted in 1898: "a certain element of politicians in Chicago . . . who claim to represent the Catholic Church . . . are the worst, most sinful, most degraded and most unscrupulous human beings in this great city." Such priests were delighted at Dunne's victory in the 1905 election. When Dunne later closed a number of all-night saloons and disreputable dance halls, the *New World* commented: "The Methodist parsons have been wanting this done for months and now a Catholic mayor has done it. . . . they will find that Catholic officials are not quite so immoral as they imagined."[42]

The league gained its most dramatic successes through its connections to the Carter Harrison dynasty within the Democratic Party. The elder Carter Harrison (Carter Harrison III) was first elected mayor in 1887. He served four consecutive terms and was reelected to a fifth term in 1893. A few months after being elected to his last term in office, he was assassinated by a disgruntled office seeker. John P. Hopkins filled his place, but soon a new Harrison was on Chicago's political scene. In 1897 Carter Harrison IV rode into the mayor's office on a wave of sympathy for his dead father. Like his father he was also elected to serve five terms as mayor.[43]

Both the Harrisons were extremely successful at winning reelection, largely because they appealed to a broad spectrum of voters. Rich, educated, and polished, they drew many voters who would normally have voted Republican. However, in building their political base, they also cobbled together a coalition of prohibition opponents, saloon owners, recent immigrants, and gamblers. The historian Paul Green argues that the two mayors did not have full-fledged political machines but merely collections of loyal followers. Appealing in particular to Irish and German voters, the Harrisons delivered low saloon license fees and loose restrictions on Sunday drinking. They won followers by allowing aldermen to control the saloons, brothels, and gambling establishments in their wards. Two of Carter Harrison Jr.'s chief supporters, for example, were "Bathhouse" John Coughlin, alderman of the First Ward, and his crony Michael "Hinky Dink" Kenna. In addition to housing Old St. Mary's Church, and later the Paulist fathers' settlement, the First Ward also contained the city's main vice district.[44]

Carter Harrison II was not Catholic himself but his wife, Edith, was. As a prominent member of the CWL, she was a considerable political asset to her husband. In fact she enhanced his appeal not only to Catholics but to elite voters as well. She was aristocratic, having been raised on a plantation in Louisiana, and was more comfortable than her husband with Chicago's most fashionable families such as the Potter Palmers and the Cyrus McCormicks. She represented an important link between Chicago's Catholic and the non-Catholic elite. She was also an author in her own right, producing books of fairy tales and romanticized stories of the antebellum South.[45]

Scholars have noted that Harrison's interest in repositioning himself as a reform candidate began in 1907, after he lost the Democratic mayoral nomination to Dunne, the reformer. In 1911 Dunne was again Harrison's opponent in the Democratic primary, while Republican reformer Charles Merriam opposed him in the general election. Harrison won his comeback bid, but he had been weakened by the length of time he had spent out of office and by the constant political infighting within the Democratic Party. Harrison needed new allies to shore up his position, and he turned to the CWL as a source of reformers with whom he already had ties (prominent non-Catholic reformers in the city often supported other parties or nonpartisan causes). He was motivated in part by the advent of women's suffrage in Illinois, where women won the vote in municipal elections in 1913. Many political analysts in the early twentieth century believed that women were strong supporters of reform, and Harrison hoped to win their votes.[46]

To bolster his reform credentials, Harrison started by appointing three CWL leaders (Tena Farren MacMahon, Helen V. Gallagher, and Florence Vosbrink) to positions on the school board between 1911 and 1914. All three women were past CWL presidents. Vosbrink was also an active member of the Illinois Women's Democratic League and served as president of the First District of Women's Clubs in Illinois. MacMahon and Gallagher would turn out to be more credible reformers than Vosbrink, because they cooperated more with non-Catholic women reformers and supported the Chicago Teachers Federation. Harrison succeeded in winning the backing of the CTF and other reformers in the 1915 election, but unfortunately, this was not enough to defeat Robert M. Sweitzer, his opponent in the Democratic primary. Sweitzer himself lost the election by a thin margin to Republican boss William "Big Bill" Thompson, who ran on an "anti-Catholic . . . anti-German and anti–Gas Company" platform.[47]

When he was elected in 1915 Thompson reportedly planned to "get rid of the army of Catholic school teachers." Soon after the election, MacMahon, Gallagher, and Vosbrink along with the rest of the school board became caught up in a dispute entailing a number of lawsuits and an intervention by the city council. The incident revealed splits among the CWL women over labor issues, and specifically over the CTF. After decades of low pay and lack of respect from the board, the teachers formed the federation in an attempt to improve their status. Led by CWL members Margaret Haley and Catherine Goggin, the board affiliated with the Chicago Federation of Labor (CFL) and soon became one of the most militant and politically active unions in the city. Haley was close friends with CWL member Anna Fitzpatrick, and a political ally of her husband, CFL president John Fitzpatrick. Haley helped Fitzpatrick when he ran for mayor in 1918 as the candidate of the Chicago Farmer Labor Party. The teachers' decision to unionize provoked stiff opposition from business groups and the conservative *Chicago Tribune*.[48]

Once on the school board, Tena MacMahon and Helen Gallagher became advocates for the teachers and their right to organize while Florence Vosbrink opposed the CTF. MacMahon and Vosbrink had been the leaders of competing factions within the CWL since at least 1909. Appointed to the school board in 1911 to succeed Isabelle O'Keeffe, MacMahon was a former schoolteacher whose father was former school-board member John

Farren. At a meeting of the National Conference of Catholic Charities in 1914, MacMahon delivered a paper echoing the *Rerum Novarum* in its emphasis on the rights of the poor. Appointed a board member in 1913, Helen Gallagher was president of the CWL for two years and also served two years as president of the Illinois Federation of Women's Clubs. Appointed to the board in 1913, Florence Vosbrink was a charter member of the CWL and had held all the offices of the league in succession. She also served as the vice president of the Illinois Federation of Women's Clubs and was active in the Illinois Women's Democratic League.[49]

In 1916 the board passed a measure called the Loeb Rule, which forbade teachers from belonging to the CTF. Soon thereafter, a segment of the board fired sixty-eight teachers, including all the officers of the CTF. In defending the teachers, MacMahon noted that many of those being fired had received high marks for good teaching. At least one of the fired teachers, Alice Keary, was a member of the CWL. Gallagher defended Keary in the meeting, stating: "I protest. That teacher has been in the service and her marks are excellent right straight through. It does seem hard to throw her out without any explanation." Standing against the teachers, Vosbrink objected when MacMahon, Gallagher, and other board members tried to prevent the vote that would fire them. The rhetoric of the meeting descended to a remarkable low point when the president of the board declared: "You cannot force me to give my reasons [for firing the teachers] if I don't want to give them." Another board member added: "Let the record show that you are turning those people out into the street without any means of support. It is a cowardly trick."[50]

As the controversy dragged on, a current of anti-Catholicism was revealed among the opponents of the CTF, which makes Vosbrink's position seem, to say the least, uncomfortable. As a former teacher herself, Vosbrink's actions on the board reflect the degree of controversy that existed, even among teachers and CWL members, concerning the wisdom of unionization. Yet politics also makes strange bedfellows; many people who opposed the CTF did so because of their hatred for Catholics. For example, a band of Nativists called the Guardians of Liberty publicly supported the firing of the teachers. One anonymous letter to the city council strangely accused Vosbrink, former president of the CWL, of being friendly with the Guardians. The leader of the Guardians is supposed to have said that "Margaret Haley and her gang [at the CTF] . . . are trying to get control of the public schools to turn them over to the Pope of Rome." Other letters accused the church of political manipulation to get Catholics installed as public school teachers.[51]

In the end the prolabor segment of the CWL ended up having far more influence than the antilabor women: those who supported the teachers won at least a substantial, though not complete, victory. The city council and a number of prominent reformers such as Jane Addams,

Mary McDowell, and Charles Merriam came out in support of the sixty-eight teachers. After a number of lawsuits and investigations by the city council, the sixty-eight teachers were rehired and the Loeb Rule was eliminated so that teachers were allowed to join the CTF. In 1917 a teacher-tenure law was passed that prevented teachers from being fired arbitrarily in the future. By the early 1920s six of Thompson's appointees to the board wound up going to jail for engaging in various forms of graft. The CTF, however, was weakened by the conflict and ended up losing a substantial amount of membership. It also withdrew its affiliation from the Chicago chapter of the American Federation of Labor, thus ending its connection to the larger labor movement in the city. Some speculated that Margaret Haley agreed to disaffiliate as part of a deal to get the teachers their jobs back. Several years later, although they did not choose to do so, the CTF won the right to affiliate with organized labor once again.[52]

MacMahon's and Gallagher's efforts on behalf of the teachers were part of a larger effort to defend the rights of city employees to unionize. Their service helped support prolabor forces within city government and thus helped shape the state. Their effectiveness was enhanced because they were able to form an important bridge between non-Catholic women reformers and Democrats like Carter Harrison IV. As scholars have noted, many Progressive reforms passed with the support of "bosses" and their constituents. The work of Catholic women reformers in creating ties among women reformers and Democratic "bosses" like the Harrisons has largely gone unnoticed by scholars. O'Keeffe's support for Ella Flagg Young and the cooperation of MacMahon, Gallagher, and prominent non-Catholic reformers on behalf of the teachers suggest that we have only just begun to uncover the real importance of laywomen's mediating role between these groups. Yet if the women formed a bridge between women reformers and Democrats, anti-Catholicism could still wash out the bridge. Teachers themselves were split about the role of Catholics in the public schools, and fomenting religious divisions was a highly effective strategy of the Thompson forces to weaken the CTF. Ironically, if Protestants were ambivalent about the role of Catholics in shaping the state, Catholics themselves were also ambivalent about the expanding role of government in the provision of social services. The latter issue would be addressed by Leonora Meder, head of the city's new Department of Public Welfare.

Expanding the State
Leonora Meder at the Department of Public Welfare

When Mayor Carter Harrison chose her in 1914 to preside over the establishment of a new government agency, Leonora Meder literally helped expand the state. As the first director of the city's Department of Public

Welfare, her work consisted of putting the department on a firm footing. She set up the department's two bureaus, one that conducted research into social conditions and another that provided direct services to the needy. Her obvious experience and professionalism helped make her work acceptable to social service professionals, and she cultivated ties to both Catholic and non-Catholic reformers. In office she worked to gain the acceptance of Catholics for an expansion of government social services, even though some feared that government would usurp the work of the church. Like the school-board members MacMahon and Gallagher, Meder served as a bridge between non-Catholic women reformers and the Democrats, and she also fostered cooperation between the department and private women's organizations. While she helped make the department broadly acceptable to as many people as possible, Meder's views shaped its work. Like MacMahon and Gallagher, she brought a labor orientation into city government, and she used her position to speak for the rights of workers and the poor.

The new department combined two of the main interests of Progressive Era social work: direct service to the poor and research into the causes of poverty. It had two subordinate bureaus: the Bureau of Employment operated municipal lodging houses for men and women, and the Bureau of Social Survey conducted research. Under Meder's watch, the department conducted investigations of unemployment, lodging houses, city parks, playgrounds, and housing in the Seventeenth Ward Italian district. The department also began compiling a directory of charity and relief agencies in Chicago for greater coordination and efficiency of poor-relief services.[53]

In explaining her work to the *New World* readers, Meder drew much of her inspiration from the papal encyclical *Rerum Novarum*, which, in the context of increasing worldwide industrial conflict, outlined the rights and responsibilities of the poor, the rich, and the government. Pope Leo XIII, the encyclical's author, tried to walk a middle line between socialism and laissez-faire economics. While prohibiting the seizure of private property by states, *Rerum* allowed for limited government intervention to provide assistance to the poor, as long as the government did not interfere with the historic charitable role of the church. The encyclical also urged governments to protect the economic interests of the working class, in order to create industrial peace and to protect family life. *Rerum* also endorsed labor organizing, as long as it was not socialist, to help secure adequate wages and working conditions. *Rerum* stressed the obligation of the rich to help the poor and noted that the poor had obligations toward the rich as well. It condemned the idea that capital and labor were naturally in conflict, arguing instead that they were dependent upon one another.[54]

Rerum Novarum taught that a male worker had a right to wages adequate to support himself, his wife, and his children in frugal respectability. He should have safe working conditions and adequate rest to preserve his health and strength, and enough time away from work in order to be able to attend church on Sundays and on holy days of obligation. Female workers, especially, were to be preserved from immoral working conditions. Ideally, married women would be spared the need to work outside the home at all because their husbands received adequate wages to support a family. Workers, in turn, were obligated to work faithfully, to avoid violence, and to refrain from harming wealthy persons or their property.[55]

Inspired by *Rerum,* as well as by Catholic thinkers such as John Ryan and Frederic Siedenburg, Meder favored government programs to alleviate poverty, particularly social insurance to relieve unemployment, accidents, sickness, and old age. She publicly supported the formation of labor unions. During an industrial downturn in 1915, the Department of Welfare opened a municipal employment bureau to counteract the city's numerous corrupt private employment agencies. Such agencies would charge a fee to find somebody a job but after a short period of time working, the person would be fired and replaced. By filling the same jobs over and over again, the corrupt agents would make a living by collecting placement fees. Meder proposed the employment bureau be made permanent, but it was dismantled after her tenure in office expired.[56]

Meder's approach to relief resembled the "paternalist" welfare states of Europe more than the "maternalist" emphasis that historians have noted among American reformers. Maternalism has been defined as "ideologies or discourses that exalted women's capacity to mother and applied to society as a whole the values they attached to that role: care, nurturance, and morality."[57] While Meder certainly endorsed the notion that government should care for its citizens, she was less comfortable with specific policies often promoted by maternalists. For example, she gave only a limited endorsement to mothers' pensions, which many non-Catholic reformers were promoting as compensation for mothers' work in producing and raising citizens for the state. Some people also favored the pensions because in theory they reinforced the ideal that mothers should remain in the home with their children, even though the pensions rarely paid enough to keep mothers out of the workforce entirely. At the same time Catholic reformers in Europe were endorsing "family allowances," allotments paid to families with young children and mothers at home in order to promote childbearing and encourage women to leave the paid workforce. Meder suggested that these pensions would be useful in the short run because they would help stop family breakups because of poverty, however, she argued that "my personal opinion of the Mothers' Fund is that it is wrong in theory. It claims to be a pension, but it is not a reward for work done, and in its essence, is charity pure and simple. . . . it will have a tendency to pauperize these families." Instead, she argued, social insurance would alleviate sickness, old age, unemployment, and widowhood without "pauperizing" families by forcing them to rely on charity.[58]

Like the paternalist welfare states in Europe, Meder focused on channeling social insurance benefits to families through male breadwinners Theoretically, such proposals could make day nurseries like the ones run by the CWL obsolete by enabling more poor mothers to stay home. For Meder, willingness to work was one of the obligations of good citizenship, especially for men. When faced with unemployment, "strong, earnest men, American citizens and fathers of families" would not beg for charity but would plead for work. Meder's vision for a municipal employment bureau would specialize in finding talented and dedicated workers, and in matching the right worker for the right job. Ultimately, she believed, the agency would not merely benefit individual workers but, by helping employers find workers more efficiently, would improve the economy as a whole.[59]

While Meder was inspired by *Rerum Novarum,* she took rights language even farther than *Rerum* did, by arguing for a right to work. Further, she argued that it was the responsibility of all Americans, through the mechanism of the state, to help individuals find work. *Rerum* argued that workers had a right to their wages because these represented private property, but the document did not mention work itself as a right. Meder, on the other hand, posed the question to *New World* readers: "Is there justice in the claim that the worker has a 'right' to be cared for by other means than [charity]? Or has the man out of employment no 'rights' at all?" The solution, she continued, was a choice: "Either we leave the worker to struggle for himself . . . turn him over to the tender mercies of bread lines and soup kitchens . . . or accept the problems of unemployment as a public burden to be shouldered by the public the same as problems of health, education, and protection." With the onset of industrialization and the closing of the frontier, Meder argued, the days of laissez-faire were over. Only government intervention could fulfill community obligations to the individual and ensure industrial and social peace. Meder advocated unemployment bureaus and job creation by government as ways that the public could fulfill its obligations toward the unemployed worker. As head of the Department of Welfare, Meder established community gardens for the unemployed, thus reinforcing the idea that citizens collectively owed individuals reasonable help in making a living.[60]

For Meder men's right to work stemmed from their roles as fathers of families, but women had a right to economic justice as well, primarily because it would enable them to fulfill their main responsibility as citizens: conformity to the church's teachings about sexuality. Meder noted that dishonest employment agents cheated women as they cheated men by providing only short-term employment and making it impossible for the worker to make a living. "What type of citizens," she asked, "are we cultivating, on both hands, and where lies the blame?" Meder went on to blame Greek restaurant owners for hiring young Polish women in conditions that encouraged sexual exploitation. Not only were the girls overworked and underpaid, which could encourage prostitution in order to make ends meet, she suggested that owners were also pressuring them for sexual favors, noting: "We are not making for a respectable and safe citizenship when we permit men to debase themselves and ruin girls' lives as they are doing [so]."[61]

Like MacMahon and Gallagher, Meder advocated a prolabor stance while fostering cooperation and ties between various groups that helped expand the role of government. As a leader in women's clubs, for example, Meder stressed cooperation between the Department of Welfare and such private organizations. In keeping with the professional standards of the day, Meder advocated prevention of social problems in her role as head of the Protectorate, and she continued to do so once she was in government. She explicitly noted that women's clubs had already been doing preventative work, and she argued that the government should follow their lead. In order to prevent crime and sexual delinquency, she recommended that the city construct more parks and playgrounds to keep children off the streets. In the city jails, she argued, young boys should no longer be housed with the adult women, many of whom were drunken prostitutes. She suggested finding other lodgings for "respectable" women who were merely poor and had no other place to sleep. She proposed that building treatment centers would be more helpful for alcoholic women than merely letting them sleep off their intoxication in jail.[62]

Like non-Catholic women reformers of her day, Meder continued to rely upon her ties to women's clubs and organizations after she entered government. In December 1914, while she was head of the Department of Welfare, the CWL Protectorate took up the issue of child labor. Meder had served on a committee that drew up a bill for the Illinois state legislature; the bill would eliminate labor by children under sixteen while school was in session. A compulsory education law would then bring the children into the schools. The Protectorate took upon itself the task of educating parents on the issue, to convince them that they should sacrifice their children's wages in order to let them benefit from additional education. Together, Meder and the Protectorate hoped to create better citizens for the state and believers for the church.[63]

Meder argued that both government and private charities would benefit from cooperation with one another. She believed that private agencies like the CWL were better equipped than government to help foster "civic feeling" among citizens, a sense of obligation to help the less fortunate. She argued that private charities would benefit as well, because government and private organizations were interdependent: "[Civic feeling] gives to people a sense of communal obligation towards those questions which were once regarded as purely charitable. Private charitable enterprises must foster this civic activity . . . because public and private agencies have become so dependent on one another that one cannot succeed if the other fails." *Rerum Novarum,* on the other hand, argued that the obligation of the rich to help the poor was a duty "not of justice (save in extreme cases). but of Christian charity—a duty not enforced by law."[64]

In her new office Meder sought to convince Catholics that they should embrace the movement of government into public welfare. Further, she promoted a broad definition of the role of government—broader, in fact, than the one proposed in *Rerum*. In a paper presented before the National Conference of Catholic Charities in 1914, she proposed that the state needed to take "an active interest in every individual citizen . . . [teach] him to lead a sane, moral life . . . [protect] him from the results of his ignorance, and . . . [shelter] him from the crushing wheels of economic abuses." Further, when help was available, church organizations should not hesitate to make full use of government funds and other resources. Even though *Rerum* endorsed a role for government, Meder encountered reluctance among Catholics to endorse an expansion of the role of government, for both practical and ideological reasons. Meder's paper at the National Conference of Catholic Charities was sharply criticized. Some of the conference participants, including Sallie Grieves Gaynor of the CWL, complained about government ineptitude and red tape. Gaynor spoke about trying to obtain mothers' pensions for mothers in the CWL day nurseries and noted that the benefits were difficult to obtain and inadequate to keep the mother in the home full-time.[65]

Other Catholic charity workers were reluctant to embrace government welfare programs, in part because of an aversion to anything that smacked of socialism, but primarily in the fear that government would usurp the role of the church. One commentator, Robert Biggs of the St. Vincent de Paul Society in Baltimore, argued that teaching people to lead sane and moral lives was the work of the church, not the state. Biggs was applauded by listeners when he argued that the church should oppose the movement to vest new powers in the state because "the Catholic Church is . . . the greatest conservative force in the world." Defending Meder from this criticism, her mentor Frederic Siedenburg noted that government was forced to step in when individuals failed to live up to the teachings of the church: "If the rich were to heed the Gospel and remember that their riches are not their absolute possession, but that they are stewards of those riches for the needs of their fellowmen, we would not need or have so much state interference."[66]

The election of 1915 illustrates the limitations faced by laywomen when they relied on the Democratic Party to achieve their goals. When Carter Harrison lost and Republican boss Big Bill Thompson won, Thompson promptly replaced Meder. She never held such high office again, although the Democrats did nominate her for municipal judge in 1922. She returned to women's club work and served as national judge advocate for the Catholic Daughters of America in 1927, as president of the Chicago Business and Professional Women's Club in 1935, and as a colonel in the Daughters of the Confederacy, also in 1935.[67]

Meder's replacement at the Department of Public Welfare was Louise Osborne Rowe, a corrupt political hack who did not share Meder's opinions about the rights of the poor. Her first act upon taking office was to establish a municipal wood yard, where poor men were forced to chop wood before they could receive shelter at the municipal lodging house. In a time of economic depression, the poor were forced to perform hard labor before they could have even a miserable cot on which to sleep. Rowe was appointed because she had been a campaign worker for Thompson. She was widely seen as incompetent by activist women of all faiths and affiliations: even Republican women begged Thompson to appoint someone else. Thompson ignored their pleas, and in 1916 Rowe was accused of demanding kickbacks from employees of the Department of Public Welfare.[68]

Meder's term in office demonstrates that, among the CWL women, those with a prolabor stance and a reform orientation achieved far more influence than those who were conservative on these issues. The prolabor women played a much larger role in the expansion of the state and succeeded to a greater extent in shaping this expansion to reflect the best interests of working class and the poor. The fact that many male Democrats, especially on the city council, already had a prolabor orientation certainly enhanced their efforts. Party politics enabled these women to achieve positions of prominence, but once they were in office they did not forget the women's clubs that had launched their careers in the first place. As Catholics, CWL members were uniquely situated to foster ties between women reformers and Democrats such as Carter Harrison. Their club work gave them ties to reformers, Catholic and non-Catholic alike, while their religion gave them more access than most reformers to the Democratic Party. The relationship was more equivocal for the Democrats: Harrison's strategy of transforming himself into a reformer did not work and he lost in large part because he had alienated his former, more colorful supporters. However, in the long run the efforts of the CWL women did make a difference to party politics. In helping overcome the reluctance of some of the faithful to see an expanded role for the state in social service provisions, the CWL played a part in creating Catholic support for programs that foreshadowed those of the New Deal.

Catholic Women and the State

The *New World* embraced Leonora Meder as soon as she was appointed in 1914, clearly delighted to have a Catholic at the head of such an important city agency. The paper framed her as a labor advocate and a civic and moral reformer, explaining that the new city department would "create new standards for the workers, for civic righteousness and public morals."[69] The paper may have been highly critical of non-Catholic reformers but home-grown reformers were another matter. Those writers who criticized non-Catholic reformers as "immoral freaks" probably viewed the non-Catholics as competing with the church for the allegiance of the urban working class. Meder and the other CWL women did not have that problem, but they did suffer another drawback from the point of view of male church leaders. They were women, and laywomen at that. None of the fictional rescue stories ever featured a woman as a powerful government official, which suggests a certain amount of clerical discomfort with women in such leadership roles. Forced to choose between conservative gender roles and applauding the civic leadership of laywomen, male church leaders chose to endorse the work of these women because it would win greater prestige for Catholics in the city as a whole. Later, priests and laymen would reclaim this public role for themselves. In the interim, however, the women's leadership was important.

Their gender may have limited the CWL reformers as leaders in the eyes of the hierarchy and the Catholic press, but gender also made possible the CWL women's role as a bridge between non-Catholic reformers and Democrats. The league women had established relationships with non-Catholic women reformers through years of cooperation in lobbying and travelers' aid work. Gender could provide an area of commonality with non-Catholic women. The efforts done in professionalizing the social work of the CWL also enabled Catholics to cooperate more closely with and be more respected by non-Catholics. The Catholic women's ties to the Democrats were more direct, including friendship, family relations, and mutual acquaintance through Catholic social circles.

It was their status as reformers friendly to the Democrats that enabled laywomen to play a role in shaping the state, helping establish a new government agency and defend the rights of labor once they were in positions of power. As a club the CWL could also appeal to the Democrats as a source of potential voters who were already organized as well as generally sympathetic to the party. Unfortunately for Harrison, they could not help him attract enough new voters to keep his position as mayor. Other Democrats would benefit more in the long term. The role of laywomen in establishing ties between reformers and Democrats, as well as the work of CWL women in convincing more of the faithful to accept an expanded role for the government social services, represented steps toward the New Deal era, in which urban Catholics came to form the bedrock constituency of such proposals. By the New Deal, however, the clerical hierarchy had firmly regained their place as the public face of the church, laywomen's organizations had been more firmly subordinated to centralized church charities, and the work of laywomen had started to be forgotten.

When one is focused upon the workings of Chicago's political system, it is easy to forget the constituency that made possible the laywomen's successes in the first place. It is easy to forget that all of these laywomen's efforts began with a plan that relied upon the labors of day nursery mothers and kitchengarten students, paid matrons and unpaid volunteers, and the pennies of little children to improve the economic standing of Chicago's Catholic community. Increased financial stability improved the lives of the poor and, at the same time, enhanced the prestige of the denomination in the city as a whole. In an era when nativism and anti-Catholicism lurked beneath the surface of public debates, every little bit helped. But winning the allegiance of the urban working class entailed more than just exhorting them to self-sufficiency. Rather, Catholic settlements had to compete for leadership on a neighborhood level. Their competitors were nonsectarian reformers, Protestant missionaries, ethnic leaders, and sometimes even parish priests.

Proprietary settlements shared certain commonalities with club-model settlements like those of the CWL. Club-model settlements had an advantage, in that they could draw upon the financial support and volunteer labor of the club members in order to function. Yet the two models were similar in that both included a political component. While the proprietary settlements would launch no female candidates into public office, they did seek to win a constituency. In competing on a local level with Protestants and others for influence over Chicago's Italians, American laywomen sought to ensure a place for themselves and their peers as leaders in the city. Thus gaining influence over a clientele, these Catholic women could make a case for greater influence both in the city's growing social welfare bureaucracy, and even within the church.

CHAPTER THREE

Sacred Space and Worldly Authority

The Guardian Angel Mission

In January 1903 a group of Sunday school teachers from Guardian Angel Mission wrote a letter describing their work. They noted that Italian immigrants had begun to move into Holy Family parish in the 1890s, and that the Irish parishioners had started missionary work among them by 1898. The teachers described the Italians as leaderless: "Comparatively few of their clergy accompany them to this new land and so, puzzled and strangely alone these poor emigrants drift along—sheer faith never dead but sadly dormant." Seeing no Italian priests, the Sunday school teachers could see no leaders they recognized as legitimate. However, the highly contested neighborhood in which the mission was located was brimming with would-be leaders. Right around the corner from Guardian Angel Mission was the renowned secular settlement Hull House, which the missionaries regarded as a competitor for the loyalties of the Italians. The missionaries also feuded with Italian ethnic leaders, including nationalists, socialists, and anticlericals, many of whom found Hull House a congenial base of operations. The missionaries blamed Italian *padrone* (labor bosses) and landlords for exploiting their poor countrymen and women. Worst of all, a number of Protestant missions dotted the neighborhood, aiming specifically to convert the Italians. The laywomen of Guardian Angel Mission viewed these other potential leaders as not having the true interests of the immigrants at heart. In contrast, they thought of themselves as "social-minded" gentry, laboring diligently for the material and spiritual well-being of the Italians.[1]

On a citywide level laywomen served as a bridge between non-Catholic women reformers and the Democratic Party. However, on the West Side of Chicago the work of the laywomen's settlements involved more intense competition than cooperation with non-Catholics. Just as each group of leaders aspired to gain influence over the Italians, each group also made their claims to authority based on their location in city space. Because their locations overlapped and their target population was the same, they could hardly fail to wind up in competition with each other. By asserting authority over the Italians, the Guardian Angel missionaries aimed to win a battle for souls, snatching victory from Protestant missionaries and others who wanted to save the Italians from the pope. Fighting this battle for souls enabled the missionaries to construct themselves as benevolent gentry, thus giving themselves a boost in status. As with the CWL settlements, the founders of Guardian Angel Mission relied upon the labor of many people, including the volunteer Sunday school teachers, in order to keep the institution running. In addition the Italians, while constructed by their would-be leaders as recipients of largesse or targets for conversion, also helped build Guardian Angel while fighting in their own way to use and define the spaces of the West Side.

Ethnic Succession and Sacred Space

The founders of Chicago's proprietary settlements resembled the more affluent heroines of the rescue stories. Proprietary settlements were run by individual women of means, who used their families' money to bankroll the settlements. While the CWL settlements hired matrons to run their operations, the wealthy women of the proprietary settlements ran the institutions themselves, recruiting help from among their friends and relations. At first the story of the proprietary settlements sounds like the typical scenario of wealthy ladies descending on the poor with largesse and Bibles, but the situation at Guardian Angel was in fact more complex. The Ambergs, the family who ran Guardian Angel Mission, were indeed wealthy, but their wealth had been recently acquired. In fact they had started out as middle-class in the Holy Family parish and had acquired their money through a combination of hard work and good fortune. Like many of Holy Family's parishioners, as they rose in social status they chose to move away from the industrial West Side in search of better housing. Yet even as they yearned to escape the dilapidated buildings and meatpacking plants of the neighborhood, the Irish of Holy Family longed nostalgically for the community they had left behind. The history of the parish became imbued with mythic significance—they came to view it as sacred space.[2] The Ambergs drew upon this founding mythology to invent themselves as gentry who could claim the authority to run Guardian Angel.

Guardian Angel Mission was founded just as the Irish members of Holy Family parish and their German neighbors began to move out of the neighborhood. Holy Family's congregation, large and thriving in 1890, had begun to shrink by 1900. In 1890 the parish owned property valued at nearly half a million dollars. It had almost 4,700 families on its rolls, comprising 21,000 individuals. Its priests performed 194 marriages and 1,181 baptisms during the year. During the 1880s and 1890s the congregation was so vast that the confirmation classes could have as many as 900 children and 40 or 50 adults. But by 1898, the year the Guardian Angel Mission was founded, the parish had started to shrink. The 1898 parish annual report shows 3,000 families on its rolls and 13,000 individuals total. By 1915 the church had only about 900 families, 225 single people, and a total of about 3,400 parishioners. By 1920 it had a mere 400 families, 130 single men and women, and a total of 1,600 parishioners.[3]

Some blamed the parish's decline on newcomers to the neighborhood, but the causes were complex. As the Irish and Germans moved out of the neighborhood in search of better housing, many "new" immigrant groups were moving in, including Italians, Poles, Greeks, and Russian Jews. Large numbers of Italian children were admitted to the parochial school, to take the seats left vacant by departing Holy Family parishioners. While some old parishioners left to escape the new arrivals, others went in search of better housing. As one observer noted: "The neighborhood had undergone little or no change from the time of the great Chicago fire in 1871. The same old shanties erected then, were beginning to show the ravages of time. . . . Just as soon as [the Irish and Bohemians] acquired the means, most of them moved away." The neighborhood also experienced economic dislocation when cable and electric car lines were built. The West Side retail district declined as people obtained easy access to the Loop. Further, some of the parish's most important institutions left to follow the old parishioners. In 1906 Loyola University moved to Rogers Park, and in 1907 the Sacred Heart Academy moved to the distant northern suburb of Lake Forest.[4]

The missionaries of Guardian Angel in many ways resembled other neighborhood Irish leaders who tried to maintain their power after their constituencies had evaporated. Longtime boss of the ward Alderman Johnny Powers, for example, attempted to appeal to the Italians—even taking on the Italianized nickname "Johnny de Pow." Hull House had tried several times to unseat Powers, pitting reformers against him and always losing. In the end, however, the Italians proved more of a threat to Powers than Hull House ever could. As political scientist Charles Merriam noted later, "only a gerrymander of the ward saved Johnny, and for his home he sought more elegant quarters outside, from which he still ruled the ward."[5]

Years after the neighborhood changed, people from Holy Family talked nostalgically about the parish's early history, when the neighborhood population was largely Irish, German, and Scandinavian. The church was founded in 1857 when, beginning as a stretch of virgin prairie, the area was a far cry from the bustling neighborhood it would become. In these early years Holy Family developed an image as a frontier church, which parishioners would remember even after the meatpacking plants moved in and people crowded into the neighborhood in search of jobs.[6] Over time clergy and parishioners maintained the frontier image by telling stories about the parish, stories that helped define the parish as sacred space and that helped create a parish identity at once Catholic, American, and specific to Chicago. Because Chicago itself was also taking shape during the parish's early years, these stories helped parishioners situate themselves in the growing metropolis and helped them steel themselves against critics who viewed Catholics as not fully American.

During the 1920s Brother Thomas Mulkerins, S.J., former sacristan of the church, wrote a history of the parish, beginning his story with Jacques Marquette, a Jesuit and the first white man to camp on the site of present-day Chicago. Mulkerins claimed that Marquette had pitched his tent within the boundaries of Holy Family parish, thus crediting the area as the original site of the city.[7] From Pere Marquette, Mulkerins moved on to another founding father in Chicago's history, the Reverend Arnold Damen, S.J. By telling stories about Father Damen, Mulkerins sought to endow Holy Family with pioneer status. Lionized as a sort of Paul Bunyan of priests, Damen built Holy Family Church from the ground up, on the virgin prairie. He first contracted for the construction of a temporary wood-frame church, to be completed in 1857. Even though the late 1850s were a time of severe depression, the permanent church was dedicated in 1860. It was a proud towering building of brick with trim of Illinois cut stone, in the Gothic style. It seemed like a miraculous thing to have sprouted from the mud of the prairie.[8]

Mulkerins emphasized Damen's great physical strength and powerful masculinity as a measure of his pioneer status, connecting his persona with a developing mythology that sacralized the parish. Mulkerins emphasized Damen's spiritual power in addition to his physical prowess. Parishioners credited Damen's prayers with saving Holy Family Church from the great fire in 1871. Damen himself said that the Virgin Mary had saved the church in answer to his prayers; in order to thank her, he always kept seven lights burning in the church before a small shrine to Our Lady of Perpetual Help.[9] This legend, along with other stories of miracles associated with Damen, helped construct Holy Family parish as sacred space in the eyes of parishioners.

Years later the resident director of Madonna Center also helped perpetuate the idea of Holy Family parish as sacred space, linking the history of the parish to her portrayal of her mother as a rescuer of the poor. Mary Amberg described her mother, Agnes, as exhibiting not only the requisite compassion for the poor and profound faith but also efficiency, drive, and determination. She compared Agnes to Jane Addams, noting that Agnes "wasted no time 'twixt rising and breakfasting, could complete her toilette for the day and be off about her business while the ordinary sort of woman should be studying the merits of two different shades of mascara." Unceasing in her efforts to help others, Agnes ran errands of mercy at night or during the early hours of the morning, even after she had spent a long day laboring at the mission.[10]

Born in Chicago in 1847 to James and Mary Hickson Ward, Agnes was a Holy Family parishioner from the early years. As an adult Agnes remembered being driven across the open prairie, every Sunday during her childhood, to attend Mass. Before Agnes was nine years old her mother died. At twelve she became one of the first boarding pupils of the elite Sacred Heart Convent School on Taylor Street, which was then under the care of the upright and formidable Mother Galway. In 1867, at the age of twenty, Agnes received her academic certificate from the convent school, a high level of education for a woman of that period.[11]

Although Agnes Amberg gained pioneer status from being an old settler of Chicago, the Amberg family did not start off as the aristocrats their daughter Mary would later portray them to be. In 1869 Agnes married a young man who was not rich but who was as ambitious as she. William A. Amberg was born in Albstadt, Bavaria, in 1847 and grew up in Mineral Point, Wisconsin. He moved to Chicago in 1865 to attend a commercial college. He founded the stationary company of Cameron, Amberg, & Co., making his fortune by inventing a loose-leaf filing system. His business suddenly became immensely successful after the Great Fire in 1871—the files of many Chicago companies had burned up and they needed to be replaced. Amberg was one of the only stationers whose stocks had not burned, so he soon became very prosperous. Active in politics and public service, he was one of the founders of the Columbus Club, a social club for laymen. For ten years he was president of the Catholic Library Association, and he also supported the Illinois Catholic Historical Society. He was on the board of St. Mary's Training School, a school for dependent children. He was also a Democrat who served as jury commissioner for the city of Chicago from 1907 to 1915.[12]

Even as a schoolgirl Agnes was described by the Mesdames of the Sacred Heart as "determined to make something of her life." As an adult, outside the long hours she spent running Guardian Angel Mission, she was also a member of the Catholic Woman's League. She belonged to the Children of Mary, the alumnae association of the Sacred Heart convent schools. In 1895 she founded a ladies' reading circle. She helped bring to Chicago the nuns of the Cenacle, an order that promoted spiritual retreats for laywomen. She was on the boards of St. Vincent's Orphan Asylum and the House of the Good Shepherd, and she ran the Chicago chapter of the Christ Child Society, which gave baby clothes to poor mothers at Christmas.[13]

Even though the Ambergs were substantially more prosperous than most Holy Family parishioners, their lives did reflect in some ways the larger experience of the parish. Agnes was of Irish descent, William was a German immigrant, and both these groups were well represented in the neighborhood's early history. Holy Family was primarily Irish, while nearby St. Francis of Assisi Church accommodated the German Catholic population. Like other Holy Family parishioners, the Ambergs also moved out of the parish when they became more affluent. Even in the 1870s the area east of Halsted, especially around Maxwell Street, was already a slum, crowded with poor people who worked in the area's shops and factories. Near the river, the parish was largely industrial, housing railroad and lumberyards, sawmills, and grain elevators. It also had stockyards, slaughterhouses, and meatpacking establishments.[14]

Like many other Holy Family parishioners the Ambergs retained ties to Holy Family after they moved. Their moves can be traced in Chicago's directory of elite families, the *Blue Book*. In 1879 the Amberg family home was on Sheldon Street, situated between a wealthy area near Union Park and a poorer one in Holy Family parish.[15] Their house seems to have been outside the boundaries of Holy Family, yet close enough that they could still socialize with members of the parish. In addition, Agnes and William sent their daughters to the Sacred Heart Convent School, further reinforcing their links to the old parish. In 1900 the family moved to a fashionable mansion on North Avenue, yet the work of the mission kept them coming back to the neighborhood.[16]

While many of Holy Family's founding legends had no doubt been told since the parish's early years, they took on extra significance in an era when so many of the parishioners were moving away. The parish had been imagined as the first site of the city of Chicago, a place of pioneers, miracles, and inspiring spiritual leaders. Like Alderman Johnny Powers, who tried to maintain his control of the ward long after his natural constituents had moved away, the parishioners of Holy Family were reluctant to let go of such a place even after they themselves had relocated. While some demonstrated hostility toward the newcomers, as if the Italians were responsible for Holy Family's decline, others realized that the influx of a new group of Catholics offered an opportunity to reconnect with the sacred space of the West Side. The Ambergs, among others, seized the opportunity to become missionaries to the Italians, a work that involved transforming the spaces of the West Side yet again. This labor enabled the new missionaries to imagine they were recapitulating the pioneering role of Damen and the others who built a church and created a community on the virgin prairie.

Origins of Guardian Angel Mission

Just as the Jesuits, the sisters, and the parishioners of Holy Family had transformed the neighborhood during the late nineteenth century by building numerous institutions to care for the burgeoning population of

Irish, so the arrival of the Italians would again reshape the spaces of the West Side. For a variety of reasons, the Italians were often turned away from existing churches. Hence, in order to missionize them, new spaces that were more welcoming had to be established. Official accounts suggest that a handful of Jesuits took the initiative, recruiting laywomen to begin the mission work among the Italians. The laywomen themselves took more initiative than the official accounts reveal, as they created worship spaces that they hoped would establish among the Italians the authority of neighborhood clergy. Even before the new Guardian Angel Mission had its own priest, hundreds of women volunteers had established a chapel and a Sunday school, in effect laying the framework for a parish and a settlement house. Intending to bolster the authority of the clergy, the women obtained some authority in the neighborhood in their own right, by establishing and running a new institution, which would then enable them to compete with local Italian leaders for influence over the immigrants, even though they sometimes failed to grasp the subtleties of the social conflicts that the Italians brought with them from Italy.

Italian immigrants were largely neglected by the American church because there were so few Italian priests in the United States at this time. The Irish clergy at Holy Family Church had done little but express contempt for the West Side Italians, so mission work was begun by an elderly Italian priest, the Jesuit father Paul Ponziglione. When the Jesuit first arrived at Holy Family in 1891, on a visit from his regular post in Wyoming, he was surprised to find almost five hundred Italian families in the neighborhood. According to Ponziglione, the immigrants "were represented to me as an entirely worthless, ignorant population, aliens, as it were to religion, their majority consisting of infidels, outlaws, gypsies, to whom no good could be done. And as there was no Priest able to speak to them in their own language they were left to themselves."[17]

Ponziglione found that many of the Italians were, in fact, very pious in their home devotions, but they had been evicted from nearby churches when they tried to attend Mass. Before his arrival, the Italians had attended either St. Wenceslaus Church (Bohemian) on Desplaines Street, the Church of the Assumption on Illinois Street, or Holy Family. The Church of the Assumption was an Italian church, but it was relatively far away from the neighborhood. The nearby churches had been hostile to the Italians because of their national origins and their poverty. They were so poor that, for the most part, they could not pay the small seat rents demanded of them, and the ushers did not like their patched clothes and ragged children.[18]

Politically, the elderly Jesuit established the tone for the future Guardian Angel Mission, setting the stage for much later conflict with Italian nationalists in Chicago. Ponziglione clashed with the nationalists because of his priesthood, his opposition to nationalist revolutionaries in Italy, and his aristocratic background. Born in a fashionable resort town in northern Italy to a noble family, he renounced his family's wealth when he decided to become a Jesuit priest. While he was studying for the priesthood in Genoa in 1848, he was captured by revolutionaries. Arrested and taken in chains aboard a warship of the King of Sardinia, he escaped and made his way to Modena, where he completed his studies and was ordained. He spent a brief period of time in Rome but was forced to flee again because of anticlerical demonstrations. Eventually, he arrived in North America and was assigned to the Missouri Province of the Society of Jesus.[19]

Conceptions of space—imported from Italy in the form of regional distinctions—shaped the conflicts of Chicago's West Side. Despite their differences, Ponziglione and the nationalists both favored an Italian national identity whereas the West Side immigrants remained more attached to their Italian regional identities. Ponziglione was separated from his parishioners because he was a northern Italian and most of them were from the South. The Italians in the Holy Family neighborhood were primarily Neapolitans, Calabrians, and Sicilians, yet Ponziglione thought of religion as the perfect tool to generate national feeling among them:

> before I entered the church . . . I heard the air resounding with the dear, and I might say, patriotic hymn of "Eviva Maria, Maria Eviva I." The sweet melody . . . was telling better than any word could express, how happy they felt in being themselves once more united, in the sacred body of religion, at the foot of the altar.[20]

The women who ran the mission would fail to grasp the complexities of Italian politics and identity, accepting Ponziglione as a natural leader of the Italians in the district. Mary Amberg noted that, for the immigrants, "The Italian-American parish priest was there like the padre in the Southern Italian village they had come from. He was not only a shepherd, but a counselor and friend." Mary Amberg also worked to incorporate him into the mythology of Holy Family, writing in her memoir about his frontier adventures among Indians in the West in a way that made him sound like Father Damen.[21] She did not consider Ponziglione's northern Italian origins, in a region that had traditionally clashed with the South. She equated the Italian bosses, or padrones, with the system of feudal exploitation that the immigrants had left behind in Italy, yet many Italians viewed the church as upholding that same exploitative aristocracy.

Despite such potential limitations the mission was reportedly very popular among the neighborhood Italians. They were probably glad for Ponziglione's attention considering the scorn they received in other neighborhood churches. Eventually, the people that Ponziglione gathered under his care formed the nucleus of three Italian parishes in the neighborhood: Holy Guardian Angel, St. Callistus, and Our Lady of Pompeii. Having founded his mission to the West Side Italians when he was already seventy years old, Ponziglione could not see his project through to completion. He died in 1900, leaving his Jesuit colleagues and a large contingent of laywomen to carry on his work. Mary Amberg credited the Jesuits with promoting a laywomen's apostolate to the Italians. She noted that in 1898 Father J. R. Rosswinkle from Holy Family recruited women for the work when he conducted a retreat for the Alumnae Sodality of the Sacred Heart Academy on Taylor Street. Father Rosswinkle reassured the affluent convent graduates that wealth in itself was not sinful—but selfishness was: the rich should use their wealth to help others. He encouraged the women to donate their time and extra funds toward helping the West Side Italians.[22]

Agnes Amberg took a leadership role in the project from the very beginning, and she and the Amberg family would later wind up running the Guardian Angel Center. At the end of the retreat, Father Rosswinkle and the other retreatants appointed Amberg to a committee to visit Archbishop Feehan and ask his blessing for a Sunday school for the Italians on the West Side. The women missionaries were enthusiastic about the work and excited about taking on a new role outside the home. Mary Amberg noted: "The social venture would be pioneering of a sort for Catholic women because the typical well-to-do Catholic matron, while fully social-minded, belonged to a very conservative tradition." She argued that these women had always had a social conscience, but they had never really been encouraged before to put it into practice. By referring to the mission work as "pioneering" for laywomen, Amberg harked back to Marquette, Damen, and the others who had built Holy Family Church. She thus placed the women's labors squarely within the pioneering mythology of the parish, rhetorically giving their new work the blessing of the parish's "founding fathers."[23]

In reaching for influence over the West Side Italian immigrants, the elite laywomen would wind up competing with local Italian leaders. Mary Amberg argued that the Italians had an "unsocial or asocial gentry." For example, she painted the labor boss padrone in colors that non-Catholic reformers tended to use for Irish political bosses:

> in spite of all his asocial ferociousness [he] occasionally found time to be good. For he was, if powerful enough, a sort of mayor in his area. He made matches, arranged betrothals, set likely prospects up in business, fought to give his people a sort of civic identity [but he] ultimately failed because he was an opportunist first and a citizen afterward. Few ever attained the status of real men of affairs in their communities.[24]

Amberg saw the padrone as a holdover from feudalism because he put his own interests ahead of those of his followers. She went on to argue that the main goal of social settlements, particularly religious ones, should be to counteract the influence of such asocial gentry; thus "social-minded," well-to-do Catholic women should vie for leadership with "asocial" immigrant men.

Agnes Amberg took charge of the mission's first project: creating a chapel as a worship space for the Italians. The missionaries literally helped reshape the spaces of Holy Family parish: they created the chapel in two rooms of the Holy Guardian Angel School at 711 Forquer Street, which had been closed by the parish several years before. The Ambergs had chosen to move the Italians out of the Holy Family basement, where Ponziglione had been ministering to them. No doubt the Italians objected to the basement as a mark of inferiority. The missionaries named the mission Guardian Angel after the school, cleaned the rooms thoroughly, acquired cast-off furniture, and created a liturgical chapel with room for seventy-five worshipers. In setting up their Sunday school and chapel, the Sacred Heart alumnae already had expertise in raising money to acquire vestments, altar linen, and sacred vessels for poor churches. Even as they established the mission, the missionaries brought their identity as Holy Family parishioners with them into the new task. One of the first decorations that Agnes Amberg acquired for the new chapel was an image of Our Lady of Perpetual Help—the same image that Damen had placed in Holy Family in gratitude because the church was spared during the Great Fire of 1871. The image would remain a source of spiritual strength for Agnes through the years, especially when the cares of the mission weighed down upon her.[25]

The mission, and especially Agnes Amberg's Sunday school, soon flourished beyond anyone's expectations. Amberg and her helpers taught catechism and Bible history after Mass on Sundays, and evening classes for people who worked during the day. The Sunday school began with forty children and quickly grew to seventy-five. Soon a number of adults began attending as well. By 1903 the school had over fourteen hundred students, more than thirty times its original size. Agnes Amberg continued to run it, supervising a corps of over a hundred volunteer teachers. The volunteers "came from all parts of the city, from all walks of life, from among the clergy and religious and lay people." The Sunday school had considerable help from the Jesuits of Holy Family, and later from the Christian Brothers and the Sisters of Charity of the Blessed Virgin Mary. Lay volunteers helped substantially as well. Unfortunately, most of the names of the Sunday school teachers are no longer available, but among the handful of names that are, one finds mostly women, primarily Irish Americans with a few Italians. One of the school's more prominent instructors, William J. Bogan, was an education activist and principal of Lane Technical High School. Other instructors included Elizabeth Smyth, Mary Mannering, Julia Garvy, Eleanor Doyle, Rose Murphy, Francis Colemen, Clio Manner, Ella Conway, Charles Doyle, and Edward Delbarco. Even after the Sacred Heart Academy moved to the remote northern suburb of Lake Forest in 1906, students and alumnae continued to commute the long distance to the West Side to serve as Sunday school teachers for the mission.[26]

The mission benefited from the strong ties of former parishioners to Holy Family parish. Even people who did not volunteer for the mission came back to the parish for special events such as the Golden Jubilee celebration of the church in 1907, and the Novena of Holy Communions, held every third Friday for nine months preceding the Golden Jubilee of the Immaculate Conception. Collections at Holy Family remained substantial, even after many parishioners had moved away. The size of the Easter and Christmas collections suggests that many parishioners returned for such holidays. Many others continued to contribute the parish through subscriptions.[27]

Transforming the abandoned Guardian Angel parochial school into a worship space enabled the Ambergs and the other volunteers to begin reshaping the spaces of the West Side to accommodate the Italians. The new chapel and Sunday school served as the foundations for a parish, establishing a base from which American Catholics could compete with numerous other would-be leaders of the Italians. Returning parishioners provided money and a supply of volunteers that would make a new church, Holy Guardian Angel, possible. In the process laywomen were encouraged to participate in volunteer work outside the home. This small step away from domesticity was encouraged by local Jesuits because the women's labor was intended to bolster the authority of the church, establishing an outpost among the Italian newcomers and bringing them under the influence of the American clergy. Ultimately, however, after the church was built, the women would end up with their own base of operations, Guardian Angel Center, from which they would challenge the authority of some local clergy. Meanwhile, the clergy of Holy Guardian Angel would find that the Italians could also be difficult to control, necessitating compromise and negotiation in their pastoral work.

Guardian Angel Church and Its Competitors

In trying to win influence over the Italians, the missionaries of Guardian Angel faced formidable competition from nearby institutions. At least five Protestant missions existed in the Holy Family neighborhood, all explicitly trying to convert the Italians. Nearby Hull House boasted vastly superior facilities and a large number of talented residents and other volunteers. While ostensibly nonsectarian, Hull House provided a base of operations for a number of Italian anticlericals and nationalists who clashed with the Guardian Angel missionaries. The Ambergs and the other missionaries experienced a certain degree of success in their competition with the other would-be leaders; because of the pent-up demand among Italians for religious services, Guardian Angel Mission became very popular and Guardian Angel Church was built in 1899. The new church obtained a pastor, Edmund M. Dunne. In the eyes of the Guardian Angel missionaries, at stake in all their labors were the immortal souls of thousands of Chicago's Italian immigrants. These would-be leaders clashed in part because they were all occupying the same neighborhood, doing similar work, and attempting to win over the same group of potential followers.[28]

A family friend of the Ambergs, Dunne became spiritual director of Guardian Angel Mission when he was still a curate from St. Columbkille's Church. Together, Dunne and Agnes Amberg built a substantial parish within a very short period of time. Soon after the pastor of St. Columbkille's died, Dunne began to devote all of his time to the mission. Only a few months after the mission opened, the congregation became too large to fit into the tiny chapel, even though Dunne said four masses every Sunday. Dunne obtained permission from Archbishop Feehan to build a church, but the archbishop could offer little financial help. Dunne canvassed his influential friends for money, and Agnes Amberg did the same. A loan was obtained, a lot purchased, and an architect employed to draw up the plans.[29]

Dunne and the missionaries intended to bring a little bit of Italy to their parishioners on the West Side: the *Chiesa del Santo Angelo Custode,* or Church of the Holy Guardian Angel, had a plain facade that was meant to suggest an Italian country church. However, Mary Amberg would later refer to the style as primarily "American economic" rather than Italian. The interior of the church was decorated to remind the parishioners of Italy, with stained-glass windows of St. Michael and St. Raphael. Placed about the interior of the church were statues of the Christian martyrs San Vito, San Rocco, Santa Lucia, and San Sebastiano. On the walls hung a copy of Raphael's *Madonna della Sedia.* The church seated five hundred parishioners, but within five years it was bursting at the seams. Dunne had originally estimated the parish would have four hundred parishioners. Instead, by 1903 there were one thousand families registered in the parish.[30]

The work of settlements was so similar to the work done by priests, it is perhaps no wonder that the two would clash in city neighborhoods. Mary Amberg noted that Dunne was educated in Rome, so he spoke Italian, including not just the language of educated northern Italians but also the Neapolitan, Calabrian, and Sicilian dialects, as well as the Italian English patois of Chicago's West Side. Aside from visiting the sick, anointing the dying, and performing his duties at the church, Dunne also helped his parishioners by "scaling down the financial exactions of the *padrone* . . . forcing elementary rights from the alderman," finding good lawyers when his parishioners needed them, and posting their bond when necessary. Amberg also noted that he could help his parishioners because he "knew most of the influential businessmen and politicians of the city." Her description of Dunne's daily ministries could easily describe the work of a settlement house as well.[31]

Hull House very quickly became the center of opposition to Dunne and the Guardian Angel missionaries. Addams herself argued that it was not the role of the settlement house to compete with religious institutions, but rather to provide a center where people with diverse views could come together to establish meaningful relationships with one another. Hull House's location in physical space, as well as its philosophical differences with neighboring institutions, placed it squarely in the middle of local controversy. Addams herself derived much of her legitimacy as a spokesperson for immigrants and the poor from Hull House's location on the West Side and her own status as a "neighbor." As she described the settlement's founding, she and her companions believed that "the mere foothold of a house, easily accessible, ample in space, hospitable and tolerant in spirit, situated in the midst of the large foreign colonies which so easily isolate themselves in American cities, would be in itself a serviceable thing for Chicago." Upon the basis of her work at Hull House, Addams built her national and international career as a writer and a leader in social movements. Further, Hull House's mission of providing meeting space for ethnic groups left it vulnerable to the controversies in which these groups took part. Finally, while Hull House itself was officially nonsectarian, the majority of its residents were Protestants, which aroused suspicion among Catholics.[32]

Hull House may not have wished to compete with Guardian Angel, but Guardian Angel was directly competing with it. As Mary Amberg said later in her memoir: "All of us looked upon Hull House as a challenge, yet we never experienced anything but kindness and thoughtfulness and cooperation from Jane Addams." The missionaries of Guardian Angel could not agree with Addams's secularism or her advocacy of birth control, even though they admired her honesty, her compassion, and her dedication to helping others. Amberg further commented that Addams was "one of the most truly Christlike individuals I have ever known." Although the Guardian Angel missionaries admired Addams and even claimed to have been inspired by her, they also made efforts to keep Italians away from the institution.[33]

The most vocal of Dunne's Italian critics was closely associated with Hull House. Alessandro Mastrovalerio was the anticlerical editor of the Italian-language newspaper *La Tribuna Italiana Transatlantica*. A resident of Hull House, Mastrovalerio lived around the corner from Dunne's church and was competing directly for authority over neighborhood Italians. The editor and the priest carried on a feud throughout Dunne's tenure at Guardian Angel Church. Mastrovalerio was an ardent nationalist and held strident anticlerical views, although historian Humbert S. Nelli has argued that his anticlericalism resulted more from resentment of Irish hegemony in the American church than from the anticlericalism of the nineteenth-century Italian revolution or Italian unification. While rivalries and infighting were common among Chicago's various Italian-language newspapers, they tended to agree on their opposition to the church.[34]

By 1905 the conflict between Dunne and Mastrovalerio had descended to name-calling. On January 14, 1905, the *Tribuna* accused Dunne and other Irish priests of making a profit from their Italian parishioners

> The Irish priests work among the Italians not to save them from sin, but through
> fear of losing fruitful clients. A dozen new churches have been built in Chicago
> for Italians under the care of Italian priests who pay the expenses by making col-
> lections among the Italians while the churches always remain as the archbishop's
> property. The Archdiocese has the best real estate office in the country.[35]

Dunne refuted the accusation and began referring mockingly to Mastrovalerio as "Don Salsiccia" (Mr. Sausage). He asserted that, without the donations of wealthy people such as the Ambergs, Guardian Angel Church
would never have been built. Church records demonstrate that Dunne did
not profit financially from his work there. Parish annual reports to the
archdiocese show that Italian donations to Guardian Angel were dwarfed
by non-Italian contributions. Dunne turned all of his salary into the
church's treasury to pay the bills.[36]

While Dunne did not get rich from his work at Guardian Angel, he did win
a promotion. In 1905 he ascended to the rank of chancellor of the archdiocese
and later became the bishop of Peoria.[37] The Guardian Angel missionaries succeeded in bolstering the authority of at least one clergyman—so well that he
quickly ascended the church hierarchy. It was also the generosity of the Ambergs that enabled Dunne to return his salary to the church. Not only did they
support the mission and the new Guardian Angel Church, they even fed the
priest. In fact, Mary Amberg portrayed her mother as the heroine of a fictional
rescue story, with her charity bestowed on Dunne:

> Well do I remember the Sunday morning preparations at our home. If there
> was to be roast chicken for dinner, it had to be prepared by ten o'clock. At that
> hour Mrs. Bentley, our housekeeper, would call old Tom, the coachman, and
> hand him a large wicker basket swathed with snowy damask. In spite of its
> covering the basket exhaled such a delicious aroma that poor Tom was all but
> overcome by the time the carriage arrived at the mission. We then watched to
> see that Father Dunne ate his dinner instead of giving it away to some poor
> immigrant who had told him his troubles before or after Mass.[38]

Despite his quarrels with Dunne, Mastrovalerio claimed to be a good
Catholic and even volunteered to teach in the Guardian Angel Sunday
school. Through the *Tribuna*, Mastrovalerio condemned parochial schools
run by the Irish primarily because he felt they were teaching Italian children "to hate their country." Yet, he did say that religion should be taught
at home. The newspaper *L'Italia* took a similar position, criticizing
parochial schools that were taught in English yet applauding when
Dunne's successor at Guardian Angel, an Italian Scalabrini father named
Manlio Ciufoletti, opened a parochial school in 1910. Presumably, the
school taught the Italian language and culture in addition to other academic subjects and religion.[39]

Even though Catholics, socialists, nationalists, and anticlericals disliked each other in Italy, the Italian priests who ran Guardian Angel Church after Dunne left—unlike Dunne and the Guardian Angel missionaries—made their peace with the non-Catholic leaders. In Chicago anticlericals fought bitterly with the American church on a number of issues. In 1905, for example, a group of Italian nationalists started a campaign to name a public school after Guiseppe Garibaldi, with Dunne leading the opposition. Garibaldi was a northern Italian republican who had been instrumental in uniting northern and southern Italy. In 1870 the Italian government that Garibaldi had helped to create occupied Rome, and the pope lost territories that had been in the church's control for a thousand years.[40]

As tensions between Catholics and anticlericals spread throughout the Nineteenth Ward, other anticlericals besides Mastrovalerio chose to use Hull House as a base of operations. Dunne's main opponents in the public school campaign were members of the Giordano Bruno Club, a vehemently anticlerical organization that met at Hull House and had Mastrovalerio as a member.[41] The *New World* castigated Jane Addams for allowing the club to meet at Hull House and accused her of proselytizing among the Italians.[42] Addams argued that Hull House's relations with neighboring priests remained friendly during the conflicts. Yet Hull House ended up on one side of the fray, in part because it was the anticlericals who chose to use its space. Addams later distanced herself from the Giordano Bruno Club because of the controversies.[43]

The Catholics also felt threatened by the presence of socialists in the Guardian Angel neighborhood and across the city. The Socialist newspaper *La Parola dei Socialisti* supported the Giordano Bruno Club and its plan to wage "An incessant campaign of anti-clericalism . . . to rid the Italian immigrant of all the superstition and ignorance in which he is kept by the papists." The newspaper also tended to dismiss the charity work done by the church in Chicago as "dismal religious propaganda." Attempting to create a forum for workers during the early 1920s the socialists even planned to open a settlement house of their own. Such plans would certainly have been perceived by many devout Catholics as a threat.[44]

The socialists also sponsored or publicized a number of anticlerical plays in the Guardian Angel neighborhood, some of which were presented in the Hull House auditorium, a fact that must have produced additional tensions between Catholics and Hull House. For example, in July 1908 the Olivia Dramatic Company performed "The Mysteries of the Spanish Inquisition" at Hull House. That same year, *La Parola dei Socialisti* noted that the Vaudeville Theatre at 379 South Halsted was putting on a number of performances for Italians. The paper commented that "The public applaud particularly when (and it happens often) priests, bosses, and exploiters are attacked on the stage." In 1918 Italian socialists put on "The Foundling of Holy Mary," also at Hull House. Another Italian-language newspaper, *L'Avanti*, noted after the performance that the audience was "rather small, but re-fined and intelligent," suggesting that the play may have appealed most to a small segment of the Italian middle class.[45]

The workers of Guardian Angel Church worried not only about secular challenges to the Italians' faith but also about the neighborhood's Protes-tant missions. Hull House itself may have been nondenominational, but a Bible study group for Italians was allowed to meet on the premises, a group that was most likely Protestant oriented. Near Guardian Angel were the First Italian Methodist Church, located at Polk and Sholto streets, and St. John Presbyterian Church, situated at 1208 West Taylor. There was also a Congregational Mission on Ewing. Attached to St. John Presbyterian Church was the Garibaldi Institute, a large settlement house that offered an elaborate range of programs, including a Sunday school, Bible study, kindergarten and play clubs, a gymnasium offering a variety of sports, sewing and dramatic classes, music lessons, mothers' clubs, English lan-guage instruction, and tutoring for naturalization. Garibaldi offered family services, including short-term relief and family visiting by social workers. During the summers they had camping trips for both girls and boys. The Reverend P. De Carlo, pastor of St. John Presbyterian Church, edited a weekly Italian-language newspaper called *Vita Nuova*.[46]

Missionaries from Halsted Street Institutional Church were quite open about the fact that they meant to win adherents away from the Roman Catholic Church. Ironically, just when the church was beginning to en-courage laywomen to become involved in mission work, Methodists re-cruited for the work a corps of women who strongly resembled nuns. Dea-conesses were single women who wore distinctive clothing and lived together in groups, and they were considered to be a particularly effective tool in missionizing Catholics:

> The Romish Church has won its victories in America far more through its white-capped sisters than its black-cassocked brethren. A Catholic priest con-verted to Protestantism said recently in a public address, "The Catholic Church does not fear the Methodist Church, nor the Presbyterian Church, nor the Mennonite Church. But it does fear these women in little bonnets with white strings who . . . go into the homes and win the hearts of the mothers. . . . They are what the Catholic Church fears."

If Catholics sometimes appeared suspicious of Protestants, perhaps mission-ary attempts like this helped generate their suspicions. German Jewish women also founded settlement houses in order to compete with Christian missionaries evangelizing among Jewish immigrants from eastern Europe.[47]

Dunne drew a portrait of the work of evangelical Protestant missionaries in the neighborhood in his book, *The Memoirs of Zi Pré*. The book is a fic-tionalized account of Dunne's own experiences in the Guardian Angel neighborhood. In the book a missionary from the "Taylor Street Mission" (probably the Garibaldi Institute) tries to lure a young Italian boy away from the church. Dunne explains that "Zi Pré" means "Uncle Priest," a familiar title given to the clergy in southern Italy. The boy, Pasqualino, is ready for his tricks, because he has met such proselytizers before. Dunne describes the Protestant missionaries:

> The feminine variety is extremely dangerous, as she usually has attractive and winning ways. . . . They offer little girls candy, clothes, and all kinds of presents, in order to entice them into their sewing circles. Some go so far as to place a cross over their chapel and hang pictures of the Madonna on the walls in order to hoodwink the simple-minded.

Even worse, Pasqualino says that a Protestant clergyman pretended to say Mass outdoors on West Polk Street (most likely at First Italian Methodist Episcopal Church). The clergyman told the assembled crowd that he was a "Catholic" priest who was not under the authority of the pope.[48]

To the Protestant missionaries themselves, work among the Italians could provide a rewarding means to serve one's fellow human beings, an opportunity to save souls, and a way to turn immigrants into American citizens. One volunteer at the Garibaldi Institute, Madge Anderson, wrote in 1929 of her work among the Italians, noting first, that "one finds the only real joy and satisfaction in life from service, and second, that the majority of our foreign neighbors are glad to learn anything that will make for better homes, lives and citizenship." Anderson wandered into the work after the death of her daughter, a teenager who had occasionally volunteered at Garibaldi. She found that the volunteer work not only helped her cope with her loss but also gave her life meaning because it made her feel needed.[49]

In the contest for influence over the Italians of Chicago's West Side, issues such as the name of the local public school, the ownership of church property, and even pictures of the Madonna on the walls of a Protestant church really stood for something larger. The real controversy was about who could claim legitimacy as leaders in the neighborhood. For the Catholic and Protestant missionaries, the salvation of the Italians was of paramount importance. Yet, for Catholics, capturing the loyalty of the Italians could also mean reclaiming a leadership role and even a vital presence in a neighborhood they believed they were losing as their neighborhood Irish moved away. Nonsectarian settlements such as Hull House also sought to win influence over their neighbors as a way to claim legitimacy as leaders and reformers. As for the Italian leaders and the American Catholics of Guardian Angel, the issue being contested was that of leadership in both the church and the city. The reputation and respectability of each group, Italians and American Catholics, were at stake within the city as a whole. Ironically, each of these two groups would try to insure its own place in the city by laboring to change the habits and values of its immigrant neighbors.

Leadership and Its Limits

Despite the friction between them, the Guardian Angel missionaries had one thing in common with the Italian and non-Catholic leaders: they all wanted to change the behavior of the immigrants. Many of the conflicts revolved around the use of the spaces of the West Side. Dunne, Amberg, and the missionaries tried to teach the Italian immigrants "American" religious practices, by which they really meant Irish American religious practices. The Italians and the Irish had conflicting views of the proper use of indoor and outdoor spaces in their devotions, in the frequency of Mass attendance, and in their style of religious processions. The missionaries' vision of proper religious behavior was also gendered: they wanted to convince Italian men to take up some of the religious habits they attributed to Italian women. Secular Italian leaders also hoped to change the immigrants' behavior to more decorous middle-class habits and a nationalist outlook. All the would-be leaders cared about how the Italian religious practices looked to outsiders, and the potential embarrassment they could cause. All these leaders ultimately found that the immigrants set limits on which changes they would embrace and which they would not. The Italians fought in the city space to retain some autonomy from the people who were competing to lead them.

The Italians and the Irish differed on the proper uses of the streets and the interior church spaces for worship and religious ceremonies. Because the Italians came from the home of the papacy, some of the missionaries viewed them as natural Catholics. Yet the missionaries disliked the fact that the Italians, especially Italian men, attended Mass irregularly and focused their spirituality instead on the large outdoor religious festivals called *feste*. Their ceremonies were more boisterous than those of the Irish, and their religious iconography more graphic. The Italians loved processions involving firecrackers and brass bands whereas the Irish preferred stately processions in which everyone maintained a more reserved decorum. The Irish favored regular attendance at Mass and reception of the sacraments for both men and women. The Italians engaged in folk religious practices that some American Catholics considered "superstitions." A fundamental difference was that the Italians did not donate money to the church, because in Italy there was no need to—it was supported by the state through taxation.[50]

As they attempted to shape the Italians' religious practices in the New World, the Guardian Angel missionaries were in effect trying to integrate the Italians into the larger American Catholic community, which often viewed the newcomers with suspicion. The mission received criticism from some American Catholics who considered most Italians criminals. In order to encourage these people to accept the Italians, Dunne equated their lot with that of earlier immigrants: "Poverty, poor crops, and excessive taxation drives him here, like the Irish, German, and Slav, to better his condition." He lauded them as morally virtuous and hardworking, argued that the number of crimes committed by Italians was vastly overstated, and noted that they were frequently the victims of police brutality.[51]

In Dunne's book about the West Side, one character in particular represents the kind of small padrones that the Guardian Angel missionaries hoped to replace as leaders of the Italians. Amadeo, father of the promising youth Pasqualino, is in a position to be a leader in his community. He runs a small bank, which is popular among his Calabrian *paesani*. He dabbles in real estate, runs a railroad employment bureau, and sells steamship tickets as well as jewelry, razors, revolvers, musical instruments, prayer books, disreputable novels, postage stamps, and homemade wine. He is callous, irreligious, and violent. On the second page of his foreword, Dunne claims that Amadeo represents "the composite embodiment of reprehensible traits which Zi Pré [the priest] had ample occasion to reprove among the male members of his flock."[52]

Amadeo's main sin is that he attends Mass only twice a year, "on Palm Sunday and on the feast of San Rocco . . . for whom he [professes] great devotion." On most Sunday mornings, he attends meetings of various Italian lodges and societies. Zi Pré urges the men to schedule these meetings for the afternoons so that they can come to Mass in the mornings, but they want to keep their Sunday afternoons free for drinking. Amadeo also refuses to give money to the church, even though he earns plenty from his various enterprises. Zi Pré jokingly refers to Amadeo one day as "Signor Tightwaddo" and tells him that he should change his name to "Amadenaro" or "Amadiavolo," because "you seem to love money and the devil more than God." Zi Pré does not believe Amadeo's professions of faith, because his Italian devotional habits do not fit the priest's criteria for being a good Catholic.[53]

Agnes Amberg's Sunday school was at the center of the missionaries' effort to reform Italian religious practices, promoting decorous behavior outside the church and more frequent attendance at Mass inside the church. The missionaries decided to concentrate their efforts on the children, preparing them for First Holy Communion and Confirmation. The missionaries claimed that, unlike their parents, the children "look upon America as their only home, and they want to be Americans not 'dagoes' or 'ginnies.'"[54] Preparation for Communion and Confirmation had the potential to address two problems. First, it was meant to head off the "Amadeo" problem of not going to church. Second, the sedate Communion and Confirmation festivities, when compared to the Italian feste, more closely resembled the public ceremonies favored by the Irish. Promoting First Holy Communion could also enable missionaries to fulfill a priority maintained by the church hierarchy. In 1910 the pope lowered the age of First Communion to seven. The idea was to promote more frequent Mass attendance and reception of the sacraments, in order to strengthen young people against the dangers of the age, which the pope defined as everything from socialism to the increasingly aggressive sexualized content of popular culture.[55]

Some aspects of the Sunday school were more likely to draw participants into the church than others. The religious education program of Guardian Angel included catechism and Bible history. The missionaries probably used the Baltimore Catechism, which was issued in 1886. This text taught religious doctrine as a series of questions and answers, which students had to memorize. Bible history may have been more interesting to students, because it consisted of telling stories instead of rote memorization. Although potentially less interesting to the students, the catechism may have been easier for the teachers because all they had to do was follow a set format (in fact, the Guardian Angel missionaries used this fact to recruit volunteers who had never taught Sunday school before). Telling a Bible story, on the other hand, would have involved creating a more extensive lesson plan.[56]

The missionaries took more care with the instruction of the boys than with that of the girls, in part because Italian women and girls were already more likely than Italian males to attend Mass regularly. The boys were taught at first by Jesuits from St. Ignatius College and later by the Christian Brothers. Agnes Amberg was grateful to have this help, because she considered teaching the boys the most difficult part of the work. At first, the girls received their instruction primarily from women volunteers. After 1907 the girls received more professional attention, from some volunteers from the Sisters of Charity of the Blessed Virgin Mary.[57]

The interior spaces of the church were also gendered to encourage religious participation by women. While male priests ran the ceremonies occurring inside, women were often responsible for interior decorations. Mary Amberg noted how neighborhood mothers and daughters lovingly made paper flowers to adorn the altar of Guardian Angel Church, and the Ladies of the Altar Society made sure the brass candlesticks were "polished to luster."[58] Because Irish American women also joined altar societies to care for the interior spaces of churches, such activities could have enabled the Italians and the missionaries to bond in a practice that was common across ethnic lines.

The First Communion and Confirmation ceremonies at Guardian Angel were quite popular among the Italians, in part because the missionaries had to make concessions to the Italians' own religious preferences. The ceremonies involved a decorous outdoor procession as well as rituals that took place inside the church. The decorousness seemed to conform to Irish

American preferences, and fathers were encouraged to attend Mass to watch their children participate in the ceremonies However, godmothers and godfathers played a more prominent role in the ceremonies for Italians than for the Irish. The hardships of the immigration experience may have made those ties even stronger in the United States than in Italy. Mary Amberg notes in her book that the godparents would sometimes immigrate with a family and live with them after arriving in Chicago. At the First Communion ceremonies, the Italians expected that one godparent would accompany each child to the altar. Dunne and the missionaries had to conduct the ceremonies in shifts, in order to accommodate so many people.[59]

Dunne recorded that his Italian parishioners felt free to ask for exactly what they wanted in other religious matters as well. They were accustomed to having long prayers invoking the protection of saints against evil, for example. Once, when Zi Pré thought that he had delivered a particularly fine sermon, a woman complained to him at the end of mass, "'Nemanco una preghiera* [Not even a prayer!]." Dunne tolerated some practices to which one might have expected him to object. For example, he noted:

> It is not unusual to see infants wearing earrings and bedecked with jewelry when brought to the church for baptism. Like the rabbit's foot with the "darkey," the ornamentation of a Neapolitan bambino would be incomplete without a charm of coral to protect it against the malign influence of the *jattatura,* or evil eye.

Dunne viewed such practices as superstitious, yet he did not bother to try to eliminate them. He was no doubt more concerned with encouraging regular Mass attendance than with eliminating the "superstitious" behaviors.[60]

Certain other religious ceremonies, particularly the Italian feste, were more difficult for the Guardian Angel missionaries to accept. These grand outdoor festivals were usually held to celebrate the feast days of particular saints. The main events of the festivals were processions, in which participants carried a large statue of the Madonna out of the church and around the neighborhood. Brass bands marched in front of the Madonna, and the faithful set off fireworks wherever she went. Behind the Madonna, women would carry large heavy candles. Sometimes penitents would walk the procession route barefoot to ask forgiveness for their sins. Other worshipers would pin money to the statue's robes or throw jewelry at its feet in order to ask favors from the Madonna. The feste also involved the consumption of generous quantities of food and drink.[61]

The fight to control outdoor religious practices was motivated in part by the attentions of non-Catholics. Of all the Italian folk religious practices, the feste were the most likely to draw attention from outsiders, who often saw the events as exotic and picturesque. The fact that the *festa* was written up in the *Chicago Tribune* suggests that non-Italians may have attended to watch the spectacle. The *Tribune* described the actual day of the procession, the candles flickering in front of the altars, and the participants dressed in Sicilian costume. At least eleven hundred Sicilians lived in Chicago at the time, most of them in the Nineteenth Ward, so plenty of people attended the festivities. The procession itself began "At three o'clock [when] the crowd of gayly dressed women and children formed in line and headed by a band, marched through Ewing, Jefferson, Desplaines, Polk, and other streets. Each child carried a large wax candle draped with flags and these they waved above their heads."[62]

Sometimes, these events could be interpreted as signs of the corruption and disorder immigrants supposedly brought to the city. The sociologist Harvey Zorbaugh echoed the idea that the feste reflected badly upon the Italian community: "When the bands march up Sedgwick during the *feste,* they always stop in front of the house of T____, the moonshine king, to serenade him." In 1905 the *Chicago Chronicle* noted with surprise that "Few arrests were made and no serious disorders occurred" at the festa of the Virgin of Mount Carmel in Melrose Park. The writer attributed the unusual good order in 1905 to extra police surveillance, as well as to the efforts of the Italian priest running the event. Yet the *Chronicle* also noted with disapproval that "All kinds of gambling games from roulette wheels to faro-bank . . . were in operation in full view of the police, who were powerless to stop them."[63]

The missionaries reacted to the festivals with ambivalence. Dunne disapproved of certain festa practices as a waste of money, particularly the hiring of multiple brass bands, and he believed that such practices would inevitably die out as the Italians become more "enlightened" or Americanized. Mary Amberg, on the other hand, lent guarded support to the feste. She described the Italian processions: "The church societies do not march in stately procession behind priest and acolytes but resemble young David dancing before the ark to the sound of firecrackers and brass bands."[64] By finding a basis in the Bible for the Italian processions, Amberg defended them as spiritually legitimate. Yet in her memoir and personal papers, she does not mention ever attending a festa.

Ironically, socialist, nationalist, and anticlerical Italian leaders also disapproved of the feste, sometimes even for similar reasons. In its protest of the feste, the *Tribuna* even made common cause with priests, who hoped to gain more control over their parishioners' religious lives by bringing their observances indoors. As the *Tribuna* noted: "In church we can have splendid festivals with music furnished by the numerous Italian bands of Chicago." They commended one Italian priest for trying to suppress the processions and even suggested that he should be made an honorary member of the Giordano Bruno Club.[65] Nationalist leaders objected to the festivals out of a sense of middle-class decorum. The *Tribuna* quoted another Italian paper as saying: "We will never tire of fighting against this humiliating religious display, this theatrical vulgarity in the streets, until this same display is conducted in a serious and decent manner, which will touch the heart." Some argued that the money spent on the events could be more useful if spent elsewhere, such as helping needy Italians.[66]

To the chagrin of the nationalists, a festa could sometimes represent Italian regional identity instead. In 1901 the *Chicago Daily Tribune* described a festa that took place in the neighborhood of Guardian Angel. Celebrated primarily by Sicilians, the festa honored the assumption of the Virgin Mary into heaven. The *Tribune* described the decorations:

> On Polk St. near Halsted, the largest of the altars was built. Five large arches were erected, covered with green branches and vines, and Sicilian and American flags . . . swung above the arches. At the end of the bower-like avenue was the altar. . . . Tiers of lighted candles flickered and flared in front of the image of the virgin, which had been brought from Sicily and set up in the open air according to the old custom.

Dunne noted in his memoir that Italians of all different regions worshiped together in Guardian Angel Church. He mentions Sicilians in the parish, but also immigrants from "Naples, Salerno, Bari, Basilicata, Abruzzi, Calabria, Cantanzaro, Le Marche, Lucca, Messina, and Palermo," and a handful from Milan, Piedmont, Modena, and Genoa. Even when these groups worshiped together at Guardian Angel, apparently they retained some separate religious rituals. As the years passed, neighboring parishes were built that tended to split up along regional lines.[67]

The degree of challenge posed to the Italians' Catholicism by anticlericals, Protestant missionaries, and socialists in Chicago is debatable. According to Rev. P. De Carlo, the pastor of St. John Presbyterian Church, by 1928 the Italian Protestant churches had about four thousand members and four thousand more people who attended periodically. Most Italians remained in the church, although the extent of their devotion cannot be determined. Certainly the large numbers of Italians who came to Guardian Angel and the rapid construction of more Italian churches on the West Side suggest that many were interested in practicing their religion. Many others did not attend Mass regularly and sympathized with the church's critics even if they continued to think of themselves as Catholic.[68]

After Dunne left the parish in 1905, the feste gained momentum with the arrival of an Italian priest in the parish. In 1910 the Reverend Procopius Chenuil netted nearly thirteen hundred dollars from sales of candles to festa participants. This represented almost a third of the church's income for the year—an income Dunne had never collected. When Dunne left Mary Amberg noted: "Our people were crushed, the old parishioners as well as the children." Yet, she added, they "were all very glad to have a pastor of their own race." The Sunday school continued to operate with Chenuil as its spiritual director, but the missionaries never achieved the same close relationship with Chenuil that they had enjoyed with Dunne.[69]

Although some Italians did slowly come to embrace more Americanized religious practices, they continued to assert their separate ethnic identity within the church. Historian Humbert Nelli argues that Italians, especially from the second generation onward, preferred to join Irish or German parishes rather than stay in their ethnic parishes. Historian Stephen J. Shaw argues that Chicago's Italians eventually adopted Irish habits and says that parishes like Guardian Angel preserved Old World traditions long enough to help the Italians make this transition. Yet historian Lizabeth Cohen notes that feste still took place in Chicago as late as the 1930s, and that they were used to demonstrate a separate ethnic identity within the American church.[70]

Although the anticlerical Giordano Bruno Club was short-lived, Mastrovalerio's newspaper, the *Tribuna,* probably affected a much larger segment of the West Side Italian population. A paper focusing mainly on the interests of the Nineteenth Ward, the *Tribuna* featured short articles written in simple language, designed to appeal to people with limited education. Nelli does not say how broad the newspaper's circulation was, but he does note that it was a major source of news for Italians in Chicago. As for the socialists, *La Parola* was "plagued by problems of small readership and inadequate financial resources." Schiavo notes that the number of Italian socialists was quite small.[71]

In order to obtain influence with the West Side Italians, each group of would-be leaders was forced to compromise in order to obtain what was most important. The missionaries of Guardian Angel compromised on outdoor festivals in order to accomplish the religious goals most important to them. They viewed rituals such as baptism, First Communion, and Confirmation as necessary to secure the Italians as firm members of the church. In order to ensure the immigrants' continued loyalty to the church, the missionaries were forced to accept activities, including the feste, which compromised the respectability of the entire Catholic community. Religious considerations could thus transcend the desire to obtain the good opinion of non-Catholics. Italian nationalist leaders were also forced to put up with the feste and with the continued regional emphasis of the immigrants. The Italian leaders were even forced, at least in the short run, to accept Irish pastors. Although these would-be leaders battled with each other continually within the Guardian Angel parish, neither group was able completely to rout the other and achieve complete hegemony over the West Side Italians.

Sacred Spaces Transformed

In the end, Agnes Amberg and the other Guardian Angel missionaries did not succeed in replacing neighborhood padrone, nor could they keep the West Side Italian immigrants from reading the *Tribuna.* But they did succeed in transforming Holy Family parish by creating new sacred spaces for the Italians. The mission attracted many people because the missionaries offered the immigrants what they wanted: a place of their own in which to worship. Guardian Angel Mission was transformed into a settlement house separate from Guardian Angel Church, and eventually the settlement house gained a new name: Madonna Center. By compromising on issues like the feste, the missionaries succeeded in ensuring the Communion and Confirmation of hundreds of young Italians every year. They were not immediately able to transform the Italians' religious habits into exact replicas of staid dignified Irish religious practices, but they did help to prevent the Italians from leaving the church altogether by welcoming them into Chicago's Catholic community.

As the Guardian Angel missionaries discovered, to control space is to exercise power. Even though they moved away from the Holy Family parish, they gained a number of advantages from returning to conduct their mission work. By winning the Italians as a client group, they could earn a place in Chicago's growing social services bureaucracy. As Guardian Angel Mission became a settlement house, its workers found themselves mediating between that bureaucracy and their Italian neighbors. Eventually, the church gained enough legitimacy as a representative of the faithful that it would play a vital role in the New Deal, taking responsibility for distributing relief funds to all of the Catholic relief applicants in the city. The settlements, including Guardian Angel, helped make this happen.[72]

Even though numerous groups competed for leadership on the West Side, it is not clear that the competition was really a zero-sum game. Although the Catholics did regain some authority on the West Side, this does not seem to have substantially injured their competitors. The anticlerical plays put on at Hull House did not noticeably hamper the work of the Guardian Angel missionaries, nor did the missionaries seriously damage the appeal of Hull House among the Italians. The feud between Dunne and Mastrovalerio appears not to have diminished the number of followers of either one. Italians could be nationalists and still consider themselves Catholics. The Protestants and socialists who tried to win the Italians away from the church were probably destined not to have much success anyway, even if Guardian Angel had never been built.

Proprietary settlements like Guardian Angel come closer than the club- or parish-model settlements to the idea of social control, for they did at least attempt to spread gentility to their neighbors. Yet proprietary settlements also gave leaders like the Ambergs a boost by enabling them to construct themselves as "social-minded gentry." Thus the Italian neighbors of Guardian Angel were not just acted upon; they also affected the people who hoped to lead them. The mission provided benefits to others as well—generating both the opportunity for Holy Family parishioners to return to their old sacred spaces and the means for them to continue to exercise some power there. For laywomen the settlements created new work for them to do outside the home, just like the heroines of the fictional rescue stories. In part because laywomen were looking for new work to do, both Guardian Angel and the proprietary model of settlements were quite popular; in the early years of the twentieth century, a mission was founded in Pasadena, California, on the model of Guardian Angel. Several Catholic settlements in Chicago also resembled Guardian Angel, at least in its proprietary aspect. One was run by Rebecca Gallery, a member of one of the most influential Catholic families in Chicago, the Onahan family. Casa Maria was founded in 1915 at Oak and Cambridge streets, a block from St. Philip Benizi Church. Gallery hoped to teach the Italian children to revere their parents, and to encourage the boys to have high career aspirations. In 1921 the settlement was transformed into a home for working girls. Another proprietary settlement was St. Mary and St. Agnes Settlement and Day Nursery, founded and run by Mrs. M. Hardin.[73]

The volunteer labor performed at Guardian Angel Mission was intended to bolster the authority of priests like Dunne. Yet as the church and the settlement house evolved into separate institutions, the women missionaries found that controlling their own space also endowed them with authority in their own right. The exhausting hours Agnes Amberg spent at the mission guaranteed that she would be viewed as a leader herself. When the mission later grew into a full-fledged settlement house with location, facilities, and program distinct from that of Guardian Angel Church, it would become a site of authority for the new resident director, Agnes's daughter Mary. When teaching catechism classes at the church, laywomen expected to defer to clergy and religious, but in doing the more secular work, the laywomen developed their own areas of expertise and even came to challenge the authority of local clergy.

CHAPTER FOUR

Leisure Culture and Boston Marriage

The Madonna Center

When Guardian Angel Mission became a settlement house in 1914, Agnes Amberg's daughter Mary moved in and became resident director. Several years later, Mary Amberg wrote a fictional rescue story of her own. Her main character was an "aristocratic but sweetly simple" settlement-house worker named Miss Dalmont. One day a little girl in the sewing class named Rosie was trying to translate into English "Signora," the Italian word for "lady." Rosie tried several different translations and finally concluded that the word meant "high-toned. . . . Just like you are [Teacher]." In response, Miss Dalmont smiled sweetly at the compliment.[1] From the time she first moved into the settlement in 1914 until her death in the 1960s, Mary Amberg labored on behalf of the denizens of the West Side. The settlement acquired a number of new programs, such as home economics courses, a kindergarten, social clubs, and a library, the purpose of which was to teach good character to the youth of the neighborhood. Ultimately, the settlement also acquired a new name, Madonna Center. As the settlement grew, Mary Amberg tried to construct herself and her family as "social-minded gentry," much like the refined Miss Dalmont. She also tried to be a good Catholic, obedient to the wishes of the clergy. However, she learned that the best-laid plans often go awry as she became caught up in controversies within the neighborhood and in the larger culture.

As the settlement grew, it gradually broke away from Guardian Angel Church, becoming a more independent institution. Control over the institution and its spaces gave Amberg un-usual authority for a laywoman: just as the CWL settlements had turned club members into leaders in politics and government, so Madonna Center turned Amberg into a leader in matters of culture. This transition was pro-foundly troubling to some neighborhood clergymen, priests accustomed to being the uncontested rulers of their parishes. They were not pleased to share their authority with a laywoman. Even though Amberg saw herself as an obedient member of the church, she and the other settlement workers clashed with neighborhood priests over issues of gender, sexuality, and leisure. The clashes between settlement workers and priests were a reflec-tion of the profound cultural changes occurring during the early twentieth century as women's roles changed, popular culture became heterosocial, and the sexuality of young women was increasingly policed by the state. Through their settlement work, Amberg and the other settlement workers gained authority unprecedented for laywomen and the autonomy to build lives as single women independent from their families. At the same time neighborhood women and girls negotiated increased access to homosocial recreation, but their sexuality also came under greater surveillance by the center's workers and the state.

The Mission Becomes a Settlement

In the early years Guardian Angel Center treated boys as a problem and girls as a solution. As early as 1903 Agnes Amberg set an agenda for the cen-ter's education program that reflected Victorian gender roles. In some in-stances the center had similar goals for boys and girls, the most important being in the realm of Catholic sexual mores. Yet, in the early period, boys had considerably more freedom than girls to roam away from their families, thus the workers of Guardian Angel saw them as more vulnerable to the temptations of crime and delinquency. The answer was to use recreational activities to teach "sound manhood," a combination of honesty, self-control, and sexual abstinence. Scouting, sports, and other activities were used to burn off the boys' excess energy, while Guardian Angel's male workers were expected to set an example of good behavior. Like other settlements of the era, Guardian Angel expected girls to learn domestic skills so they could help their families survive in the slums. Rosie, the little girl in the Madonna Cen-ter sewing class, was a stock character not just in rescue stories but in all kinds of writing about settlements, both fiction and nonfiction. Thus, while boys' leisure was defined separately from work, girls' activities were defined in ways that combined the categories of labor (activities performed to benefit others) and leisure (activities done for one's own enjoyment). By the time Mary Amberg took over as resident director of the settlement, this gendered vision of leisure had already begun to change.

The mission took on secular education programs early in the twentieth century, opening a summer vacation school in 1904 for the neighborhood children. Housed in the Dante Public School, the summer program offered the same gender-specific activities that were later adopted by the mission year-round. For girls there was a home economics course, featuring washing and ironing, light cooking, infant care, and hygiene. For the boys the school had sports, hikes to the lakefront, and handcrafts. In an era when some believed that Protestant churches were becoming "feminized," Catholics emphasized competitive sports for boys as a way to demonstrate that religion was compatible with masculinity. The Guardian Angel missionaries thought of the school as an enjoyable alternative to the rigors of the academic year, even though the girls' course looked more like work than recreation.[2]

Guardian Angel Mission actually became Guardian Angel Social Center in 1912 when it moved to the abandoned St. Francis School on Newberry Street, just south of 12th. At first only two rooms of the St. Francis School were used: one as an apartment for resident worker Catherine Jordan, and the second for everything else. Two other resident workers, Don Kearins and Margaret McGivern, lived nearby. None of these three drew a salary; they were probably supported by their families. Forty-eight non-resident volunteers helped run the center's activities. Soon the center also had an auxiliary to raise money, and several years later it incorporated and gained a board of directors as well.[3]

Moving into the settlement in 1914 as resident director gave Mary Amberg both an independent home of her own and a career for the first time in her life, at the age of thirty-eight. In her memoir Amberg suggested that her mother disapproved of her moving out of the house, at least until she accepted the benefits Mary could provide the settlement as resident director. Because settlements were intended to be homelike, moving into Guardian Angel provided Amberg with a comfortable home of her own as well as a career. Living in the settlement house empowered her to find personal autonomy, self-fulfillment, and companionship in a community and an era that accorded little status to single laywomen.[4] Despite these benefits, Amberg wrote in her memoir that she was at first reluctant when a friend suggested in 1913 that she take over the mission work to relieve her aging mother. She wrestled with a series of doubts about the mission, likening her struggle to the experience of Christ in the garden at Gethsemane and calling it her "dark night of the soul." She feared that she could never live up to her mother's strength and ability, worried about the center's lack of secure funding, and became discouraged by the proximity of Hull House, located a mere two blocks away. Eventually, she decided that a Catholic settlement had more to offer than a secular one like Hull House ever could.[5]

After she became resident director, Mary had to carve out a niche for herself in an institution that carried her mother's stamp. She invented herself as a combination of genteel role model and best friend to the center's children, and she often performed the crucial settlement task of sitting inside the front door, greeting the people who entered and directing them to the appropriate clubs, classes, and activities. She noted years later: "I thought the way these things were done gave tone . . . to a whole institution: that so much depended upon graciousness." With her quiet patience, she succeeded in making friends with many of the children; some even trusted her enough to bare their souls to her. One young man wrote to her in 1917:

> dont think for one minute that I dont appreciate all the time and patience you spent with me. . . . And yet you never tried to make me feel as though I owed it all to you. . . . I wonder if all this mess I keep writing bores you. I hope it dont for it relieves me greatly and then again, who can I tell it to, that would understand?

In another case, three young boys who had been exiled briefly from the center for misbehaving pleaded with Catherine Jordan to let them come back, saying "we feel lomesome [sic] without you and Miss Amberg."[6]

Program by program the center continued to grow. The kindergarten for children aged three to five was added in 1914. The average attendance ranged from twenty to forty-five. There was a paid worker and also some student assistants from the National Kindergarten and Elementary College. The teachers were paid a total of $625 for the year, divided between them. One of the summer kindergarten teachers, Frances McElroy, wrote to Mary Amberg about how much she enjoyed the work:

> I hate to think of the time when I will have to give it up and go back to the wealthier class of children as these are such dear kiddies and so affectionate. . . . I have had numerous invitations to visit them, that is, they add, "If your Ma will let you come—Wont you ask her if she would let you visit me?"

The kindergarten fed the children snacks of milk and graham crackers and provided extra milk and eggs to sick children whose families could not afford such luxuries. The center also added a play club for children aged five to nine.[7]

Employment continued to be a focus as the center expanded. It had offered employment programs as early as 1903, when a night school for vocational English opened in the basement of Guardian Angel Church with five hundred students in attendance. Neighborhood youth usually started working as soon as the law allowed, at age fourteen. Sometimes they would give the center as a reference when looking for work. Others took the center's classes, like the sewing class, hoping this would lead to a job. The center's workers sometimes drew upon their friends in business to find jobs for these children, and sometimes mediated disputes with their employers.[8]

For boys, the center promoted "sound manhood," which was similar to the nineteenth-century ideal of "manliness"—an ideology stressing the need to master one's emotions and passions.[9] The center's goal was to keep the boys away from temptation and to foster honesty, self-control, and sexual abstinence. The center's spaces were gendered on the assumption that adolescent males would be the hardest to lure inside. In 1914 the center opened a poolroom for the young men, in order to keep them away from commercial pool halls, where they would learn about drinking, gambling, and prostitution. The poolroom was located right inside the front door, to enable the boys to slip in and out easily. It was supervised by a young male volunteer who sometimes visited the boys at home, taking them to confession and warning them to stay away from "bad women."[10]

The center also taught boys discipline through the Boy Scouts, an organization founded in 1908 by Sir Robert Baden-Powell. An officer in the British Army, Powell had trained soldiers in various techniques of wilderness survival and later translated these techniques into a program for boys. A nonsectarian organization, the scouts required members to fulfill the obligations of the church to which they belonged. The scouts also taught other values that were attractive to Catholics especially "the military virtues, such as honor, loyalty, obedience, and patriotism." Mary Amberg noted in a letter that, because of the scouts, "Our rough, undisciplined little chaps have improved . . . in manliness, courtesy, [and] self-control." In 1916 the Boy Scouts performed a first-aid drill at the city's annual Arbor Day celebration. Although hampered by lack of funds, the center also tried to sponsor summer camping trips for the boys.[11]

Honesty was another crucial component of manhood, a standard against which many of the center's boys would come to measure themselves, even when they failed to live up to it. In January 1917, for example, one young man wrote to Mary Amberg to apologize for a series of mistakes. He had played hooky from work for two weeks and lied to his mother about it. In the end he ran out of money and repented:

> I am sorry for not obeying you and letting you have all this trouble. . . . I really did not use my brains to tell you the truth. . . . So now I am . . . going to take away all the sins I have done. I am going to confession to-night at 7 oclock at the Jesuit Church. . . . I am going to Communion tomorrow morning and receive the [sacred] heart. And then I am going to work right along and keep straight all the time.[12]

The center treated boys as bundles of energy that needed to be kept out of trouble, but it viewed girls as workers whose help was crucial to their families' survival in the city. The family can be viewed as a haven from the exploitation of the workplace and the hardships of migration, or as a hierarchy that placed unequal demands upon its members. The centers' workers and neighborhood Italian families placed heavy demands upon daughters to contribute to the family income and perform housework. When the girls were young, they did industrial home work to bring in money for their families. They would string beads, crack nuts, and manufacture artificial flowers in order to bring in a few pennies from contractors. They cared for younger children and cleaned, and when they were older they would work outside the home for wages. On Chicago's West Side girls were employed as store clerks, errand runners, and candy makers in a major caramel works. Boys worked as well, but they had more leisure time because they were not expected to contribute as much to home chores. Girls had limited opportunities for recreation, but they could justify going to the settlement because they made clothes for their families.[13]

The center sponsored a comprehensive home economics course for girls that included not only sewing but also cooking and cleaning. In the Newberry Street location, the center spent $350 creating a domestic science room, with tables, pots, and pans, twenty-two gas rings, and two stoves. Students from the Lewis Institute helped teach the classes. One can view such classes as patronizing and culturally inappropriate.[14] It is true that the center's cooking class was more Irish than Italian when it focused on "the hundred and one ways to prepare potatoes."[15] However, Amberg and her coworkers came to value the healthfulness of Italian staples such as broccoli, tomatoes, olive oil, beans, and whole-wheat pasta. Other skills could also be extremely valuable in slum neighborhoods. Many West Side families were bereft of basic clothing items, let alone white dresses for the girls' First Holy Communion. Cleaning advice might have been helpful for those living in overcrowded apartments in a filthy city, where bad personal hygiene could spread disease. Even Italian newspapers complained that some immigrants were dirty, although they tended to blame bad conditions rather than the immigrants themselves.[16]

In addition to domesticity, Mary Amberg also used clubs to teach the girls "refinement" and generosity to those less fortunate, in effect training the girls to be little ladies like herself. Interestingly, some of the clubs also sponsored activities that were heterosocial, in an era when Italians often preferred to segregate children strictly by gender. At least some girls accepted Amberg's instruction in gentility. In 1918 one young woman asked Mary Amberg for a job recommendation as a nursemaid to a baby. She addressed her letter to "My Dearest Big Sister," saying, "Oh, I'd love to work for such lovely fine people . . . Miss Mary, like your family is, nice an refine [sic]. . . . I am learning to be very quiet an gentle like you like me to be . . . an I also want to be a grown up young lady." For the older girls Amberg used clubs like "The Sorority" to teach genteel habits. Some of the activities of the club were actually leisure-oriented. The Sorority sponsored an annual cotillion, usually held at some posh location such as the West End Catholic Woman's Club. Members invited young men and women from the center, in addition to adult friends, well-wishers, and board members. Because most of the girls worked, they were also able to save their money and give some of it to charity.[17]

By 1914 the center had begun to provide girls not just with training in housework but also with a few leisure activities intended primarily for their own enjoyment. Summer vacations are the most important example. In 1914 two of the center's girls got to take a trip to Pottawatomie, Michigan, staying with two women from the center in a cabin near a lake. One of the center's workers wrote back: "I can't begin to tell you how much the girls are enjoying it. . . . Of course the lake is the chief attraction and the direct threat that I can make is to tell a girl that unless she does as I ask she can not go in bathing."[18]

Even though running the center gave Amberg and the others some authority within the neighborhood, as laywomen they were frequently reminded of their subordinate status within the church. In 1916 they were told by Archbishop Mundelein that they needed to move: the abandoned parochial school on Newberry Street where they were housed was opening again. While they believed the order to move was unfair, they also believed in obedience to church authorities, so they found a new location in two empty store buildings at 927–931 West Polk Street. Despite the move, the center's work continued to thrive with a staff of four full-time workers and an unspecified number of part-time volunteers. During the year 1918–1919, the center had a total of 1,404 people registered for its clubs and classes and an average daily attendance of 230. The sewing and play clubs had the most children (537) while the kindergarten had 136. Groups for boys included the Holy Name Society Juniors and the Boy Scouts, which had 164 and 68 registrants, respectively. There were 57 Junior Girls, and the Working Girls' Club had a membership of 42. The settlement was heavily used by girls and women, but there were also many boys and young men registered for center activities.[19]

By 1916 Mary Amberg and the girls of the Guardian Angel Center were branching out beyond their previous experiences. After a lifetime in the shadow of two strong-willed parents, Mary had gained both authority in the neighborhood and autonomy in her own life. After endless hours spent cooking and sewing, neighborhood girls finally began to enjoy some leisure activities intended for their own recreation and amusement. They were participating in recreation that had been available for boys from the beginning. Such changes would not go unnoticed in the parish and would engender a backlash among Holy Family's more conservative clergy.

War, Sound Manhood, and the Girl Scouts

World War I proved both a shock to Mary Amberg's family and a precipitating factor that changed the center's vision of gender. Worrying about the war hastened the deaths of Mary's parents, which bolstered her autonomy but left her bereft and lonely. The war provided a test for the center's boys and their "sound manhood" and put women such as Amberg's friend Marie Plamondon in uniform. At about the same time, the center started a controversial Girl Scouts troop in the neighborhood. Opponents viewed the Girl Scouts as a challenge to the gender identity of male soldiers; uniforms in particular were believed to make the girls seem masculine. In addition critics worried that recreational activities such as scouting would enable girls to spend more time enjoying themselves and less time laboring on behalf of their families. Although the Girl Scouts were approved by the archbishop, a local priest was among the people who disagreed heartily with young girls engaging in this type of activity. The ensuing controversy highlights not only changes in early twentieth-century gender ideology but also the enormous gendered power differential within the Catholic community between female laity and male clergy. A settlement house that created positions of authority for laywomen within a parish was acceptable only as long as the laywomen did not challenge the authority of the local priests.

The priest in question, F. X. Breen, was a Jesuit at Holy Family and an advocate of a militaristic version of "sound manhood," which he taught to the center's boys. Until his feud with Mary Amberg, and especially with her friend Marie Plamondon, he was involved extensively in helping the center. Breen helped the Ambergs during the move to West Polk Street in 1916–1917. He was a teacher at St. Ignatius College, and at the center he ran the Exempla Club for boys. When Amberg provided him with an office in the center's new location, he thanked her and called her "a real friend of mine." Many of the center's boys eagerly embraced his vision of masculinity—several enlisted because of it. In 1917 one of Breen's former club members wrote Amberg a letter from his post in the U.S. Army, saying, "You mentioned Father Breene [sic]—how I wish I could shake him by the hand and hear his 'God Bless You' again before I go over . . . he is my idea of a real man." Breen drew a connection between faith, patriotism for the United States, and ethnic pride: "The Italian American who is not a Catholic is a traitor to his God and to the most sacred traditions of his noble race . . . I want nothing to do with such a class of people. They are a menace to the Nation."[20]

While the center's boys were gone, others also served the war effort. The girls worked in a way that did not challenge Breen's vision of proper gender roles, such as knitting and sewing bandages for wounded soldiers for the center's Red Cross Auxiliary. Ninety girls enrolled in the auxiliary, and the average attendance at meetings was twenty-five or thirty. Apparently Red Cross Headquarters always gave the supplies generated by the center good marks for quality. A number of the center's male workers went off to war: Don Kearins volunteered for an ambulance squad, and Charles Gardiner died in the service.[21]

The war exhausted Mary Amberg's parents and hastened their deaths. On top of her already busy schedule, Agnes Amberg wrote numerous letters to the young men from the center who had gone overseas. William, normally a warm-hearted and jovial man, became depressed when Americans of German descent were suspected of disloyalty to the United States. In September 1918 he died at the family's summer home on Mackinac Island, Wisconsin. Agnes kept working at the mission for a time, yet she was visibly weakened by William's death and she died in November 1919.[22]

After her parents died, Mary turned increasingly for companionship to her lifelong friend Marie Plamondon, who became more involved in the center's work. Plamondon's parents were also killed during the war; they were aboard the *Lusitania* when it was sunk by the Germans. Plamondon had found a sense of purpose during the war by working for the Bureau of the Water Corps Service in Chicago, yet she found herself adrift again after the war ended. Her family was wealthy enough that she did not need money, but losing her parents had forced her to reevaluate her life. Her brothers and sisters were all married and had families of their own. She had spent most of her adult life in high society, attending parties, traveling, and riding horses. The settlement offered her both companionship and a sense of purpose. As she explained to an old friend: "with Daddy and Mother way up in Heaven . . . I have been finding comfort and content and a degree of satisfaction I had not dreamed possible in a little Center right over in one of the most appalling districts of the city. Some change from horseback canters along the Drive."[23]

Plamondon was tailor-made to offend the strict gender ideology of F. X. Breen. Even when active in high society she had always dressed in masculine-looking suits, neckties, and stiff straw hats. She was known in society circles as "the Duchess," which probably reflected her rather imperious personality. During the war her job had made her an expert in auto repairs and also entailed wearing a uniform. While Amberg continued to teach "refinement" to the center's girls, Plamondon herself refused to conform to such gender conventions; she continued to wear man-tailored clothing at the center.[24]

Plamondon's work at the center also stretched Breen's vision of appropriate gender roles. She soon became a leader of the boys' clubs, a job most settlements commonly reserved for men. She was very fond of the boys, and it seems they loved her as well, in part because she made copious use of slang. As a friend wrote to her in 1924: "Your conversation has all the sprightly stimulus of a well-made highball." She even smoked and swore. As Mary Amberg later wrote: "Marie's well-fitting grey serge jacket, her Sam Brown belt, her capacity for rendering a hearty 'Damn!' when things did not go exactly right, all awed and impressed the younger male elements in our midst. Poor lads, little did they know that her heart was pure gelatine [*sic*], and she would even have given them her Sam Brown belt if it meant adding anything to their happiness."[25]

Even though Plamondon was a strong supporter of the Girl Scouts, it was Amberg who was chosen by the archbishop in 1921 to organize the

Girl Scout movement among the West Side Italians. Amberg claimed in her memoir that she had often hoped the center could have had a Girl Scout troop before its Boy Scout troop, because she believed the neighborhood girls were usually much more confined than the boys.[26] The Girl Scouts were modeled after Sir Robert Baden-Powell's Boy Scouts. Baden-Powell himself created an organization for girls named the Girl Guides, which offered some of the same activities as were offered to the Boy Scouts but which also emphasized housekeeping skills. In 1912 a wealthy widow from Savannah, Georgia, organized the first troop in America and called them Girl Scouts.[27]

Breen's response to the formation of the Girl Scouts troop was to tell the congregation at Guardian Angel Church that "there is nothing uplifting in the Scouts. It just makes a girl mannish." He objected in part because the Girl Scouts enabled girls to have recreation away from their families, claiming that girls ought to spend their free time at home with their mothers. Even though Girl Scouts were being promoted by the archbishop, Breen did all he could to prevent a troop from forming in his parish, even telling parishioners not to let their girls join.[28]

"Mannishness" was one of Breen's main reasons for disliking Marie Plamondon, and he referred to her in conversation as "that Plamondon creature." He criticized her for smoking and swearing and for her "spunky nerve." He believed she was gossiping about him behind his back, and he even preached a sermon making thinly veiled references to her in which he argued that lay people who criticized priests were committing sacrilege. For her part, Plamondon was quick to lash out whenever she felt insulted. Two hot-tempered people, Plamondon and Breen disliked each other in part because they were so much alike. Most of all Breen was angry that two laywomen would challenge his authority in the parish. In private he said that "if the old maids [at the center] did not stop interfering with his doings he would go to the Archbishop who would see that protection was given his priests." He also worried that the Girl Scouts would detract from the parish's sodalities, which were under the direction of priests. Like the Girl Scouts, these organizations also afforded girls some recreation away from their mothers, but Breen justified this by saying that sodalities were under the direct supervision of the church.[29]

The developing controversy with Breen highlighted the fact that the settlement had given Amberg and Plamondon a position of authority in the neighborhood—a situation the priest ultimately could not tolerate. Neighborhood girls even used the center's endorsement of scouting to justify their own interest, saying to Breen that the Girl Scouts "must be all right because Miss Mary, Miss Plamondon and Miss Jordan are with us." Despite Breen's objections, the center did form a Girl Scout troop. At first eighteen girls signed on, but they all stayed away from the orientation session after Breen began to preach against the movement. In order to restore enthusiasm for scouting, Amberg resolved to take the girls to the West Side scouts rally and scoured the manual to find tests that the girls could pass easily, hoping that they could win merit badges.[30]

The Girl Scouts most likely appeared "mannish" to Breen in part because of their uniforms. Breen was not the only person to disapprove of uniforms for girls: when the Girl Guides were first founded in England, their uniforms were purposely made blue instead of the Boy Scouts' khaki because khaki was associated with the military. In the United States, the Girl Scouts adopted a khaki uniform. One of Breen's former protégés, a soldier during World War I, highlighted the connection between uniforms, masculinity, and concepts of honor, writing to Mary Amberg that, "to wear the khaki today is an honor, equal to the cause we are fighting for, to crush Autocracy." Catholics across the nation were suspicious of the Girl Scouts. One writer in *Catholic Charities Review* suggested that some people believed, erroneously, "that Girl Scouts had to wear knickers and act like boys or be trained for military duty." The Girl Scouts were controversial also because, instead of completely subordinating girls' activities to the needs of their families, the program encouraged neighborhood girls to strive for personal achievement. The Girl Scouts promoted a combination of Victorian and modern gender roles, teaching girls to become accomplished housekeepers and to uphold traditional sexual mores but also encouraging them to reach for less traditional achievements. The center's scouting program taught the girls to sew, embroider, and cook. Supporters of the Scouts also wanted to teach the girls to respect God, obey their parents, and train their immigrant mothers in American cleaning techniques. Yet the girls also participated in rallies with other Girl Scout troops, wearing uniforms and even marching in formation, while the Girl Scout handbook encouraged them to train to earn a living.[31]

The center also challenged neighborhood gender mores by providing married women in the neighborhood with recreation outside their homes. Researcher Louise Odencrantz noted in 1919 that Italian mothers "had no recreation."[32] In the same year the Girl Scout troop was founded, the center sponsored two Red Cross classes for women and girls, one on home care for the sick and one on home hygiene. Breen objected and nobody came to the first class, but later, thirty-two women and girls, including eleven married women, received diplomas for the Red Cross courses. The women attended the class but did not come to the final awards ceremony at which the diplomas were distributed.[33]

As the center constructed its Girl Scouts program, the controversy with Breen raged on. Mary Amberg found herself in the middle of a war she had never intended to cause, trying to soothe two hotheaded combatants. Breen moved out of his office at the center, and when Mary Amberg tried to pay the rent for his new office he refused to cash the check. He eventually became interested in a new settlement house run by an Italian woman, the Countess Lisi Cipriani. Plamondon went on vacation for a while but continued to fume about Breen. Amberg tried to calm her: "Such a letter as was awaiting my return . . . last evening was unworthy of you . . . but you are ill, depressed, lonely. . . . Oh! Pal Dear, why can't you learn that such intense resentment . . .

accomplishes nothing — & but exhausts you? . . . I believe we pay a physical price eventually for such riots of arrogance & resentment."[34]

Even though Amberg and Plamondon could not hope to prevail against a neighborhood priest, without the authority gained by their settlement work they would never have been able to challenge him at all. The archbishop had indeed promoted the Girl Scouts, but his commitment to the movement was weak. He refused to publicize his support or give the movement any money, in contrast with the tremendous support he would later give to boys' work through Bishop Bernard Sheil and the Catholic Youth Organization. Amberg retained the friendship of several other influential clergymen, including Frederic Siedenburg, the founder of the Loyola University School of Social Work, which was enough backing to keep the center open but not enough to keep the center from having to move.[35]

The center gave Amberg and Plamondon not just the authority and courage to challenge a priest but also the opportunity to forge a partnership. Amberg may have chosen Plamondon as a companion, yet the quarrel with Breen demonstrates she was not going to let Plamondon make decisions for her. Amberg had never thought of herself as brave, yet with quiet dignity she decided to pack up the entire center and move rather than keep fighting. She chose a location outside the boundaries of Guardian Angel parish, away from Breen's territory. Plamondon objected to running away, but Amberg gave her a choice: "'He went about doing good' was said of Him Marie Dear for whom all our work should be done. I, too, mean to go about doing good & I cannot if I dwell on . . . the past . . . I do not wish to hurt you . . . but—you must know the essentials of our going on together."[36]

Mary and Marie at Madonna Center

As a result of Mary Amberg's decision to withdraw from the fight with Breen, the center moved in 1922 away from the two parishes that had meant most to it: Holy Family, the parish that had created it, and Holy Guardian Angel, the parish it had helped build. The new center was considerably north and west of the old location, on Loomis and Spruce, partly because Italians from Holy Guardian Angel parish were beginning to move in this direction. In cutting ties with the old neighborhood, a new name was chosen, Madonna Center. Removing them from the direct control of Holy Family priests, the move gave Mary Amberg and Marie Plamondon the freedom to build their lives together. While Mary's and Marie's sexual orientations cannot be determined, their relationship can best be described as a Boston Marriage, a committed same-sex life partnership similar to ones documented among many women reformers of the Progressive Era. Just as secular settlement workers built networks of caring relationships, Madonna Center enabled Marie Plamondon and Mary Amberg to build close ties with each other that sustained their work and fortified them to construct a new relationship with their neighbors.[37]

Children play on the rooftop playground of De Paul Settlement House. Archdiocese of Chicago, Joseph Cardinal Bernardin Archives, Chicago, Ill.

above—Neighborhood children, Guardian Angel Center, n.d., ca. 1915. Madonna Center Collection, Department of Special Collections and University Archives, Marquette University, Milwaukee, Wisc.

below—De Paul Settlement House—Rooftop playground with children and nuns. Archdiocese of Chicago, Joseph Cardinal Bernardin Archives, Chicago, Ill.

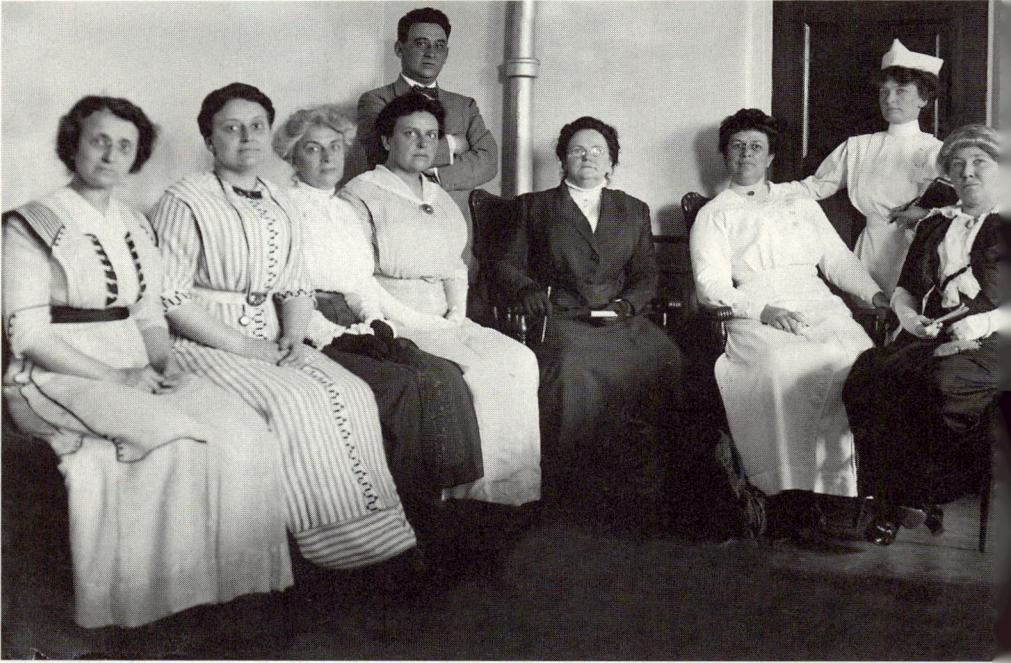

Although they posed together for this photograph, Catholic Woman's League officials and school board members Tena Farren MacMahon and Florence Vosbrink fought on opposite sides of a controversy over the Chicago Teachers' Federation. Leonora Meder, the first director of Chicago's Department of public welfare, is also pictured. Meder and Vosbrink were rivals for the presidency of the CWL. Seated from left: Minnie Low, Dr. Clara Seippel, Florence Vosbrink, Gertrude Howe Britton, Leonora Meder, Tena Farren MacMahon, and Dr. Anna Dwyer. *Chicago Daily News*, Chicago Historical Society, DN-080956.

left—Agnes Amberg was a talented and ambitious woman who knew from an early age that she would make something of herself. She was one of the main founders of Guardian Angel Mission, later renamed Madonna Center. Loyola Press, Chicago, Ill.

right—Mary Amberg said that reading religious books inspired her to work with her mother and become resident director of Guardian Angel Mission, a position that she held from 1914 until her death in the 1960s. Loyola Press, Chicago, Ill.

above—Girls' Dancing Class, Guardian Angel Center, Christmas 1916. Madonna Center Collection, Department of Special Collections and University Archives, Marquette University, Milwaukee, Wisc.

right—Sewing class for ten-year-olds, Guardian Angel Center, ca. 1910. Volunteers provided countless hours of labor in leading settlement clubs and classes. Sewing classes were a staple of settlement work and provided both domestic training and clothes for neighborhood girls. Madonna Center Collection, Department of Special Collections and University Archives, Marquette University, Milwaukee, Wisc.

right—Reading Room, Guardian Angel Center, 1915. The center featured a number of activities designed to appeal to boys and men, including a reading room and a billiard room. Madonna Center Collection, Department of Special Collections and University Archives, Marquette University, Milwaukee, Wisc.

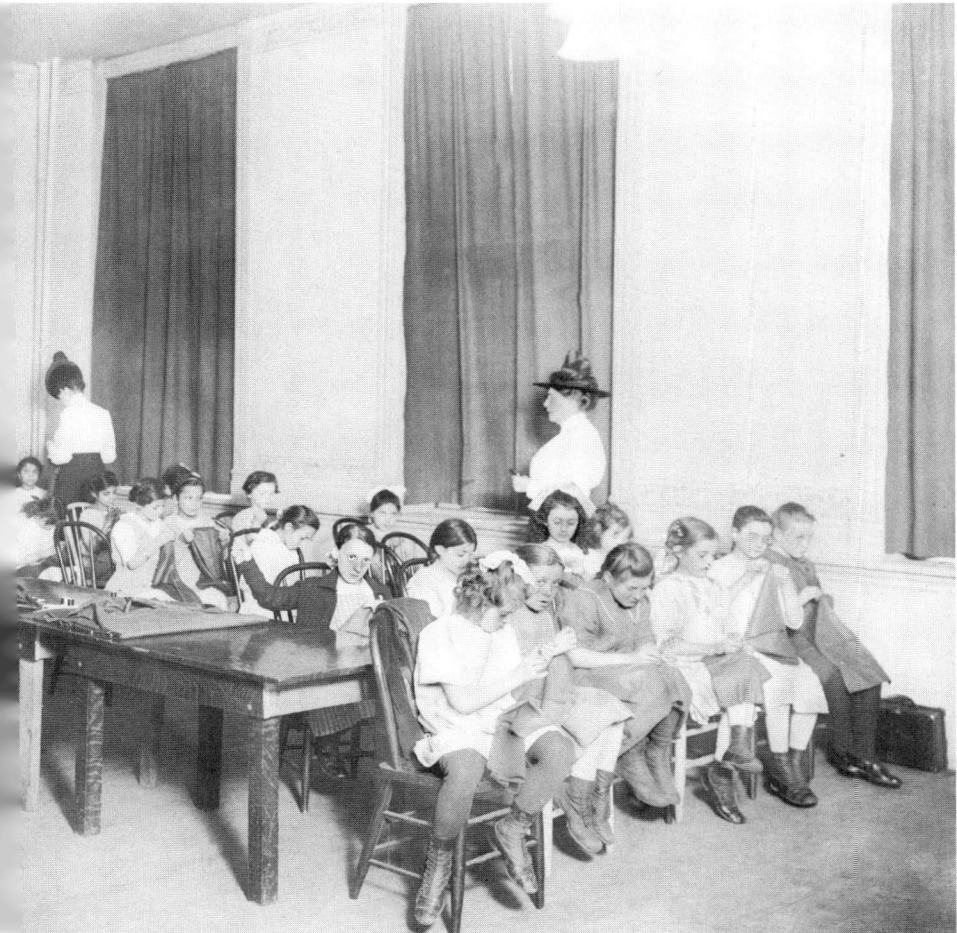

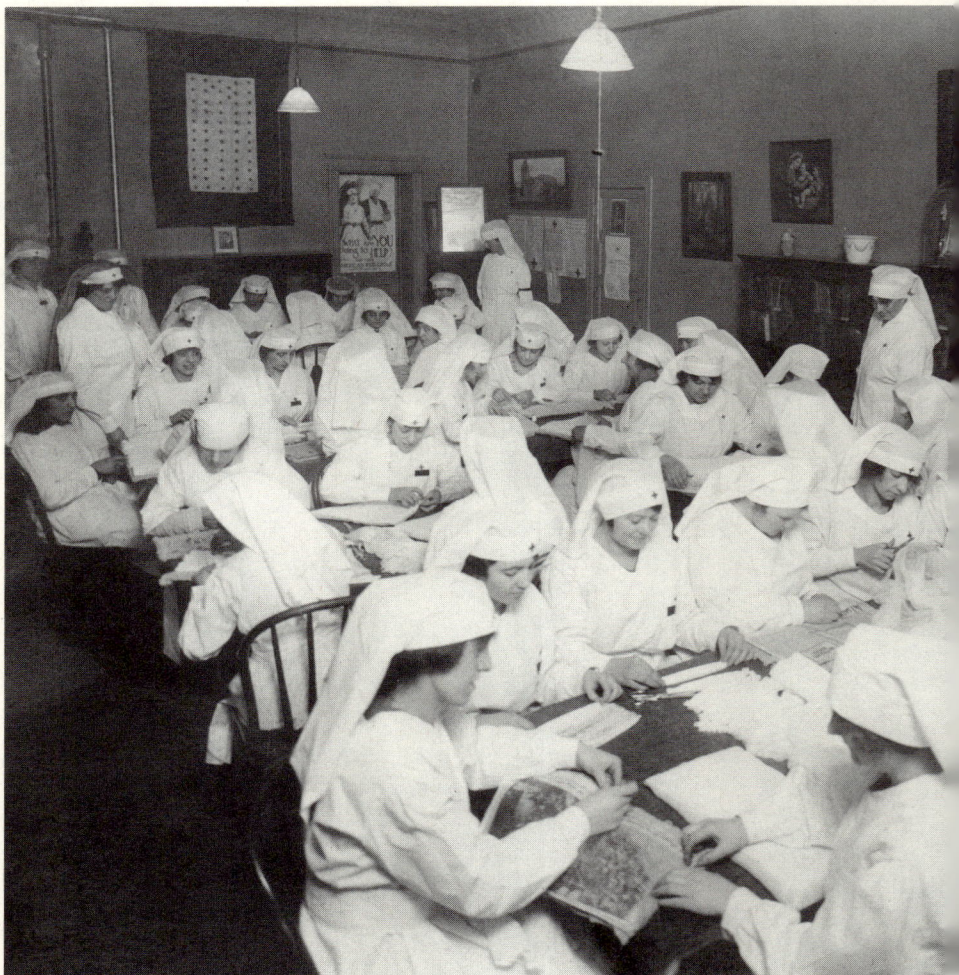

above—Red Cross volunteers from Guardian Angel Center rolling bandages, ca. 1917 or 1918. During World War I, settlements often coordinated volunteers, who were an important source of supplies for the war effort. Madonna Center Collection, Department of Special Collections and University Archives, Marquette University, Milwaukee, Wisc.

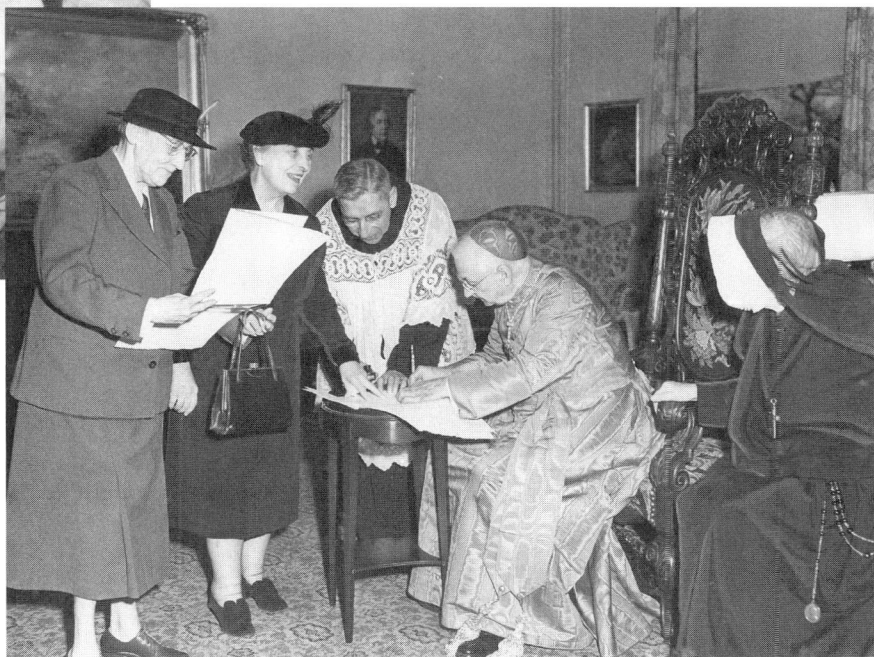

below—Mary Amberg and Marie Plamondon rece.ve an award from Cardinal Stritch for their work at Madonna Center. Archdiocese of Chicago, Joseph Cardinal Bernardin Archives and Records Center, Chicago, Ill.

left—An unnamed sister greets a family at the door to the day nursery. Daughters of Charity Archives, Mater Dei Provincialate, Evansville, Ind.

below—Sisters Louis O'Connell and Agnes Hart on rooftop playground with children. This photograph is rare because it caught the sisters' faces in an unguarded moment of enjoyment—according to the rules of the order, sisters were supposed to hide their faces from the camera. Daughters of Charity Archives, Mater Dei Provincialate, Evansville, Ind.

In her book about Madonna Center, Mary concealed the real reason for the center's move, saying instead that more space was needed so that Marie could move in. The "Italian" children who attended the center were now mostly American-born, and they called Mary the "boss," and Marie the "chief."[38] The new center was located not far from the Ambergs' former home on Sheldon Street, and it included three buildings: a "big house," a smaller house, and a garage that became a gym. A chapel and a medical clinic were created. Originally built by David Bremner Sr., an old friend of the Ambergs, the house fell into the hands of an Italian businessman named Lespina when the neighborhood changed. Reputed to be a member of Al Capone's gang, Lespina was murdered in 1922, and his widow offered the house to Amberg. Several other residents moved into the main building with Mary and Marie, including Catherine Jordan and an older woman whom everyone called "Mother Quigley." The center's director of boys' work lived in one of the other buildings.[39]

Like many of the women of Hull House, Mary and Marie had a relationship that sustained their work for over four decades, yet their story is noteworthy in part because they were Catholic. During the nineteenth century Protestant women took part in a "female world of love and ritual," in which intense friendships among women were commonplace. Mary's and Marie's letters demonstrate that some Catholic women also enjoyed such a "female world of love and ritual." Further, like many of the Protestant women in Chicago's reform circles, Mary and Marie's relationship lasted well into the twentieth century, ending only with their deaths during the 1960s.[40]

Although their love for each other fills their correspondence, there is no evidence as to whether Mary and Marie had a sexual relationship. The only discussion of homosexual sex in Madonna Center's records concerns a young Italian boy.[41] Ironically, if Mary and Marie were lovers, the church might actually have facilitated this relationship to a certain degree. Scholars have noted that, during the early twentieth century, Catholic preoccupation with policing heterosexual behavior may have deflected some attention from the policing of homosexual acts.[42] Marie's love for Mary was filled with admiration for her spirituality. In 1924 she wrote Mary a brief and tender letter, to be read at the end of the day: "Good-night dear heart. May God bless & keep you as you are, for I think you're as perfect as people do [other than] your own little self." To others Marie spoke with pride about Mary's spiritual state: "her lily soul has . . . been whitened after a long standing." Mary met frequently with her confessor, attended Mass at least once a week and sometimes more often, maintaining a secret fondness for taking Communion before breakfast.[43]

Due in part to Marie's fragile ego, her love for Mary also had an element of jealousy. One particular incident in the autumn and winter of 1924 illustrates the problem with painful clarity. They were having trouble paying off the center's mortgage, and Mary suggested they rent out a few rooms in the house. Faced with the prospect of sharing her "boss," Marie responded as though she had been asked to move out. She took an extended trip away from Madonna Center for at least three months.[44] In the middle of her trip, she wired to Mary her resignation as secretary of the center's board. Mary responded with patience and humor: "Your resignations as Secretary submitted, but were absolutely scorned, and you were unanimously reelected." Later she reassured Marie the plan was not meant as a separation. After receiving assurances of Mary's love, Marie conceded: "I guess dear you do love me but not 1/2 I think as much as I love you and never will." She returned to the center after Mary and the board abandoned the rental scheme.[45]

For her part Mary behaved as though she was surprised and pleased to receive so much attention, admiration, and love. In July 1925 she wrote, poetically: "Marie Dear, Your letter . . . was awaiting my return this morning, and I don't need to tell you that I loved getting it. Even though I did choose the state of single blessedness, I do love a love letter, and you certainly know how to write one." Mary was clearly touched by Marie's affection. Despite the love letter, Mary may not have had an exclusive claim to Marie's affections. In 1922 Marie was away from the center, possibly involved in a romance with a man. Mary wrote: "Please be . . . careful about trotting around with that old beau of yours, for quite unfounded gossip has often traveled farther than Hot Springs." Mary added that she was destroying Marie's letters, presumably the ones that dealt with this romance.[46]

Mary and Marie's relationship was recognized by others as a partnership, although the nature of their relationship does not appear to have been questioned. When Marie went away again in 1925, this time spending time with a different man, Mary wrote how hard it was to be alone, saying: "Even Mr. Moore of the linen department of Field's asked for you the other day. So many can't seem to understand seeing me trodding around alone, and it is a lonesome business." Mary was despondent when she thought Marie was going to leave her: "You know, years ago, I pictured a great big Settlement, and me with you . . . and when I see that such a thing is impossible, it has made me feel pretty blue & heartbroken." Mary's heart mended again soon, when Marie came back again for good.[47]

Authority and Liberalization, 1922–1930

If Madonna Center gave Mary and Marie the autonomy to build a loving partnership together, it also strengthened their authority over the people in their new neighborhood. With less trouble than before from local clergy, they planned to continue emphasizing the center's old goals, including self-control for boys, gentility for girls, and job opportunities and recreation for everyone. Even though she promoted the Girl Scouts, Mary Amberg in particular seemed eager to continue picturing herself as a model of gentility and encouraging the center's girls to emulate her. Yet as they moved to their new location, the settlement women also found themselves working in a changing culture with a new generation of young people. As second-generation Italians became increasingly Americanized, they began to distance themselves from their parents, to demand the same recreational opportunities as other Americans, and to be attracted by the more aggressively sexualized content of 1920s popular culture. To a certain extent the settlement women tried to put the genie back in the bottle, attempting to use the authority of the center, and even the authority of the state, to reinforce the authority of parents. Yet this process necessitated a complicated negotiation among all the entities involved including the church, popular culture, parents, the state, and even the young people themselves. The Madonna Center women actually fostered the emerging heterosocial leisure culture of the early twentieth century by providing chaperones and an air of religious sanction to heterosocial activities.

Even after the move the center still had a conflicted relationship with neighborhood priests, although they were never again forced to move. As early as 1914, the Reverend Charles Fani, pastor of Our Lady of Pompeii Church, had asked the center to open a night school of Italian to compete with the one at the Methodist Episcopal Church on Polk Street. The class never materialized, even though Fani offered to teach it himself. Fani soon claimed that the center skimmed off his best parishioners, his "leaders," and diverted them from parish work. In 1924 Fani's new church was to open with a High Mass, a parade of twenty-five Italian fraternal societies, and five brass bands. Yet Amberg does not mention she planned to attend the festivities and only hoped that Cardinal Mundelein would pass in front of the center during the procession. Our Lady of Pompeii Church had its procession and festival every year in October, yet none of the center's workers ever mentioned attending. Fani even considered doing social work at his church; Amberg heard rumors of this and worried for a time that the center would no longer be needed.[48]

As the precipitating factor in the center's move, the settlement workers' vision of gender continued to evolve in the new location. Mary Amberg continued to think of herself as "social-minded gentry," modeling "refinement" to the girls and even writing stories to that effect. Yet by the 1920s neighborhood girls were changing, new opportunities were becoming available to them, they were becoming less obedient to their parents and more likely to experiment with sex. No longer were girls viewed as primarily servants to their families and now the settlement began to treat them more like boys: as problems and potential embarrassments to the Catholic community. In the 1920s the tight control that Italian parents had maintained over their girls began to slip. Italians had always tended to guard their daughters closely, which explains why Italian girls were underrepresented in the population of foreign-born prostitutes. However, the rates went up among the second generation.[49]

Evidence shows that the club girls took many initiatives to gain new pleasures for themselves. The Pollyanna Club's dance in 1924 raised enough money to help pay for vacations for ten of the girls. They even had money left over to purchase tickets to the movie "Days of the Golden West." Further, almost all of the clubs sponsored parties. Like dances, card parties were popular among the girls. The clubs also put on plays, generating more funding for the clubs and entertainment for other young people.[50]

In dealing with the stress between the generations, Madonna Center's first impulse was to attempt to reinforce the authority of parents. Many parents wanted to strictly chaperone their daughters, and the daughters increasingly wished to go out in the evenings like non-Italian girls. Catholic writers often stressed how laudable the Italians were for guarding their daughters so closely, and the center tended to side with parents even in situations that today would be considered abusive. In 1925 the center described Philip M. as a "high-type Italian," because he had some education. Yet they described him as "strict" with his children because he beat and kicked them when they did not do what he wanted. Madonna Center found a place for his oldest daughter in St. Joseph's Home for the Friendless but ultimately advised her to go back home, even though she was still afraid of her father.[51]

In order to appeal to the young people themselves, however, the Madonna Center women also promoted new activities (some of which mixed boys and girls) and even enabled neighborhood girls to redefine themselves as modern. One middle-class mother, trying to find a job for her daughter at the center, explained this new "modern" young woman best, insisting that her daughter was "a peppy, up-to-the-minute girl—but NOT a flapper."[52] The term *flapper* had connotations of immodestly dressed young women who flouted sexual convention. A "peppy" girl was modern, in contrast with the sedate nineteenth-century young lady, but Catholics expected both to give no hint of sexual impropriety.

Promoting physical vigor among young women, the center began to offer camping and athletics, including a girls' basketball team. For the center's girls, going to camp was a highly prized activity. When one mother wrote a permission slip for her two older daughters, she noted that her younger daughter was crying because she wanted to go too. A series of letters in 1924 reveal the high spirits, even "pep," of the girls at camp. They pulled pranks such as filling each other's beds with dried beans and rice. They went swimming and rowing and ate huge quantities of food. One girl wrote to Mary and Marie, describing her favorite activities: "There isn't anything I enjoyed as much as the hike we took this morning after Mass. We played 'follow the leader' for a while and then when we got tired we sat down and composed two songs, which we hope to sing to you when we all meet in September."[53]

Even the center's devotional clubs began to sponsor a measure of recreational programming. In the mid-1920s, for example, the Little Flower Club (named after St. Theresa) sponsored an outing to Lincoln Park and a Christmas party. Outside of pure recreation these clubs were designed to teach Irish American devotional styles to the Italian children. The members of the Agnes Ward Amberg Communion Guild took Communion regularly in a body in memory of Agnes Amberg and occasionally on behalf of other members of the Amberg family. They also performed other spiritual activities, such as novenas and prayer novenas, taking Communion or reciting certain prayers every day for nine days.[54]

During the 1920s the clubs started to reflect other changes in the circumstances of neighborhood girls. The Business Girls Club demonstrated that an increasing number of Italian girls were entering white-collar jobs. The club sponsored musical events, lectures, study, social events, and the ubiquitous domestic science and sewing classes. The center also attempted to establish a club for young married women, targeted specifically at members of the Sorority who had married. Because these young women had grown up in the center's clubs, they were more receptive to socializing outside the home than their mothers might have been. The center also started a mothers' club.[55]

While the center's girls became peppy and modern, the center tried to continue teaching "sound manhood" to its boys as it always had done. The basketball, baseball, and football teams were used to teach good sportsmanship, defined in part as the control of anger. In 1925 the center's baseball team became involved in a dispute with another team, and Amberg wrote to the captain of the center's team, advising him: "Whatever you do, Joe, don't get into any argument with the other side. If they try to make any trouble about yesterday's game . . . tell them in a very gentlemanly way that they should take it up with your managers."[56]

The center's boys' clubs continued to be popular during the 1920s, largely because of the companionship they offered. One boy stated on his membership application that he wished to join the Frata Club "To get in with a good bunch of fellows." A different applicant added that he was "very interested in the welfare of this club, and will strive to boost it." After reading such applications, members of the club would vote on whether to admit the applicant.[57]

The records of the boys' clubs reveal that the boys were aware of what they stood to lose from challenging the mores of adults, while some of the boys appear to have internalized the center's moral teachings and policed one another's behavior. Young people prone to rebellion probably avoided the settlement altogether. With certain notable exceptions, the Nic-Con Camping Club was a group of wholesome young men who had become too old for the Boy Scouts. In 1923 one of these young men ran away from home, probably with a young woman. The club wrote to him, hoping to make him go home: "Probably it has never occurred to you that your leaving your homes and families kind of casts a black shadow over the morality of the Club. . . . Can't you see that what you have done will make your mother . . . feel that by going camping we have put such a notion into your solid heads?" When not disciplining one another, the young men went camping twenty-four times a year and took Communion together regularly in memory of Agnes and William Amberg. They went camping with the Boy Scouts and also took Communion with them. They held raffles to raise money and used some of the proceeds to buy food for poor families.[58]

One of the center's most important roles was to mediate between parents and children, although they sometimes helped enlarge the gulf between the generations even as they hoped to shrink it. The center's help sometimes led to upward mobility for its young neighbors, which could benefit their material standard of living while confusing them culturally. One former boy scout, Frank Mentone, became the center's director of boys' work, and the center's workers helped several other young people get through college, in one case finding someone willing to pay a young man's tuition and in another case finding a job for a young man so he could work his way through college. One young woman felt that education had made her different and cut her off from the people in the neighborhood.[59]

The center's recreational programs also challenged the authority of parents by promoting a heterosocial, albeit heavily chaperoned, youth culture in the neighborhood. Many young people appreciated such recreation; as one commented, the center "was the only place you could go for diversion." Some parents objected, however, especially when the center's activities involved liberalization of gender roles. The center sponsored activities that promoted social interaction among boys and girls, including dances and even the library. The center provided well-chaperoned dances, designed to let the young people meet one another in a highly controlled atmosphere and to keep them away from sleazy commercial dance halls. The young people of the center responded enthusiastically. Eventually, the young people's clubs at the center even began to sponsor their own dances.[60]

Parents were not always pleased about the mixing of boys and girls. For instance, Petrina L.'s mother, Rose L., would not let Petrina play with the other girls in the neighborhood, let alone attend the dances at Madonna Center. Rose even stopped letting Petrina use Madonna Center's library, once she found out that boys also went there. This was very difficult for Petrina—she had spent most of her time reading because she was not allowed to play with other girls. She even considered becoming a nun in order to escape this strict supervision. Ironically, even though the center's workers were very careful to keep books deemed unsuitable out of the library, they were unwittingly helping liberalize social mores in the neighborhood.[61]

Madonna Center occupied a middle ground between its neighbors, the emerging popular culture of the era, and the growing coercive apparatus and social services of the state. At no time was that middle ground more evident than when the center became involved in attempts to control the sexuality of the neighborhood's young people. One might criticize female reformers for gaining salaries and prestige by taking authority over people of other classes and races, but these same reformers labored under a system they did not create, one that provided a decent living only to those who had authority over others.[62] In our examination of the work of Mary and Marie, rather than see them imposing their values upon their hapless neighbors, it is more useful to view their work as constant negotiation between attempts to assert authority, the limits of that authority, and maintaining functioning relations with the state and dominant culture.

Parents, the center, and representatives of the state all wished to prevent unmarried young people from engaging in sexual activity, although case records indicate how difficult a job this was. Like the leisure culture that surrounded them, some of the second-generation Italian girls were developing a new openness toward sexual matters and a concern for their own pleasure, along with a great deal of guilt as well. For example, Minnie M. felt guilty about having sex outside of marriage and went voluntarily to the House of the Good Shepherd, an institution run by sisters for "fallen" women and girls. Mary Amberg and the Chicago Big Sisters arranged to keep her from having to go to court, in order to spare her family the publicity. Yet Minnie also suggested the idea, newly popular in the 1920s, that women were not passionless but desired sex like men did. She wrote to Amberg, thanking her for her kindness and asserting: "I pray hard for strength to resist future temptations."[63]

During the 1920s the center's growing cooperation with the juvenile court gave the center a powerful tool for disciplining girls.[64] Carmella W. came to the center's attention because of some kind of sexual misconduct with a boy. In an attempt to keep the young woman out of an institution, Marie Plamondon became her probation officer. Carmella was forced to sign a contract, in which she promised to meet Marie twice a week and report all her activities to her. She also promised

> that I will never be on the street at night after dark unless she gives me permission to be. I further agree that I will attend church every Sunday and go to communion every Sunday. I will keep company with only such girls as [Miss Plamondon and Miss Amberg] are willing that I should keep company with. I will keep company with no boys or men. I will always tell the truth to my mother and to Miss Plamondon.

The injunction that Carmella was to go to church and take Communion every Sunday was designed to enhance her self-control. Communion was considered a powerful spiritual tool against the power of sin. Most likely, Plamondon also required Carmella to go to confession regularly as well, where a priest would question her about her behavior. Despite all this pressure, Carmella failed to live up to her agreement; the next letter she wrote Plamondon was from the House of the Good Shepherd; most likely she had been committed there by the court. In veiled defiance, Carmella apologized for giving Plamondon so much trouble but also reminded her that she would be eighteen soon and free to do as she pleased: leave the House of the Good Shepherd and marry the boy who was the source of her troubles.[65]

While Carmella W. was coerced out of activities she clearly enjoyed, Madonna Center could also help protect young women from sexual exploitation. The young women in Madonna Center's neighborhood could experience substantial coercive pressure from young men to have sex. The protection of the Madonna Center women, even though it posed the danger of incarceration in an institution, may sometimes have been preferable to various forms of sexual abuse. At the very least the center and the House of the Good Shepherd could sometimes provide alternatives, if difficult ones, to intolerable situations.[66]

Young women in the Madonna Center neighborhood faced sexual victimization both from boyfriends and from strangers. The most serious case at the center involved Anna E., whose family was highly dysfunctional. When Anna was thirteen, Madonna Center sent her to the House of the Good Shepherd as a "preventative case," because she was malnourished, of sub-par intelligence, filthy, and her family abused her. Anna's time in this institution may well have been the most peaceful of her young life. After she was released a few years later, an unsavory young man named Ferdinand first coerced her into having sex and then, when her menstrual periods stopped, warned her not to tell anyone he was the boy with whom she was having sex. When Ferdinand was discovered, the couple married. Soon Ferdinand and his mother were both abusing Anna, and eventually Ferdinand tried to divorce Anna and keep the baby for himself. Madonna Center stood by Anna for years, accompanying her every time she went to court. Eventually, they placed Anna's two children in an orphan asylum, saving them from an abusive father and a mother who loved them but who was not mentally competent to care for them.[67]

Strangers in the Madonna Center neighborhood could be just as bad as boyfriends in exploiting young women, and the law was often no help. In the case of the D'A. family, for example, one son was put on trial in a case of gang rape. Yet because the young woman in question was over seventeen, the age of consent, all the young men in the case were acquitted. In another case two young girls reported that a Greek man in the neighborhood had repeatedly exposed himself to them when they were at his home visiting his wife.[68]

Madonna Center workers sometimes could use their connections to the juvenile court coercively, but they were limited in their ability to do this by their need to maintain the trust and respect of their neighbors. The center's workers tried, for the most part, to keep girls away from the court, both to spare the girls an ordeal and to preserve Madonna Center's relationship with its neighbors. Even Carmella's "probation" under the care of Marie Plamondon was meant to keep Carmella away from the court; a valuable form of protection because, once in court, girls were much more likely than boys to be committed to an institution. Further, even girls who went to court for nonsexual reasons were subjected to humiliating interrogations about their sex lives and physical examinations to prove their virginity. Sometimes Madonna Center did participate in legal proceedings, particularly if the court asked them to intervene; often their intervention served to reinforce the authority of parents. For example, Mary D.'s parents took her to court not because of any alleged sexual infraction but because she refused to pray and go to Mass with them. The court asked Madonna Center to try to exert religious influence on the girl. Usually the center refused to testify in court against any of their girls. Sometimes the center did participate in a girl's commitment, but they did their best to hide the fact, for fear that their neighbors would no longer trust them.[69]

While the center regulated the sexuality of its girls with external controls (either protective or coercive), it continued to focus on teaching its young men to internalize self-control. The center's workers adhered to the commonly accepted idea that the male sex drive was overpowering; yet they believed that young men could overcome it through religious and moral education. The center even took a few steps toward sex education, although it lagged behind non-Catholic institutions. Sex education was still highly controversial among Catholics. In 1928 the center arranged to have a "social hygiene" class taught by Dr. John Suldane, a doctor who had for years given free medical care to the center's neighbors. The students were a small group of handpicked young men, most in their early twenties. The center did not offer sex education for girls until 1933.[70]

Two cases illustrate the ideal of self-control taught by the center—and its limitations. The case of Mario, written up by Mary Amberg in her memoir of the center, presents the self-control ideal. He started in the center's day nursery in 1925 and continued at the center for years. Even though he eventually fell in with a group of tough young men, Mario's early religious training stayed with him. One night Mario was with them when they went out to commit a gang rape. On the way they happened to drive by Madonna Center. Seeing the familiar building Mario repented and made his friends stop the car and let him out. That night the other gang members were arrested, but Mario was at the center instead. Even at the center Mario still wrestled all night with his overwhelming desires; the center's male worker had to restrain him forcibly from leaving to rejoin the rape. The worker prayed with him, and in the end Mario broke down, confessing that he had fantasized about the rape for weeks and sobbing that he was just as bad as the rest of the gang.[71]

While any sexually active young woman could be prosecuted by the juvenile court, young men's sexuality usually only came to the court's attention when some sort of abuse was involved. The case of Tony B. illustrates the severe limits of the center's ideal of self-control. In 1929 he was twelve years old and a dependable and conscientious boy scout. Two years later he learned that the people who had raised him were not his "real" parents. Tony had been burned in an accident when he was two years old. His mother did not want to care for him, so she gave him to her childless sister-in-law. This aunt and her husband had raised Tony and supported him in comfort. Despite his aunt and uncle's kindness, Tony decided that he needed to go live with his birth mother. His new home life was characterized by filth, violence, cruelty, and sexual abuse. Tony's older brother, Edward, beat him up, and the center's social worker even suspected he had tried to abuse him sexually. Tony complained to center workers that he no longer had "raviola" on Sundays and never had a bag of peanuts anymore. He was unhappy that nobody washed his clothes for him. Worst of all Tony once shouted to his mother: "I won't go back to sleep in your house because you are a bad woman—you run around with the men on Taylor St." Madonna Center concentrated on trying to reform Tony's behavior, but they could not heal his fundamental problem; the discipline of the Boy Scouts could not help a young man who had been let down so much by the adults in his life. The center's workers tried sending Tony to various institutions, yet he always returned home. In 1934 he and his brother were arrested as members of a gang accused of committing more than a hundred robberies and at least one murder.[72]

Like the center's relations with young people, case records demonstrate that its dealings with adults could range from friendship, to protection, to coercion. The center began doing more casework early in the 1920s, hiring a trained social worker until 1928. Sickness and unemployment topped the list of reasons why Madonna Center's neighbors received material aid: 31 percent of families in the case records experienced sickness, and 31 percent experienced unemployment. About 12 percent were widows and 2 percent widowers. A few families were extraordinarily large, but the average was only 4.7 children; 7.5 percent of families experienced substance abuse; 6 percent had a problem with juvenile delinquency; 4 percent had family members in jail. The center gave meal tickets, clothing, and tickets for ice during the summers.[73]

Poor families came to the center's attention in a variety of ways. Occasionally, a mother would visit the office herself to ask for help.[74] Most of the time the supplicants were genuinely in need, but occasionally someone would ask just out of curiosity. In 1923 Loretta P. told the center worker that she "Just came over because her mother saw we helped others last year and [we] would like to get something, too."[75] This strategy could backfire, however. In 1927 one of the center's workers called the mother of the B.

family "a pest" because she asked for too much help.[76] In order to avoid such criticism, some families would write letters or send their children to ask for help.[77] Other "cases" would be referred to the center by a priest, schoolteacher, or politician. Some "cases" started out as members of Madonna Center clubs, others were referred by neighbors. A handful started out as employees of the center.[78]

Before giving assistance, center volunteers would often visit families at home. Families could be disqualified if their homes displayed evidence of prosperity or if they owned their homes. Sometimes neighbors would inform on families if they believed the people did not deserve help.[79] Alcohol use also disqualified a family for help. Notably, center workers seemed to regard alcohol as a luxury while Italians viewed it as a staple and evidence of prosperity. Families would buy loads of grapes to make their own wine, which they would store in barrels, in a cellar if possible. Most families would keep wine for their own use, but some also sold it. A family was considered poor if they had only two barrels of wine, but comfortable if they owned twenty; Italian neighbors used the number of barrels owned as evidence that a family did not need charity.[80] Center workers were indignant when one mother said she could not afford milk for the baby because her husband insisted on having wine.[81]

The center used casework to foster its version of sexual morality among neighborhood adults, encouraging people to be married in church and discouraging divorce, birth control, and abortion. For example, in 1926, one of the center's volunteers found a former Guardian Angel girl who had been divorced because her husband cheated on her. Mary Amberg herself had prepared Mrs. Minnie A. for her First Holy Communion. Nevertheless, the volunteer noted with disapproval that Minnie joked about the divorce with a friend. With the help of volunteer doctors, the center also worked to check the spread of "birth control propaganda" in the neighborhood. Later in the 1930s, when their neighbors were suffering from the hardships of the depression, they began to run into cases of women trying to obtain abortions, which they would discourage.[82]

Even though the center promoted conservative values with regard to marriage, in cases of domestic abuse they helped women challenge, to a degree, the power their husbands had over them. Mary Amberg was especially concerned with "easing the burden of suffering for other women and girls." The settlement's housekeeper, Katie H., was an example. The settlement stood by Katie for many years while, abandoned by her husband, she sued for child support, and they later tried to help her daughter Mary, who had married an abusive alcoholic. They wrote letters to Mary's husband, warning him to treat her well while she was pregnant, and provided a summer vacation for one of the couple's daughters, a temporary refuge from the violence in her family. The center also occasionally provided assistance to men with violent wives.[83]

The center's staff worked hard to create opportunities for the neighbors and to improve their lives, but they did not consider them equals. Amberg and Plamondon sometimes used ethnic slurs to refer to their neighbors, although never to their faces; rather, they would do so in a joking way with members of their own class. They could even be condescending toward their high-achieving neighbors, showing little awareness that this might have been insulting. A friend of Marie's once tried to pay a compliment to one of the center's Italian workers but in doing so managed to portray him as a noble savage. He wrote: "I liked your friend immensely. I found him utterly unspoiled and . . . lovable."[84]

Over the years, the women of Madonna Center increased their authority over the neighbors through relief programs and cooperation with the juvenile court; yet their ability to use this authority was limited by the need to preserve their legitimacy among the neighbors and their desire to protect some neighbors from the state. While their inclination was to bolster the authority of parents, they also challenged the authority structures of neighborhood families and gender inequities in recreation. They provided options for abused women, recreation for Italian women and girls, and helped transform the belief that defined "leisure" for girls primarily as work for their families. The center also helped usher in a heterosocial leisure culture by creating opportunities for young men and women to socialize together. Hence, although the intentions of the Madonna Center women were conservative, they helped tug their neighborhood in the direction of modernism, promoting the relaxation of extremely strict ethnic standards of mixed-sex interaction, while mediating between their neighbors and the expanding authority of the state.

The Apex of Laywomen's Autonomy

In one sense, proprietary settlements like Madonna Center fit the model of the genteel rescuer of the *New World* stories better than club-model settlements. In proprietary settlements, wealthy women were more likely to work directly with neighborhood children and adults. Yet doing settlement work also gave the leaders of proprietary settlements a boost, in a manner the rescue stories could not have foreseen: they gave the settlement women authority within city neighborhoods. These settlements required backing from the hierarchy in order to survive, yet their mere existence as relatively autonomous institutions within parish boundaries set the stage for conflict with local clergy. The heroines of the rescue stories did not challenge gender inequities either, or modernize leisure, yet the settlements did. The heroines of the rescue stories were not supposed to be political, yet the settlements helped create a role for laywomen in mediating between neighborhood Catholics and the growing social services and coercive apparatus of the state. The rescue stories were not designed to encourage dramatic change in women's domestic relationships, but living at the center gave Amberg and Plamondon, for example, a unique degree of autonomy for single women of their class and the opportunity to forge a remarkable life partnership, notable for its longevity regardless of whether their relationship was sexual in nature.

If proprietary-model settlements gave laywomen cultural authority in neighborhoods and an increased role in mediating between Catholics and the state, parish-model settlements were designed to take back these prerogatives for the male clergy. By encouraging the creation of parish-model settlements, priests sought to harness laywomen's labor while limiting their independence and subordinating them to priestly authority. Ultimately, many of the programs pioneered by women would later be incorporated into parish structures and into the growing bureaucracy of Catholic charities. In this the Catholic settlements resembled non-Catholic ones, many of whose programs were ultimately incorporated into the structures of city government. While one of the goals of parish settlements was to prevent laywomen's involvement in activities that the church viewed as undesirable (such as politics), parish-model settlements were more than just devices for controlling laywomen. In fact they enabled Catholic women to redefine themselves as modern, by providing them with opportunities outside the home, which many parish women embraced with enthusiasm.

CHAPTER FIVE

Aspiring Politicians

The De Paul Settlement Club, 1910–1920

In a speech in 1923 Father Francis McCabe recalled the founding of the De Paul Settlement Club, a laywomen's group established in 1914 to raise money for a settlement house in St. Vincent's parish. McCabe thanked the members of the club, especially "that faithful old guard that wanted to be politicians at one time, and wanted us to coach them in voting. We wouldn't do it, and they finally came and asked, 'Father, isn't there something good to be done?'" Like the members of the hierarchy who promoted noblesse oblige among laywomen, McCabe hoped that benevolent work would keep his female parishioners away from politics. He also recognized that the labor of laywomen could be a great asset, as he struggled to lead a parish becoming increasingly poor and divided by ethnicity. The settlement club thus appeared to serve both his goals at once. McCabe was fully aware of the work laywomen had been doing in Chicago since the CWL opened its settlements in 1893, and the De Paul Settlement and Day Nursery was inspired by their efforts.[1] Just as city government adopted some programs begun by settlements, Catholic parishes across the city were also influenced by women's settlement work. Parish-model settlements were different from other settlements, however, in that they aimed to capture the benefits of women's labor while limiting their ability to challenge the priests' authority.

To a certain extent McCabe's efforts succeeded. The settlement club members resembled, in some ways, the heroines of the *New World* rescue stories: pious and domestic, they took on the work of the club with enthusiasm. The De Paul Settlement Club also helped the parish cope with an influx of poorer parishioners, by working to establish ties between better-off and poor Catholics in the face of socioeconomic and ethnic change. McCabe's plan to limit the political activities of St. Vincent's women failed, however. If it had not been for the political connections of certain women in the parish, in fact, the settlement itself would never have been established. Further, laywomen themselves received a substantial boost from settlement work and other parish activities. They demanded professional and educational opportunities, as well as opportunities to do benevolent work, within their parish. The priests of St. Vincent's met many of these demands, as a way to keep the women's labor at home. Settlement work also enabled parish laywomen to craft a new self-image as modern. Without openly challenging domesticity, they portrayed themselves as competent, energetic, and efficient—worthy of respect. While reassuring St. Vincent's more conservative parishioners, defining themselves as modern enabled the settlement club women to take on expanded roles outside the home.

Education and Opportunity at St. Vincent's

When Francis McCabe first came to St. Vincent's as its pastor in 1910, he faced a huge debt on the church and college buildings. At a time when money was badly needed, an influx of poor immigrants from various ethnic groups would spur the parish's better-off Irish parishioners to move further north. At the same time laywomen were beginning to press for Catholic educational opportunities; they were also entering white-collar jobs. McCabe was well aware that he needed to muster all of the parish's resources to meet these challenges. Even though McCabe disapproved of women's political involvement, he did recognize their potential to make a real contribution to the parish. Thus the priests and nuns of St. Vincent's parish began to promote education and career opportunities for parish women. McCabe planned then to recruit these women to do volunteer work for the parish. Ultimately he hoped some of them would train as social workers at the university while gaining professional experience at the settlement house. McCabe's female parishioners responded enthusiastically to his attention because it provided them with new opportunities. McCabe understood what women's shift to white-collar work could do for the parish in terms of increased money and prestige, but he also cautioned them that new opportunities should not cause them to lose their focus on domesticity. He hoped to capture their energy while shaping its expression.

Working women could bring substantial resources to a parish. Before the De Paul Settlement was opened, McCabe was told that instead of building a day nursery he should "build a working girls' home and you will bring those into your parish who will contribute to your parish." Working girls' homes were generally not moneymakers for the nuns and laywomen who ran them, but they did attract hardworking, enterprising young women to a parish. McCabe refused to build a working-girls' home; he claimed charity should be about helping others, not enriching one's own parish. Nevertheless, he did not hesitate to seek contributions of money and labor from the working women already in his parish.[2]

St. Vincent's had once been prosperous, but by the early twentieth century it needed an infusion of energetic workers to help solve its problems. A decade before McCabe's arrival, Lincoln Park, the neighborhood in which St. Vincent's was located, had contained a population mixed in both ethnicity and class. Immediately surrounding the church was "the most prosperous Irish neighborhood of the northside," composed of two-story brick duplexes clustered around the church at Webster and Sheffield avenues. Also in the neighborhood were German, Irish, and Polish laborers who worked in the factories located along the north branch of the Chicago River. East of the church, in a section dominated by German Presbyterians, there were lower-middle-class people who lived in boardinghouses and worked in the Loop.[3]

St. Vincent's parish covered most of the neighborhood, extending from the river on the west, east on North Avenue to Halsted Street, north on Halsted to Armitage (then Center Avenue), west to North Lincoln Park West (then Lincoln Park), north to Wrightwood, and west again to the river. Although, as a territorial parish, St. Vincent's was open to all Catholics living within its boundaries, it catered primarily to the neighborhood's Irish. The neighborhood's Germans attended St. Theresa's nearby, and its Poles attended St. Josaphat. St. Vincent's parish was blessed with a handsome church building, built in 1895 at a cost of one hundred thousand dollars. The Sisters of the Blessed Virgin Mary ran two schools in the parish, a coeducational grade school and a girls' high school. In addition St. Vincent's College (which became De Paul University in 1907) offered both high school and college courses to boys and young men, most of whom lived in the neighborhood. Founded in 1898 the college was run and staffed by the Vincentian fathers, who also ran the parish.[4]

The Daughters of Charity of St. Vincent de Paul, who would later run the De Paul Settlement after it opened in 1915, operated two institutions in the neighborhood: St Joseph's Hospital and St. Vincent's Infant Asylum. They were the sister order to the Vincentian Priests. Both orders had a long history of dedication to benevolent work and education, which may have helped make them receptive to new ideas in charity. This order of nuns also ran another settlement house in Chicago; first known as the Catholic Social Center, its name later changed to Marillac House after Louise de Marillac, patron saint of the order.[5]

In the interval between the beginning of the century and World War I, Lincoln Park saw the arrival of growing numbers of working-class immigrants, including "Poles, Slovaks, Serbians, Rumanians, Hungarians, and Italians." Many of these would later place children in the day nursery. As the neighborhood became more economically and ethnically diverse, St. Vincent's major institutions remained under Irish control. The parish newspaper, called the *Vincentian Weekly,* attained a circulation of between thirty-two and thirty-six hundred copies weekly, reaching into approximately two thousand homes every Sunday. The university also continued to cater to Irish Americans.[6]

From the moment of his arrival in Chicago, Francis Xavier McCabe demonstrated a gift for motivating people, largely because of his unflagging energy and good humor. He was a flamboyant orator and had spent ten years honing this skill at St. Vincent's College in Los Angeles, first as professor of history and oratory and later as vice president of the college. After Los Angeles he spent four years as a missionary in the Southwest. In Chicago he quickly turned his skills to the benefit of the parish, working to reduce the debt on the church and to raise money for his projects. Unafraid of controversy, he started running the College Theatre for a profit, showing plays and later films as a source of revenue for the university. McCabe himself was a talented performer with an attachment to Shakespeare. He encouraged student productions, gave readings and lectures, and would even sing for his audiences.[7]

Early in the twentieth century, women had begun to petition the hierarchy for higher education opportunities in Chicago. Inspired by their demands, McCabe crafted a plan for coeducation at De Paul University. At the request of Cardinal Quigley, he made plans for the university to incorporate the girls' high school. Amid great excitement the girls were moved into one of the university buildings in 1911, and the seniors even started taking certain university courses. The plan to create a separate women's college within De Paul ultimately failed because of the opposition of Cardinal Mundelein, but the university continued to offer certain courses to women. The Teachers' Extension offered college courses in the afternoons and during the summers for city teachers, and the College of Music attracted many women students. For the young men McCabe added a college of law and a college of commerce in 1912.[8]

Even for young women at St. Vincent's who did not aspire to a university education, many other opportunities were available in the parish. For example, the editor of the *Vincentian Weekly* asked the high school girls to submit stories for publication. One student responded happily: "Girls, do your best. With such encouragement, we may some day become famous." A De Paul High School student followed this advice and wrote an article, which was published in the *Record-Herald.* A high percentage of the high school students passed the Normal Exams, which would enable them to go to the State Normal School for free training as teachers. Even young women who did not finish high school could take advantage of new opportunities. For example, the telephone company advertised in the *Vincentian Weekly* that it would pay five dollars a week to young women over sixteen while they were training to be telephone operators.[9]

Young women at St. Vincent's openly expressed their enthusiasm for the new opportunities being made available to them. In 1911 the sisters of the high school opened a commercial course that trained parish girls to work as typists and stenographers. With a sense of excitement one high school student remarked: "It only remains to be seen what St. Vincent's business women can do." While the majority of St. Vincent's women probably did not parlay clerical work into more powerful positions, anything seemed possible when opportunities were expanding on every side. Catholic education did primarily equip young women to remain subordinates in the workplace. But if it had been merely disempowering, laywomen would not have petitioned for it and flocked to it when it was offered.[10]

Even though the parish was helping propel its young women forward, St. Vincent's priests and the young women themselves moved to reassure themselves and other parishioners that the changes were not going too far, too fast. As if to assert that they would not stray too far from domesticity, the high school girls claimed in 1911 that "there are no incipient suffragettes among the young ladies of De Paul." Yet in 1913, when women in Illinois won limited suffrage, a number of St. Vincent's women would enthusiastically take up the vote and other forms of political work. Playing upon the anxieties of young women who were moving into white-collar occupations, the *Vincentian Weekly* sternly warned: "Arrogance is always an intolerable trait in woman, for it gives evidence of either a poorly trained or a coarse mind." Thus the parish newspaper encouraged St. Vincent's women to achieve, but also to beware not to make anyone else uncomfortable about their achievements.[11]

The De Paul Settlement Club and the Modern Catholic Woman

Before the De Paul Settlement Club was established in 1914, women had been traveling outside St. Vincent's parish to do settlement work at a number of other institutions in Chicago. The club was intended to woo such women back and recruit the labor of others. While its membership included both married and single women, the club would draw its leadership from a core group of married women, many of whom became involved in parish affairs during large fund-raising bazaars held in 1910 and 1913. Benevolent work enabled these women to define themselves as modern by emphasizing their own self-confidence, achievements, and even competitiveness. Like the mother at Madonna Center who insisted that her daughter was "a peppy, up-to-the-minute girl—but NOT a flapper," St. Vincent's women could be energetic while still embracing piety and domesticity.[12] This new, more modern gender identity being created by these women was acceptable to McCabe and others at St. Vincent's because the women did not openly challenge existing gender hierarchies or the authority of the clergy. Yet the settlement club did enable laywomen to gain a certain influence in the parish, especially in the affairs of the settlement.

Before the settlement club was founded, St. Vincent's women had to travel outside the parish to do this kind of work. In 1913 a Miss McKeon of St. Vincent's parish was running the day nursery of St. Philip Benizi Church. St. Patrick's Church had a settlement club, which may also have appealed to parishioners at St. Vincent's. An ad for the settlement club in the parish newspaper even noted: "Some of our charitably inclined have been going a long distance into other parishes to assist in settlement work, and schools of this, that and the other thing, when right here in the University building, on every other Monday night, we have what promises to be the best Settlement Club on the North Side, if not in the city, in the near future."[13]

The first steps toward bringing such women back to the parish for volunteer work were the 1910 and 1913 fund-raising bazaars. These bazaars were not a new idea; both Catholics and Protestants had used them since the 1850s. The bazaars at St. Vincent's were unique, however, in how they galvanized the parish women who would later be central to the settlement club. A poem in the *Vincentian Weekly* entitled "The Last Shall Be First" named many parish women who later became active in the settlement club. The poem noted:

> Mrs. Sullivan with a smile so bland,
> [was] the most amiable lady in the land.
> Directed by [this] lady fine
> We were soon marshaled into line . . .
> Mrs. Kolb in the corner [who] had a stand—
> presided o'er by a merry band—
> The "Teddy Bears" were the attraction here
> And people came from far and near
> To see Mrs. Navin and Mrs. Stack . . .
> Carrying the "Teddies" forward and back.

Those women who did not run stands could still make substantial contributions to the event. Some donated prizes, both secular and religious, to be auctioned off. For example, "Mrs. Burke a chest of silver gave, / The winner, our pastor, Father McCabe," while "Mrs. Piries presented a statue of St. Anne, / Which was won by Mrs. Navin's man." Some women sold raffle tickets: "Mrs. Pierce sold series on a picture fine." Others with good luck took prizes home: "John McGillen's watch to Mrs. Sullivan sent / Swelled our treasury many a cent." And finally, the married women enlisted trained single women, including the help of "Miss Handley, our Secretary, so bright— / [who] Made note of every thing quite right."[14]

The *Vincentian Weekly* never printed large numbers of rescue stories as the *New World* did. A few articles focused on charity, including several written by female students at the parish high school. The stories focused on the obligation of the rich to help the poor and emphasized the happiness that can come from helping others. Others stressed the positive ties that acts of charity can create between rich and poor. The stories in the *Vincentian* thus echoed themes that were common to the *New World* rescue stories.[15]

While the fictional tales in the *Vincentian* echoed the *New World* rescue stories, St. Vincent's women wrote about their own benevolent work in a different voice. During the bazaar, for example, the women embraced the idea of competition. For the 1910 bazaar McCabe divided the parish into three separate districts, each with its own colors. Each district had a team of women whose job it was to collect items to sell or raffle off at the bazaar. They made many of the items themselves and also went door-to-door asking for donations, each group competing to collect the best prizes. Demonstrating their competitive spirit, their loyalty to Father McCabe, and their knowledge of the Bible, one group claimed they were working "like bees" and then nicknamed themselves "the McCabees" (Maccabees is part of the apocryphal scriptures, included in Catholic Bibles but not Protestant ones). The bazaars offered women the opportunity to use their domestic skills such as sewing, decorating, cooking, and baking skills for a public purpose and also gave them the opportunity to move beyond the limits of domestic ideology. As the domestic ideology could not, competition allowed them to unleash an element of creative aggression.[16]

When the teams set out to gather prizes and sell raffle tickets, they described themselves in terms appropriate for hard-hitting salespeople. The women of the Southwest district claimed: "Though this district is the smallest . . . it makes up in activity, push and strenuosity [*sic*] . . . hustle is the watch-word. The workers are anxiously waiting for some of their friends to come forward with an automobile and a house and lot; they are looking for big game." The women described themselves with the personal characteristics of successful entrepreneurs—determination, energy, and aggression. The drive to win led the teams to boast to each other about their prowess. When the Central District was ahead in 1910, the Eastern District claimed to be catching up fast and bragged that it was going to "put one over." This competition paid off in financial terms. The 1910 bazaar, for example, netted the considerable sum of ten thousand dollars to help relieve the parish's debts.[17]

Further promoting achievement, the bazaar even generated a few career opportunities for single women, though it created more for young men. Everyone in the parish, even the schoolchildren, was supposed to participate in the fund-raising. Young men, particularly students at the university, could work as secretaries to a particular district or promoters for some of the bazaar's many events. St. Vincent's young men were encouraged to regard parish social activities as assets to a career in business. Young single women could sometimes find opportunities in running parish events as well, especially if no young man was available to fill a position.[18]

In addition to promoting achievement among women, the bazaar also helped knit the parish together in spite of the demographic factors that were pulling it apart. For nonperishable goods, the bazaars set up a system of exchange within the parish community wherein people donated things they did not need anymore and spent small amounts of money to win other things that they might not be able to afford to buy. While there were some grand prizes, most were quite modest. The *Vincentian Weekly,* for example, proudly noted that one young woman had won a fur collar. Meals offered another opportunity for parishioners to come together. Refreshment tables and banquets offered a variety of delicacies, from home-cooked hot dishes to hot dogs, pickles and relishes, tea and coffee.[19]

Parish women's enthusiasm about the bazaars transferred quite easily to the settlement club. Shortly after the club was established, members noted in the parish newspaper that "when you mention De Paul Settlement Club every one is interested." The club's first meeting was held on August 17, 1914, and within a year it had ninety-eight active members, plus twelve honorary members who paid dues but did not attend meetings. The honorary members even included four men. At least thirteen, and possibly as many as twenty, of the original settlement club members had been active in the bazaars of 1910 and 1913.[20]

The substantial club membership challenges the notion that laywomen were not interested in settlement work. Although they did not move into settlements in large numbers, through the club many of St Vincent's laywomen became enthusiastic supporters of settlement work. Many either could not afford to devote themselves to full-time unpaid work or had husbands and children. Settlement clubs allowed them to participate in the movement without neglecting their other responsibilities. Further, the settlement club women lived in the area and were already participating in the life of the neighborhood even though they did not live in the settlement. Finally, we should not assume that all the residents in nonsectarian settlements were actively engaged in social work. Some residents regarded settlements as little more than a cheap place to live.[21]

Parish women not only supported the day nursery, they played a vital role in establishing it. Agnes Nestor was a member of the parish who started working as a glove maker at a young age and rose to become president of the Women's Trade Union League. Nestor was a strong supporter of the nursery and helped obtain a building to house the work. At the behest of Woodrow Wilson, she also served as chairperson of the Women in Industry Committee of the Council of National Defense. Promoting day care was one strategy for ensuring that the nation could benefit from women's labor during the war.[22]

Other women at St. Vincent's also took the initiative in establishing the new day nursery. Soon after the club was founded its president, Mrs. Sullivan, appointed a committee of three women to visit the settlement club in St. Patrick's parish to ascertain how much money was needed for the project. Other club members took excursions to price linens and baby clothing at retail and wholesale stores. A third committee scouted possible locations for the settlement. Collecting baby furniture, outfitting the settlement's chapel, and hemming towels for the nursery kitchen, all gave members a sense of accomplishment. When they hosted the nursery's formal opening in December 1915, they noted proudly that "Visitors from almost every nursery and children's hospital in the city came during the day and declared the De Paul Day Nursery was furnished and equipped as well as if in existence for five years." One member taught a "fancy-work" sewing class to parish children and charged ten cents a lesson to raise money for the nursery. Members also took personal satisfaction in making sure that the nursery building met state requirements, and in making it comfortable and homelike.[23]

Even though the settlement club fostered piety and utilized members' domestic skills, McCabe overestimated the club's ability to keep parish women away from politics. Several women from St. Vincent's were actively involved in political work and even ran for office after Illinois women won the right to vote in 1913. After chairing the Women in Industry Committee in Washington, Agnes Nestor came back to the parish to deliver a lecture to raise money for the nursery. She also sought the Democratic nomination for the Illinois House in 1928. Veronica Walsh, a former resident of St. Vincent's parish, worked for a number of years as a stenographer for a judge and ran for office herself after Illinois women won the vote. McCabe even urged St. Vincent's women to register after they won the right to vote in Illinois in 1913, probably hoping to balance the votes of Protestant women. It may be that McCabe objected not so much to women voting, especially after they had won the vote and he could not stop them, but to their participation in political clubs. By 1920 local politicians had begun to use women's clubs as labor in their campaigns, and club women were even trying to influence political decision making. McCabe nurtured parish women's interest in the wider world, by attending the club's meetings regularly and giving talks on subjects as varied as schools, the meaning of citizenship for Catholics, charity and settlement work, threats to public morals, and later the war.[24]

As they interpreted the work of the De Paul Settlement to the public, the settlement club women interpreted themselves to the public as well. In promoting their various fund-raising events, the women perpetuated the rhetoric of competence and energy that they had taken on for the bazaars. For one event they proudly announced in the *Vincentian Weekly* that "the line . . . waiting [for] tickets Monday night . . . would put to shame any one who would say the settlement members were not hustlers." (Obviously, club members were not using the word *hustler* in its modern connotation of "prostitute.") Even McCabe emphasized the women's "energy," when he called them "many of the most energetic ladies, married and single, in the parish." The club's more private activities reinforced this image. Besides furnishing pleasant social occasions, card parties sponsored by individual members offered them a chance to demonstrate fund-raising ability. When earnings were substantial, they could be announced in club meetings and greeted with a round of applause.[25]

Yet even as they crafted a new self-image as modern, energetic achievers, St. Vincent's women wrestled to reconcile their new identity with a nineteenth-century belief in feminine humility. One young parish woman named Ursula Kelly provides an example. After she died unexpectedly in her sleep at a young age, her friends extolled her work as head of the St. Vincent's Altar Society, describing her as an "inventive genius with executive ability and business sagacity of a high order." They noted in another article that "she worked on for years in a subordinate position, content to be near the Tabernacle. . . . when she was finally forced into leadership, she quietly transformed the . . . old-fashioned easy-going altar society . . . into a progressive church organization with scores of active members and . . . financially a big asset of the parish."[26] Even as they praised her success, Kelly's friends took pains to point out that it did not come at the cost of her humility. Kelly was not a member of the settlement club, but she did benefit it posthumously. After she died, her friends started a fund in her honor to buy milk for the day nursery children. Her situation—the need to balance achievement with humility—was shared by leaders in many of the women's organizations at St. Vincent's.

Framing the settlement club women's work in terms of energy and competence could reassure traditionalists that they were not dangerous like "New Women" or feminists. However, the settlement club did gain real influence in the parish, especially over the settlement and over the religious sisters who ran it. Historians have argued that laywomen viewed settlements as an opportunity to achieve administrative positions in a field that had long been dominated by nuns. While this was true for proprietary settlements like Madonna Center, at the De Paul Settlement Club women seemed content to let the Daughters of Charity retain administrative control of the agency most of the time.[27]

Even though the settlement club women were usually content to let the sisters set policy for the settlement, when they disagreed with any given policy the laywomen's opinions carried weight. For example, when the settlement was incorporated in 1929, the sisters wished to change the institution's name to Marillac Center. Mrs. Burke, the president of the settlement club, objected that "such a change of name would at this time . . . be almost disastrous; that De Paul Nursery was now well and favorably known throughout the city; that it took years of hard work to make it so." Because of the club's financial importance, Mrs. Burke was able to keep the settlement from changing its name. The Sister Servant (superior) of the settlement explained:

> As perhaps you know, De Paul Settlement Club was organized quite a while before the opening of the Nursery. The ladies had collected funds for the beginning of the work and have been true, loyal, sincere friends ever since. [They have] . . . never been dictatorial in any way . . . turning all funds in and never questioning the disposal thereof. We cannot afford to antagonise [sic] them, as we could not exist without them, so [we] have concluded . . . that under the circumstances, it is best to retain the old name.

The settlement club was a crucial source of income support for the settlement throughout the 1920s. A core group of dedicated members kept the club alive until sometime in the late 1950s. In order to promote the longevity of the club, in 1915 the women formed an auxiliary for girls aged fourteen and under.[28]

Like the heroines of the rescue stories, the settlement club women valued domesticity, piety, and humility. Yet they also used a language of energy and competence to define themselves as modern, which allowed them to gain roles outside the home and genuine influence in the parish. The club provided other benefits as well, such as opportunities for prayer and fellowship. McCabe may have hoped that establishing a settlement within a parish could steer women away from activities to which he objected, while limiting the challenge to clerical authority posed by proprietary settlements such as Madonna Center. It is true that the settlement club members never posed a great challenge to the authority of any of St. Vincent's priests, yet they still managed to gain influence with the Daughters of Charity and stay involved in politics as well. By providing recreation and volunteer opportunities, the settlement club would also help establish ties between parishioners of all classes.

Creating Community:
The Club and the Parish

Because the De Paul Settlement was located in a parish, the settlement club had unique opportunities for fostering ties among people in the neighborhood. As some parishioners began to move into white-collar occupations, the settlement club could offer them appealing reasons to stay in the neighborhood, even as a newer and poorer population moved in. Like other parish organizations, the club could offer fellowship and spiritual benefits for members. The settlement club also gained prestige from its connection to the university, and from the amount of attention the club received from McCabe. Genteel entertainment could appeal to the more financially secure parishioners and could skim off a little of their surplus wealth in order to help the poor immigrants moving into the area. The club's devotional and volunteer opportunities could help reinforce ties among parishioners of all classes. Social events promoted interaction among the better-off, while the work of the settlement itself could bring these more affluent Catholics in contact with their poorer neighbors. The efforts made by club women to define themselves as modern could have led to divisiveness in a parish that expected domesticity from women, but their energy and competitiveness were acceptable because these qualities were used to benefit the parish as a whole.

A closer look at the club's membership will demonstrate why genteel entertainment may have appealed to some club members. A number of the members belonged to families that appeared to be climbing into the middle class, having members in both blue- and white-collar occupations. Settlement club members were primarily lower-middle-class or high blue-collar. Eleven of these club members were traceable through the 1914 and 1915 city directories, which provided some occupational data on the group. Two of these members were widows; three belonged to families whose members had political or city jobs, including one alderman (Patrick Carr), one investigator from city hall, and one fireman; two members belonged to families that owned their own businesses. Out of a sample of 112 active members from 1914 and 1915, 83 were married, 18 were single, and the marital status of 11 could not be ascertained.

Many families had both white-collar and blue-collar members. This was the case with the one single woman of the group, Anna Costello, a clerk who lived with a number of relatives. Another member had a daughter who was a bookkeeper and who appeared to be the only employed person in the family. Of the two blue-collar breadwinners, one was a bartender. Another member was married to a laborer while her two daughters were clerks, thus her family had both blue- and white-collar workers. Several other families also had members in both categories. Mrs. Adams's husband was the investigator from city hall, while her two sons were box makers. Mrs. N. Gannon had a fireman, a clerk, and a stenographer in her family.[29]

Some parishioners objected to the settlement and steadfastly refused to acknowledge that the parish had so many poor people who needed help, but the growing prestige of the settlement club helped mitigate such objections. As the president, Mrs. Burke, said in 1929: "having the same name as De Paul University added prestige to the Nursery." To borrow prestige from the university setting, club meetings were held in the university building. The settlement club also sponsored many educational lectures in accord with the educational mission of the university. During one fund-raising effort, parishioners who donated money to the settlement would receive a certificate of thanks made to look like a college degree. The settlement club also drew many of its members from the Men's and Women's University Club of De Paul University, probably a group founded to raise money for the university. The University Club disbanded in 1914, and its female members joined the settlement club, while the men went elsewhere. The new settlement club members were not university students, although some had children who were. Rather, they were parishioners of St. Vincent's eager for a greater connection with the university.[30]

McCabe warned parishioners that there was no such thing as a "fashionable" Catholic church, yet during his tenure as pastor St. Vincent's took on certain fashionable pastimes. McCabe was winning attention in the secular press for his dynamic speaking ability, and the settlement club women encouraged this by sponsoring him in lectures that gave him additional publicity. Other members of the parish also worked to make it fashionable. For example, the choir, with a reputation for excellence since early in the century, began sponsoring operatic performances. These could entertain music lovers and demonstrate the parish's good taste at the same time.[31]

The club gained enhanced prestige and public-relations opportunities from its connections with the clergy. One *Vincentian Weekly* article described an event "in which many prominent clergy of the arch-diocese will take part," including vocal selections in French by a well-known priest. The more important or high-ranking the member of the clergy who participated in an event, the more glory fell upon the hostesses. In 1916 the settlement club hosted a formal opening of the De Paul Settlement at which the settlement's chapel was dedicated by the archbishop of Mexico, who was visiting Chicago at the time. And, of course, the ladies thoroughly enjoyed the settlement club's ongoing connection with Father McCabe. McCabe repeatedly condemned individuals who performed acts of charity in order to receive favorable publicity, yet public relations was actually one of the tasks the settlement club set for itself in its by-laws. They publicized their social events and lectures in newspapers both secular and religious. They paid to have the De Paul Settlement's name included in a list of day nurseries. They handed out flyers at the church door after Mass, describing the work of the settlement and recruiting members for the settlement club.[32]

The settlement club gave its members individual and group benefits, but by redistribution it also helped hold together a parish that was becoming more stratified by class and ethnicity. Club members literally collected surplus from the parish's more affluent members for the benefit of its poor. The club members gathered crucial items such as cribs and baby furniture, toys, and clothing from parishioners who no longer needed them. Even damaged goods such as old rubber items could be recycled for the benefit of the nursery. Parishioners' extra food could help feed the nursery children.[33]

During World War I, collecting surplus food from better-off parishioners was crucial to the settlement, as rampant inflation pushed up the cost of staples. Before one club meeting, members were asked to bring any soap or flour they could spare. Another time the club charged members one potato, "short on eyes, but with a good sound heart," as the price of admission. The club also held frequent "pound parties," open to the whole parish, which required guests to bring one pound of some scarce commodity, and "food showers," which accepted any food that could be spared. Another strategy during the war was to keep the nursery in the public eye by appealing to people's patriotism: "Like our sailors and soldiers, the babies, who will be the heroes of the future, are loved by everyone; so we must not overlook their needs in our loyal patriotism." The settlement club also sponsored a lecture about the war and used the profits of the lecture to support the nursery.[34]

The club's social events could also bind parishioners to each other. Exchanging modest luxury items (a tea set, a doll's fur set), and winning small amounts of money from each other at card games like Euchre and Cinch, not only kept members coming back but also ensured that their houses would be filled with each other's things. While the actual items exchanged were similar to those won at the bazaars, the settlement club differed in that the exchanges took place within a small group of people who knew each other intimately. To preserve the rough equality of exchange, the people who organized events took pains to make sure not only that the prizes were desirable but also that there were enough to go around.[35]

The settlement club meetings offered members a number of social and spiritual benefits that could encourage piety, provide genteel recreation, and foster fellowship among members. Settlement club meetings often gave members the opportunity to perform for one another, singing songs, playing music, and reciting speeches and poetry. Club meetings usually began and ended with prayer. The club also had masses said for the benefit of members both living and dead, and also for favored clergy. Other prayers were organized as the need arose, to benefit sick members or sick clergymen, and to console parishioners who mourned lost loved ones. Club members were also prayed for daily by the Daughters of Charity of St. Vincent de Paul, the order that ran the settlement. McCabe's lectures on spiritual topics added structure to the settlement club's spiritual dimension. The priest urged settlement club members to promote the Devotion of the Miraculous Medal.[36]

The settlement club fostered cooperation and exchange with other parish organizations as well. The club contributed funds to the Altar Society and received contributions from the Sodality of the Blessed Virgin Mary. It sponsored social events along with the Knights of Columbus, and with the Ladies of Isabella (who funded the settlement's kindergarten). Because of McCabe's emphasis on charity, the parish's organizations had more in common as they focused increasingly on charity work. For example, after McCabe arrived at St. Vincent's, many organizations began to plan their social events as charity fund-raisers. The Knights of Columbus, the Ladies of Isabella, and the Catholic Knights and Ladies of America are all examples. Through the intervention of Father McCabe, the settlement club also secured the cooperation of the Teachers' Extension of De Paul University. The settlement club had further connections with other parish organizations in that some of their membership overlapped.[37]

Some parishioners feared that the settlement would supersede the parish's earlier charity organizations, but in reality they cooperated well. McCabe reassured the other parish charities that "no one of these organizations need conflict with the work of the others," and he urged the organizations to cooperate with each other. At least one member of the Society of St. Vincent de Paul, a laymen's charity, supported the day nursery from the beginning. The society members, all men, typically supplied needy parish families with food and, if necessary, rent. The nursery did not eliminate the need for the society, but it reduced the society's expenses by enabling mothers to earn money. The Ladies of Charity, a laywomen's organization, also helped by doing volunteer work at the nursery.[38]

The settlement itself also brought parishioners of various classes and ethnic groups in closer contact with one another, although not in relationships of equality. The day nursery ran an employment bureau, which advertised in the *Vincentian Weekly,* saying: "If you want a woman for work by the day, leave your name and address at the Day Nursery and tell what day you want her." Although the parish contained many small businesses that could have employed day nursery mothers, it is also probable that the mothers were doing domestic work in the homes of other members of the parish. One brochure for the day nursery said that the nursery mothers "go out by the day washing, scrubbing, waiting tables, etc." Nearby small businesses that could have employed day nursery mothers included grocery and dry-goods stores, stationers, ice-cream parlors, laundries, and tailors' shops.[39]

A few details will help reveal the settlement club's involvement with those who used the settlement. Encouraging some parishioners to work in the homes of others may have highlighted inequalities in the parish, but the settlement also tried to lessen such inequalities by including day nursery mothers in parish social events. By the 1920s, for example, the settlement sponsored a mothers' club for the nursery mothers. Eventually, at least one nursery mother even joined the Ladies of Charity in order to sew for "the poor."[40] These remedies probably succeeded in incorporating some nursery mothers into parish life on a more egalitarian basis. This no doubt worked best for American-born or Irish American mothers, who had something in common with the middle-class and upwardly mobile members of the settlement club.

Volunteer activities also brought settlement club members into contact with their less affluent neighbors. For the most part, they appear to have been content to raise money, while allowing the sisters and their paid assistants to look after the little children. Yet the sewing class taught by one of the club members would have brought her in contact with nursery children. Further, the club also encouraged all interested persons to visit the nursery, hoping that spending time with the little children would convince people to make contributions. If they were making such offers to the general public, settlement club members were most likely spending time at the nursery themselves.[41]

Several major events caused the settlement club to decline in numbers after a few years of operation. When the United States became involved in World War I, for example, club members found their efforts were being stretched in several directions at once. The war gave them the opportunity to sell Liberty Bonds and do Red Cross work but also made it harder for the club to obtain supplies and money for the nursery. Further, departing servicemen occupied their time, energy, and money, especially since a number of the settlement club women had sons in the military. As a result of all these different claims on their attention, some club members became indifferent and forgot to pay their dues. However, the club also gained some new members during the war, electing a German American vice president and possibly some additional German American members as well. German Americans had begun to assimilate into St. Vincent's parish, probably in response to the stigma carried by German ethnicity during the war.[42]

In 1920 the settlement club was dealt a harsh blow when McCabe was transferred away from St. Vincent's to another post. A few stalwart settlement club leaders carried on with the work, but they would no longer have the prestige of being the favored organization of a beloved pastor. The new pastor of St. Vincent's, Father Levan, was technically the new spiritual director of the club, but he neglected it in favor of other priorities. With McCabe gone, the club was less able to resist a number of other setbacks. By the 1920s settlement work in general was no longer as fashionable as it had been before the war. Parish organizations focusing on traditional domesticity and personal piety became more popular during this decade. Starting in the 1920s the club also faced competition from the De Paul Settlement's Auxiliary. Not to be confused with the De Paul Settlement Club Auxiliary of young girls, the settlement auxiliary was composed of "some of the most prominent and wealthy women in Chicago."[43]

During its heyday the De Paul Settlement Club did for St. Vincent's parish some of the things that the Catholic Woman's League was trying to do for laywomen in the city as a whole. Genteel entertainment could appeal to the parish's upwardly mobile members, giving them a reason to stay in the neighborhood and to contribute some of their resources toward helping the area's needy. Capitalizing on the prestige of De Paul University could help the settlement club gain members and raise money. Fostering cooperation between the parish's many social and charitable organizations could further strengthen bonds between parishioners. In addition, generating ties between day nursery mothers and families in the neighborhood with more resources could help bring some of the parish's more marginal members closer to the church. The settlement club gave a boost not just to its own members but to everyone in St. Vincent's parish.

Laywomen and Parish-model Settlements

The parish-model settlements made laywomen's participation dependent upon the approval and support of parish priests to a greater extent than either the club-model or the proprietary-model settlements. Hence parish-model settlements were unlikely to give laywomen an independent power base from which to challenge the authority of the clergy. Because it was organized in a parish, the settlement club relied so heavily upon McCabe that it suffered a grave setback when he left the parish in 1920. It was the Daughters of Charity who ultimately made possible the survival of the De Paul Settlement. However, the club members did manage to gain a certain authority in settlement affairs, and to retain their interest in politics. Like the CWL members, their work helped keep the upwardly mobile involved in the community and helped establish closer ties among members of various classes. Like the heroines of the rescue stories, settlement club members embraced piety, domesticity, and humility while still seeking a larger role for themselves outside the home. Defining themselves as energetic, competent, and modern allowed them to expand their options without posing too much of a challenge to the parish's conservative gender ideology. If the rescue stories sketched new ways of being a good Catholic woman, the laywomen at St. Vincent's tailored the outline to fit their own needs and their own vision of who they were.

As in the club-model settlements run by the Catholic Woman's League, the laywomen in St. Vincent's parish appear to have done relatively limited volunteer work in the settlement itself, preferring to leave such work to the sisters and the settlement's paid staff. This reliance upon paid staff suggests a professionalization of social work that was beginning to take place in Catholic charities overall, combining contemporary social work ideas with Catholic doctrine and priorities. In St. Vincent's parish, the De Paul Settlement Club helped underwrite these changes by its work to acquire funding and supplies for the De Paul Settlement. Ultimately, McCabe intended this professionalization to benefit and uplift the parish as a whole, helping the parish adapt to economic change. The crucial labor necessary to accomplish this plan was to be supplied by day nursery mothers and by the Daughters of Charity of St. Vincent de Paul.

CHAPTER SIX

Unexpected Rescuers

Day Nursery Mothers and Nuns

As part of an effort to professionalize the charity work conducted at St. Vincent's, the priest Francis McCabe set out in 1914 to change one of the parish's long-standing traditions. In the year before the settlement was established, McCabe went to war against the annual practice of giving Christmas baskets to the poor. Every year at Christmastime, a parish laywomen's group called the Ladies of Charity had hosted a "pound party," for which the price of admission was a pound of nonperishable food. The ladies arranged the food in baskets, which needy families could then pick up at the church. In 1914 McCabe criticized this practice, saying: "It has been the custom to have those in need call for their basket, [but] many times . . . those who [call] are not so deserving as others. They come and take away what should be given to others more deserving."[1] McCabe's idea for reforming the practice was to institute a system of screening. He asked his parishioners to send in the names of "deserving" poor people, so the parish could deliver baskets to their homes.

McCabe's parishioners at first misunderstood his plan. Instead of sending in the names and addresses of "deserving" people, they sent the people themselves to pick up baskets. Frustrated, McCabe explained again in the parish newspaper: "Do not send the people to us—we will go to them. In this way, deserving ones are reached. These bear their trials in silence and do not come out. The army of professionals that are applying summer and winter would require the U.S. Army Commissariat to supply their demands." The neighborhood poor themselves also misunderstood McCabe's instructions on how to be "worthy." Instead of hiding their Christmas baskets in shame, they let their neighbors know that baskets were to be had.[2] More than any other pastor of St. Vincent's, McCabe used the terms *deserving* and *undeserving* to segment the parish's poor. Historians have identified this terminology as pertaining to the Charity Organization Society (COS) movement of the late nineteenth and early twentieth centuries. It has been criticized as needlessly cruel language used to stigmatize the poor, yet these terms were also associated with the emerging profession of social work. Using the power of the pulpit, McCabe combined COS language with theology to create a professionalized, yet Catholic, way of doing social work.

As a parish-model settlement, the De Paul Settlement and Day Nursery was subordinate to a pastor's authority in ways that Madonna Center and the CWL settlements were not. A powerful preacher and author of a regular column in the parish newspaper, McCabe set out to become the public voice of the settlement. Defining the nursery mothers as the "worthy poor" served a similar function for poor women as the rescue stories did for the more affluent: both aimed to rouse the energies of women to improve the economic condition of the Catholic community. The nursery mothers were expected to work in order to feed their children, and the nursery was also intended to provide professional opportunities for upwardly mobile laywomen. Hence, the labor of the mothers was intended to give a boost not just to their own families but also to the community as a whole. Along with the day nursery mothers, the nuns and laywomen who ran and staffed the nursery provided vital labor to improve the economic status of St. Vincent's parishioners. While the rescue stories focused primarily on volunteers like those who belonged to the De Paul Settlement Club, the nuns, lay workers, and nursery mothers can all be viewed as unexpected rescuers. None of these women had a public voice in the way that a priest did, but their actions reveal that they viewed themselves and their work differently than the images promoted by McCabe.[3]

Theology and Professionalization

Many of St. Vincent's parishioners were reluctant to acknowledge that the neighborhood was changing, and that more should be done for the impoverished newcomers. Hence McCabe needed to convince his better-off parishioners that others needed help. In order to demonstrate his expertise in this area, he incorporated contemporary social work ideas into his professional identity as pastor of St. Vincent's Church. He combined the language of professional social work with theology, notably the doctrine of the Mystical Body. This doctrine taught parishioners, poor and rich, that they were all members of Christ's mystical body and hence were interconnected one with another. McCabe promoted charity as an important part of this interconnectedness. The doctrine of the Mystical Body could be used to persuade better-off parishioners to be more generous to the newcomers. However, the use of theology also represents McCabe's power as a priest. He commanded specialized knowledge that the settlement women did not, and he also had the authority to speak to his parishioners as the voice of the church. McCabe thus set the terms for charity in the parish, though the women also had agency since they were the people who actually carried out the work.

McCabe's power as the voice of the church at St. Vincent's was amplified by his reputation as a flamboyant and persuasive orator. One reporter for the *Chicago Record-Herald* described his preaching style, saying: "When the very reverend father warmed to his work you could have heard him a block down the street—trolley cars clanging by and groups of small boys halloeing from corner to corner notwithstanding." His style was to strike terror in the hearts of his audience in order to send them running to the confessional. Once they were there, he would treat them gently so they would be more likely to repent and atone for their sins.[4]

McCabe's authority as pastor did not shield him or the settlement-house project from criticism by parishioners. As he noted in 1914: "We are aware of the fact that there are some . . . [who] do not think it advisable to start such a work. Pray tell us, who asked your advice? We are coming in daily contact with the misery and trials of those who, if we had a good settlement house, would be able to take care of their little ones and would be independent." Parishioners could deny the changes in the neighborhood, but they could not stop them. In 1900 the parish had about five hundred families comprising about thirty-five hundred people in all. By 1910 it had fifteen hundred families comprising about five thousand people. The parish had gained fifteen hundred people, despite the fact that the parish boundaries had been redrawn in 1908 to cover a smaller area. McCabe also noted in the parish newspaper that times were hard for many of his parishioners.[5] Further, the newcomers were mostly non-Irish.

Historians have long noted the association of the terms *worthy* and *deserving* with Charity Organization Societies (COSs). These institutions shared a number of common principles, which have come to be referred to as "Organized Charity" or COS ideas. The core belief of Organized Charity was that almsgiving provided an incentive for individuals to become impoverished. Hence COS followers believed that poverty could be prevented by giving as little material assistance as possible, and that charities should keep records and coordinate their efforts to ensure that only the worthy poor received help. The worthy poor were thrifty, sober, industrious, and too proud to ask for help, whereas the unworthy were not. Giving alms excessively could spoil the worthy, luring them into lives of dissolution and

sloth. COSs used home visitors to spy on the behavior of the poor and refused aid to all but the most blameless and morally upright poor people.
One could argue that COSs employed their language of worthiness for pur-
poses of social control, in order to shame the poor into working for low wages
rather than accepting charity, or to penalize drinking or sexual unorthodoxy.
Some Catholic charities had adopted COS methods by about 1915, yet other
Catholics objected to COSs, largely in the belief that Catholicism itself was a
trait that some Protestant reformers would view as unworthy.[6]

In some ways COSs deserve their reputation as agencies of social control,
yet they also represent a stage in the professionalization of social work. We
may view the terms *worthy* and *unworthy* as a professional or semiprofessional
language. At the turn of the century, people were widely acquainted with this
terminology as a sign of expertise in charity work. An official of one COS once
noted that people would visit his office seeking help for their neighbors. Often,
when such people were telling their stories, they would

> bring in the word "worthy" or "deserving," doubtfully, as if not exactly accus-
> tomed to use it when talking of their neighbors, but as if thinking no other
> classification would be quite in place in a charity organization office, just as
> we half unconsciously drop into the use of such semi-technical words as
> "acute" and "chronic" when speaking to a physician, or "believer" and "unbe-
> liever," in a clergyman's presence.

McCabe's use of this terminology thus served not only to compartmental-
ize his needy parishioners but also to claim professional expertise in charity
for himself.[7]

Even as McCabe claimed this professional expertise for himself, he also
planned for the De Paul Settlement to train others in the parish to become
professional social workers. Social work education would not only help St.
Vincent's parishioners compete in the job market, it would also help St.
Vincent's parish institutions compete with similar Chicago institutions. In
a speech in 1923, McCabe noted:

> a long time ago . . . I had a vision of the future. I looked to this building to do
> in Catholic lines what the Hull House is doing in its line. . . . I had hope of
> seeing this place made the sociological center of the University . . . the center
> for the visiting nurse . . . a center for a bureau of child welfare work[,] for the
> gathering of the mothers' clubs, for the teaching of Christian doctrine . . .
> works all near and dear to the heart of the Divine Master.

Such an institution might persuade reluctant parishioners to regard the set-
tlement house with pride instead of resisting it. Further, it would give De
Paul University an edge against its main Catholic competitor in Chicago,
Loyola University.[8]

In attempting to overcome the reluctance of some parishioners to accept the settlement house, McCabe stressed that all the faithful had responsibilities toward each other as members of the Mystical Body of Christ.[9] In particular, the rich had special obligations to the poor.[10] As McCabe told his parishioners, the doctrine of the Mystical Body "makes clear our social responsibilities and gives practical meaning to such utterances as this from Christ, our Head: 'As long as you did it to one of these, the least of my brethren, you did it unto me.' (Matt. XXV, 40) This is to show what Charity and union there should be among co-members of Christ." While individuals remained responsible for their own salvation, they could not ignore other members of the Mystical Body and still expect to go to heaven. Incorporated into the Mystical Body through the sacrament of baptism, church members could renew this tie by partaking of the Eucharist. Symbol of membership, the Eucharist also functioned to reinforce the authority of the clergy, because only a priest could perform the ritual. In the early twentieth century, a movement to increase the authority of the clergy paralleled the movement toward greater clerical control of church charities, including settlements and day care.[11]

McCabe's attempts to professionalize charity work at St. Vincent's could provide expanded services and new professional opportunities for parishioners, as well as reinforcing his own authority. Using COS language could make him appear to have expertise in charity, while incorporating the doctrine of the Mystical Body helped him distinguish the charity work to be done at St. Vincent's as Catholic. Further, because the doctrine of the Mystical Body of Christ relied upon sacraments such as the Eucharist McCabe reinforced the importance of priests like himself, the only ones authorized to deliver the sacraments. In the process of defining himself as a charity expert and religious authority, McCabe would also redefine St. Vincent's parishioners. Turning De Paul University into a center for social work training would enable upwardly mobile parishioners to acquire professional training for their children. Such financially secure parishioners were obligated to help the poor, but the poor themselves had obligations as well. To be defined as "worthy" poor, parishioners had to conform to McCabe's expectations, which included not asking for a Christmas basket, and sending mothers out to work.

Creating the Worthy at the De Paul Settlement and Day Nursery

By referring to some of the neighborhood poor as undeserving, McCabe seemed to be excluding people from full membership in the parish community, but in fact the day nursery actually expanded the number of people who could receive help. In a community that was deeply ambivalent about working mothers, the nursery enabled McCabe to create the worthy poor as a rhetorical category: by valorizing poor mothers for going out to work, he named them as worthy. McCabe also hoped the settlement would create the worthy, literally, in the younger generation, by educating nursery children for hard work and economic success as well as for morality, faith, and obedience to authority. The children's education was even aimed at inspiring their parents to work harder and become more pious. While tending to encourage conformity, McCabe's rhetoric eventually aimed not to marginalize and exclude but to include the poor more closely in the life of the community. As McCabe exercised his voice as pastor of St. Vincent's, numerous women worked hard to establish the institution he was trying to define. Nuns from the Daughters of Charity of St. Vincent de Paul and hired laywomen created a settlement house and day-care center on North Halsted Street and labored to live up to the professional standards for nurseries that were emerging by the 1920s.

According to Sister Camilla of St. Joseph's, the nursery was in demand from the moment it opened on December 9, 1915. She wrote to the motherhouse of the Daughters of Charity: "I think Fr. is at his wits end as he & *seven* women were trying to manage *their* [*sic*] children the morning of the opening." At first, the motherhouse was not able to permanently assign sisters to the De Paul Settlement, but they did arrange to "lend" one sister from St. Joseph's Hospital and another from St. Vincent's Infant Asylum. Sister Alicia and Sister Irene came to the nursery every morning and returned to their lodgings at the hospital each night. A group of women volunteers from the settlement club helped arrange the furnishings for the house and chapel.[12]

The nursery consisted of two buildings, one at the front of the lot and one at the rear. The rear building had sleeping rooms on the top floor for the young women employed at the nursery, and a sleeping room for the children on the bottom floor. The other building held a chapel, and later a dormitory for the sisters, a community room, refectory, and a small office for the "Sister Servant" or sister in charge of the community. Sister Camilla noted that the house was plainly furnished and looked "settlement-like." She described it as clean and comfortable, and she particularly extolled the virtues of its steam heat. The first floor contained a meeting room, small office, kitchen, bath, and store room. The second and third floors had a nursery, playroom, dining room, and a room used to bathe and dress the children.[13]

Because of the shortage of sisters, a lay matron was at first hired to run the institution. Mary Ahern had previous experience as a matron before taking over at the De Paul Settlement. Laboring hard for low pay, women like Ahern provided crucial support to the plan to bolster the economic standing of Chicago Catholics. Protestant reformers tried in vain to interest educated middle-class young women in day-care work, but they were primarily attracted to more prestigious jobs in school teaching and kindergartens. Most likely a widow, Ahern was able to use the nursery job as an opportunity to educate her teenaged son at De Paul University while they lived together in two rooms on one of the nursery's upper floors. As matron, Ahern would supervise all the nursery's cooking and laundry and take charge of the lay staff. The nursery also employed a number of "girls," probably unmarried young women from the neighborhood.[14]

The nursery opened with about nine children and soon cared for an average of fifty-three children per day. On an unusually busy day there might be seventy-five. The nursery reflected the great diversity of the North Side: it cared for children of at least twenty-seven different nationalities. In 1922 (the only year for which detailed ethnic statistics are available), the nursery admitted a total of 168 children from eighteen different groups. Children listed simply as "American"—most likely children of Irish or German descent—made up 22 percent of the nursery children. Perhaps because of the large numbers of Germans on the North Side, Germans represented 19 percent of the children, and the Irish only 18 percent. Hungarian children made up 11 percent; Swedish were 5 percent; Italians, Austrians, and Poles each made up about 3 percent of the children admitted. Scottish, Norwegian, Finnish, and English children made up about 2 percent. French, Swiss, and Jewish children (nation of origin not specified), as well as Canadians, Assyrians, and Russians were less than 1 percent.[15]

While Catholics were deeply ambivalent about working mothers, they realized that women's labor was sometimes necessary to support their families. McCabe played upon these mixed feelings when he portrayed nursery mothers as torn between their duty to feed their children and to care for them. He described nursery mothers as "honest" saying they "wanted to keep their self-respect . . . to get out and work, and not be objects of charity." Using the nursery became in itself a proof of willingness to work. In fact some COSs used nurseries as a form of work test. McCabe noted that women were often caught between their need to work versus their children's need for care. Nursery supporters also invoked the specter of family breakup to plead for help: "Wouldn't you be willing to . . . help the struggling little mother who is trying so desperately to keep her baby with her?"[16]

While women at St. Vincent's had often been seen as entitled to some financial help from the parish, needy men had traditionally been viewed as suspect. Hence day nursery supporters mentioned fathers as little as possible in the parish newspaper, even though it is clear that at least some of the day nursery families had fathers present. A 1920 survey of twenty Chicago nurseries showed that fathers were present in over 38 percent of families. While the De Paul Settlement was not one of the nurseries surveyed, parish records do reveal that forty of the forty-five families who received aid from the laymen's charity the Society of St. Vincent de Paul had two adults in the household. Surely fathers made up a significant number of these adults. Many of them were probably sick. Twenty people in these families required medical care, and twelve were hospitalized. To avoid stigmatizing fathers who could not support their families, supporters of nurseries had long had to tread carefully, generally emphasizing illness or involuntary unemployment. During the early twentieth century, many men were unable to support their families for reasons beyond their control. In 1900 nearly 20 percent of children worked for wages. These numbers had declined by 1930, and there is some evidence that women's workforce participation increased as that of children declined. The "family wage" may have been a working-class ideal and a goal of progressive church leaders, but it was not yet a reality.[17]

Some nursery supporters believed that these institutions could even reform unworthy parents. St. Vincent's parish newspaper argued that parents would become inspired to greater "faith, hope and encouragement" because of the loving care given to their children. In a Catholic nursery, such inspiration could be both work-related and religious. The *St. Vincent de Paul Quarterly*, the journal of the Society of St. Vincent de Paul, noted in 1899: "The mother gains fresh courage and continues her work, and it oft-times happens that she is so invigorated . . . she finds . . . she has time to attend to Mass on Sundays . . . and what is better, the idle or, more frequently, sick husband at home, is encouraged to do something for himself and those dependent upon him."[18]

An even better way to avoid a sense of stigma was to leave the parents out of the matter altogether and to focus attention upon the innocent children. This strategy can be seen during the early 1920s, when the Daughters of Charity decided to expand and renovate the nursery building. They took advantage of their political connections and moved the nursery operations to an abandoned police station across the street. Jokes about little children "in jail" further distanced nursery adults from the spotlight. When a group of wealthy women decided to raise money for the project, the *Daily News* wrote that "Society folk are determined to take the stigma of wrong environment from the youngsters." Charming photographs of wealthy women giving gifts to poor children routinely graced the society pages in newspapers of the day.[19]

While McCabe and the nursery supporters worked to portray nursery families as worthy, the nursery was training the children to survive in an industrial economy. McCabe believed that if poor children could have the best care that modern science had to offer, they would "get at least an even break in the fierce struggle of modern times." The *Vincentian Weekly* argued that industrial competition led to poverty, noting that when life became a struggle for survival, the strong would flourish but the weak would necessarily fall by the wayside. The parish newspaper also told parishioners that "Vice and depravity" were often the effects of poverty rather than its causes.[20]

The nuns and laywomen who ran St. Vincent's aimed from the start to meet the highest professional standards in caring for the nursery children. From the time the settlement opened in 1915, visitors from other Catholic institutions remarked on how well-equipped the nursery was. The De Paul

Settlement served the children nutritious meals, something that many day nurseries did not do in the early decades of the twentieth century. A 1916 budget for the settlement shows expenditures for high-protein foods such as meat, poultry, fish, and eggs, noting that the nursery served the children milk, bread and butter, fruit, and vegetables. In contrast, many turn-of-the-century nurseries were often haphazard in the food they served the children. Historian Emily Cahan says that, in one early nursery, a child had to be sickly before he was given milk regularly, and the milk had to be prescribed by a physician. Amy Jane Leazenby's 1920 survey of Chicago nurseries noted that one nursery routinely served the children black tea, while others haphazardly served whatever food they had on hand. To reach out to older children, the De Paul Settlement also offered programs for school-aged youngsters, including sewing classes, hot lunches, and an after-school program for children in the local public and parochial schools.[21]

Leazenby's study was part of a movement to professionalize day care that started in the late 1910s. On December 28, 1917, Chicago's city council passed an ordinance regulating day nurseries and requiring them to be licensed. Enforcement was lax, but the regulations themselves were a step in the right direction. They required a minimum amount of cubic air space per child, hot and cold running water, clean toilet facilities, isolation rooms for sick children, and separate combs and towels for each child. The De Paul Settlement seems to have succeeded in complying with the law, and in some cases even exceeded its requirements. They bathed the children when other day nurseries did not and separated the dormitory and the playroom, so that sleeping children could have quiet. Some Chicago nurseries did not even put the children down for naps at all during the day. The De Paul Settlement also had access to the services of doctors and nurses from St. Joseph's Hospital and isolated sick children from the general nursery population. They sent nurses to visit the families of the sick poor and provided some relief services such as clothing. The nursery did fall short, however, in accepting children as young as two weeks old. Day-care professionals discouraged this practice because it made breast-feeding impossible although many mothers probably had no choice. The nursery may also have had a fairly high number of children per adult staff person, at least in the beginning.[22]

The settlement had a kindergarten, which was established by a number of volunteers in June 1916. Most nurseries at the time limited their work to providing "minimal forms of care and protection for the children." The volunteer teachers might have come from the settlement club, or perhaps they were members of De Paul Council No. 14, Ladies of Isabella, which had volunteered to "take care of" the kindergarten. In any case the kindergarten continued with volunteer teachers for a little over three years, until the sisters decided this plan was no longer practicable. The children became confused by the lack of continuity because they had a new teacher every day, each using a different method. They became almost "impossible to discipline," so a salaried kindergarten teacher was hired in September 1919, for both morning and afternoon sessions.[23]

McCabe hoped that the nursery would give the children citizenship training, grounding in their faith, and respect for authority. He may have believed they needed citizenship education because of their diverse parentage. He believed the nursery could shape the futures of children because, "at the impressionable age, having the symbols of religion impressed upon their minds, hearing the words of prayer and the little hymns" would influence them as they grew older. Avoiding the imaginative play advocated by the kindergarten movement, he envisioned didactic lessons to inculcate the children with patriotism and religious faith. McCabe saw the nursery as a cure for social unrest of all kinds; he was distressed by what he saw as "that restless spirit that at the present day threatens to overthrow what law and order we have in our country, as well as the rest of the world." He hoped that shielding very young children from sin could keep them on the right path as they grew older. The alternative was the youth culture of St. Vincent's neighborhood, to which McCabe strongly objected. He urged parents to use firm discipline and scolded them for allowing their children to roam the streets, write graffiti on the walls, pick up bad language, and learn about sex.[24]

Similar to his plan for the De Paul Settlement Club, McCabe sought both to control local children and to empower them to succeed. In fact, he viewed the attempts to control and shape their behavior as key to their ultimate success in life. The ideal of the worthy poor functioned in much the same way, controlling nursery mothers (or at least steering them along a certain path) and empowering them too, by enabling them to find employment. The labor of the Daughters of Charity and lay workers such as Mary Ahern made the new system possible, while other laywomen provided assistance as volunteers. After the settlement was established, other options for the poor were downplayed, such as the St. Vincent de Paul Society, whose provision of food and rent might have enabled mothers to stay home. Thus the nursery did, to a certain extent, limit women's choices by pushing them into employment. However, like the women of the settlement club, the day nursery mothers accepted the benefits offered by the nursery while resisting attempts to fully control their choices.

The Agency of the Worthy

Before the nursery opened, McCabe wrote in the pastor's column of the *Vincentian Weekly* that he hoped it would aid "The real poor who struggle to keep up a brave front . . . because they will, if helped, try to get on their feet as soon as possible and begin to help others."[25] Day nursery mothers were encouraged not merely to become self-sufficient but to act as rescuers

for others, because the economic uplift of the parish required the most efficient use of every possible resource. The day nursery empowered mothers
to earn money, while unfortunately encouraging their status as underpaid
marginal labor. The voices of poor women such as the day nursery mothers
are notoriously difficult to find; they do not leave letters, diaries, or collections in archives. These voices are more silent still when an institution has
no case records that give any glimpse into their clients' personal lives. The
day nursery mothers at St. Vincent's are nearly as silent as McCabe was ver-
bose. Nevertheless, their actions do give some insight into their lives.
Neighborhood mothers made enthusiastic use of the day nursery, when it
suited their interests to do so. They also set limits on the degree to which
their choices would be governed by McCabe and the nursery.

As soon as the nursery opened, neighborhood mothers flocked to use it.
Mothers appeared particularly enthusiastic that their children would be in
the care of sisters, trusting them to keep the children safe. Before the nursery even opened, about twenty neighborhood children were known to
need its services. After it opened, Sister Camilla wrote to the motherhouse
that "many applications have been made as to [when] the Sisters would
take the children. Every day there are *new* children brought to the nursery
and as I am writing—*nine* are there today." Even Sister Camilla was pleas-
antly surprised at "the confidence with which they give their little ones to
the Sisters." DSPC members also noted that the mothers "seem contented
when the children are in the care of the good Sisters." The mothers had
good reason to welcome the nursery; their child-care options were often
limited. If a mother had no relatives to care for her children, she might be
forced to leave them alone during the day. Jane Addams notes that several
children in the Hull House neighborhood were crippled in accidents while
left alone. In summers when it was too hot to keep children locked indoors, parents might send them out to roam the streets. Sometimes parents
would have "older" children, who could be as young as six or seven, care
for the younger ones.[26]

Neighborhood mothers also used the nursery as an employment agency.
Sister Camilla reported that she "did not think before the work started it
would be so flourishing—but the calls are numerous—women asking for
work & applications made for women to work." At first many such calls
were referred to McCabe himself, but the settlement then took up the work.
Soon the employment bureau was matching workers with an average of
eighty positions per month. It found work for men as well as women and
could even find jobs for parishioners who had no children in the nursery.[27]

The nursery's employment bureau often found jobs for mothers that
were laborious and low-paying, but which offered the advantage of flexible
hours. Mothers often worked by the day doing domestic work in the homes
of other parishioners. This work could have included cleaning, scrubbing
laundry, or even (ironically) child care. As marginal laborers, women were

relegated to physical labor with low pay, usually with no possibility of promotion. However, some mothers also preferred work that was close to home and offered flexible hours, so they could get home easily to be with their children. Some women also derived their sense of status from being mothers, rather than from paid work. Home responsibilities prevented many mothers from taking better-paid, steady jobs.[28]

The mothers of the De Paul Settlement were certainly not willing to be pushed into the labor market under any and all circumstances. In May 1916, the De Paul Settlement Club noted in the *Vincentian Weekly* that "An employment bureau has been in operation for some time past in connection with the Day Nursery. . . . It seems that this fact is not generally known or our people do not require the work, as we have more positions than applicants. Especially does that apply to women." Parish residents were either unwilling or unable to fill the demand for labor resulting from an increase in production because of the outbreak of World War I in Europe. While some women viewed providing for their children as part of their mothering role, others would take wage work only in times of financial necessity, and they viewed such work as an extension of their home responsibilities, another way of taking care of their families. At a time when labor demand was high, mothers may have been reluctant to take wage work because their husbands were more likely to be employed.[29]

In other studies of day nurseries, nursery mothers exhibited similar agency, using the services of nurseries but refusing to conform to the expectations of matrons and staff. In Philadelphia, for example, mothers

> expressed gratitude for nursery care, suggested that the nursery was different from charity, fought with nursery workers over a child's future, asked them to intercede with employers or creditors, lied about their situation in order to get help from the nurseries, relinquished control over their children's future to the guidance of the nursery workers, and used the nursery as a negotiating tool in their own struggles with other family members.[30]

Nursery mothers may have been grateful to have a safe place to leave their children when they went out to work, but this does not mean that they resigned control over their families to nursery workers.

Domestic work in the homes of other parishioners could have helped older parishioners get to know newer ones, albeit not on an equal footing. A certain amount of ethnic conflict may have also resulted from these working situations. Nursery statistics suggest that only 18 percent of the families using the nursery were of Irish descent, although a number of the children listed as Americans could have had Irish forebears. Ironically, the Irish women who had long scrubbed in the homes of Protestants may have started to become mistresses themselves. While many Irishwomen learned middle-class manners while scrubbing Protestant women's homes, they may have then taught such habits to their own employees later.[31] The Irishwomen may have seen this as giving poor women a chance to get themselves on their feet. Yet conflict may have occurred, especially if mistress and employee came from different ethnic groups.

While very little information about most day nursery mothers at De Paul has survived, the life story of one mother named Donna F. illustrates how crucial the nursery could be restoring a poor woman's agency. Not only did the nursery enable Donna F. to feed her many children, it also enabled her to help others within the parish, including the Daughters of Charity. Donna was an immigrant from Ireland, born in County Mayo on February 2, 1884. She began to use the nursery in 1915 because of "adverse circumstances" in her marriage. Not only were her seven children raised in the nursery, she herself was employed there for over fifty years. She did volunteer work out of dedication to the sisters, scrubbing, sewing, cleaning, and maintaining the chapel. She sponsored regular fund-raising events when she made special bread and invited people over to reminisce about Ireland and incidentally give dollars to the settlement. She joined the laywomen's organization the Ladies of Charity and worked in the resale shop they opened for the benefit of the nursery. Her contact with the nursery lasted for over sixty-three years. In 1973 the Daughters of Charity honored her by making her an affiliate member. The sisters noted Donna's particular devotion to Mary the mother of Jesus, understandable perhaps because Donna was a struggling mother herself.[32]

As Donna's case demonstrates, the nursery did succeed in binding some mothers more closely to the parish. It is difficult to tell whether her experience is at all representative of the experiences of other day nursery mothers. The mothers' club founded by the settlement in the 1920s probably helped bring some mothers, particularly if they were Irish, more fully into the life of the parish. Germans began to join in parish events after World War I, and some of them may also have taken advantage of the mothers' club. Mothers from other ethnic groups were probably less likely to join in such activities, and particularly if they were not Catholic.[33]

If day nursery mothers left few clues as to their feelings about the nursery, their children were even more silent. Nursery supporters said the children enjoyed playing with the nursery toys and the other children. For example, the *St. Vincent de Paul Quarterly* told of "A small child, a little boy, [who] strayed away from home, and when the mother met him returning, asking, 'Why, John, where have you been?' he responded that he had just walked down to look at the nursery." Another boy, kept home from the nursery for a day, said, "I feel so lonely, Mama." The De Paul Settlement's equipment included dolls and stuffed animals, child-sized furniture, tea sets, tricycles, and other things that could have been very tempting to children who probably had few toys of their own. Beyond publicity photographs of them playing with nursery toys, very little information survives about how the children experienced the nursery. Certainly it was safer than being left alone all day and provided companionship and learning activities.[34]

The experience of Diane Durante should provide a cautionary note against the assurances of adults who claim to understand the experiences of children. Although Durante is much younger than the people who attended the De Paul Day Nursery during the 1910s and 1920s, she did attend a Daughters of Charity day-care center in Chicago decades later. In an interview, she recalled that the nuns kept a number of animals in order to entertain the children, including a large parrot. Instead of being delighted by the animals, Durante recalls that the parrot always made her cry—she felt sorry for him because he had to live in a cage.[35]

As for the Christmas baskets, parishioners seem to have caught on to McCabe's new plan for their distribution. He no longer had to lecture them to suffer in silence. Perhaps he succeeded in making them ashamed to ask for help, or maybe they simply learned better than to ask at Christmastime. Of course, angry, disgruntled, or indifferent parents left no record of their lack of enthusiasm. Some may have just stayed away from the nursery. Yet the nursery actually expanded the options of poor families for assistance. The parish's other charities continued to operate as before. Even though it received less attention than the nursery in the parish newspaper, the Society of St. Vincent de Paul continued to help poor families with groceries, coal, medicines, and rent. The sisters of the parochial school continued to educate poor children free of charge, and the Ladies of Charity continued sewing First Communion outfits for them.[36]

The mothers of the De Paul Settlement labored long and hard for their families, for the most part living up to their role as the laborers who would uplift the entire parish. Yet they demonstrated that they also had agency.[37] Although McCabe and the settlement tried to pull them into the labor market, they could still refuse employment if they did not need or want it. The success and popularity of the nursery, however, suggest that these mothers often did require employment and they were glad to have a safe place to leave their children. As the life story of Donna F. demonstrates, "adverse circumstances" in a marriage could make paid work a dire necessity, especially with the decline of child labor. Yet Donna F. also demonstrates that the day nursery mothers were more than workhorses. In fact, over the course of her lifetime she came to resemble the heroine of a rescue story: volunteering at the settlement, enjoying a meaningful devotional life, even sponsoring fund-raising social events, she was a woman who continued to focus on the needs of the community even after her own hardships had begun to ease. Donna F.'s success was made possible by her own dedication and by the assistance of the Daughters of Charity of St. Vincent de Paul.

The Daughters of Charity

Publicity was central to the phenomenon of rescue stories—this new way of being a good Catholic woman was debated in the newspapers even as laywomen strove to shape the ideal to fit their own lives Yet privacy had always been central to the main model of service offered to women by Catholicism: religious orders. Even those sisters who labored in the world were expected to be apart from it. Scholars have noted that the self-sacrifice and self-effacement required in religious orders were similar to—and reinforced by—the gender conventions of the nineteenth century. These gender and religious conventions still influenced the Daughters of Charity in the early twentieth century. One speaker at the dedication of a new building in 1923 described the sisters' work with domestic and gendered imagery: "The building . . . is solid and with a plain exterior. . . . I think it typifies well the humility of the good Sisters and the little children that will occupy it. The interior, however, is bright and warm, which is also typical of the charity that will govern in this building." The need for humility often meant that the tremendous amount of labor performed by the sisters for the settlement went largely unrecognized. The role of nuns, in general, deserves more attention in work on settlements, which are often viewed as primarily a laywomen's activity. In some cases, rather than providing a wholly independent niche for laywomen, settlements enabled laywomen and sisters to cooperate in institution building. The Daughters of Charity also provide a fruitful contrast to McCabe's vision of professionalization, for COS ideals were not the basis of their professional identities.[38]

Like a secular settlement house, the De Paul Settlement was both a residential community and a social service institution. The sisters lived on the premises and valued living in community for the strength it could give to individual members. The first sister arrived to take charge of the house on February 15, 1916. On March 16, a seminary sister (or sister-in-training) was sent to assist the first sister. These two at first ate and slept at nearby St. Joseph's Hospital, until arrangements could be made for them at the settlement. They placed a great deal of importance on the first meal they shared together at the settlement on April 3, 1916. By August 24, 1919, a third sister had arrived, making the little group into a real community.[39]

The sisters were primarily from working-class backgrounds and were not particularly young when they took up the work. Six sisters who worked at the settlement between 1915 and 1930 can be traced. Three were from urban backgrounds and three from rural families, two with fathers who were farmers and one whose father was a miller. Among the urban sisters, one's father was a waiter, one's was a printer, and one's was a waterworks inspector. Their average age upon beginning their vocations was thirty.[40] The sisters made the nursery possible in part by working for next to no money. In 1916 the salary for two sisters was $50 apiece, a total of $100. In contrast the amount spent on lay staff in the same year was $477. It is not clear how many lay staff members there were, but what is certain is that the sisters' salaries were small. The settlement's food budget for the year was over ten times what the sisters made.

One nun in particular, Sister Mary Barbara Regan, exemplified in her own life the professional expectations required of the Daughters of Charity, illustrating the balancing act necessary between strict communal discipline and the good humor required to care for small children. In overseeing the other sisters, Sister Mary Barbara placed a great deal of emphasis on "mortification," the act of denying oneself pleasures and accepting pains in dedication to God. For Sister Mary Barbara, coming to the De Paul Settlement was itself a form of mortification. She had risen to the rank of first assistant of the St. Louis Province and assistant superior of Marillac Seminary; hence her posting at the settlement was actually a demotion. According to all reports she accepted the change, saying: "I have always been made a great deal of in the Community, certainly more than I deserve, and God wanted me to see, and wanted others to see, that I wasn't very important, after all."[41] Sister Mary Barbara served as the director of the De Paul Settlement from 1930 until her death in 1941, so her tenure as Sister Servant of the De Paul Center began shortly after the ending date for this work (1930). Nevertheless, she had been an educator and administrator in the Daughters of Charity for many years before she came to De Paul Center. Her instruction of the sisters at the center is likely to have been very similar to the one the sisters of the order had lived under for at least the previous decade.

We can learn something of what was expected of the sisters in their daily lives from a talk delivered at a retreat shortly before Sister Mary Barbara's death in 1941. The sisters were to practice strict discipline, and to give the outward appearance of modesty and dignity, particularly in front of outsiders. Sister Mary Barbara told the other sisters to say their communal prayers piously, slowly, and "nice and loud" so they could be heard. She admonished them to read a biography of a deceased Daughter of Charity every Sunday, and to cover themselves thoroughly when they went to sleep at night. She commented: "The Holy Habit is very attractive, so we have to be careful how we act in the presence of externs and other religious; modesty is absolutely necessary for us." The habit was also quite distinctive. The headgear of the Daughters of Charity was a large white starched cornette, similar to the head covering worn by the actress Sally Field in television's *Flying Nun* series. The robe worn by the sisters was long and black. Together, these garments must have made chasing after little children particularly difficult. Among the other rules for sisters' behavior, they were forbidden to use slang (a fault she suggested was a particular problem in Chicago). Even when writing to their parents, the sisters were to make sure their letters were not "worldly" but had an "air of religiousness" about them.

The sisters were not only supposed to set an example for outsiders, they were also to regard the outside world as spiritually dangerous. Sister Mary Barbara once cautioned one of the sisters: "Remember . . . that the world can give you nothing, but it can take away all you have. You are a Spouse of Christ, so never take externs into your confidence; do not be familiar with them." Even visiting friends and relatives could be dangerous. Sister Mary Barbara cautioned that they were not to eat candy at relatives' homes, saying that this was against the idea of mortification.

Sisters were expected to mortify themselves, welcoming suffering joyfully for the love of God. Nevertheless, the nursery does not seem to have been a joyless place. Apparently Sister Mary Barbara had mortified herself to the extent that she sometimes appeared unsympathetic to other sisters who were suffering physical pain. Yet she could be deeply sympathetic to laypeople and exhibited great compassion toward nuns whose pain was emotional. One of the sisters who knew her commented that she was "always ready for a laugh." Another sister noted that she was particularly sensitive to the needs of little children. In one incident, for example, she found that the nursery staff had piled up all the furniture into the middle of the playroom in order to clean. The problem was that the children were still there! She scolded the staff: "The children are not for the nursery . . . the nursery is for the children." Sister Mary Barbara liked bringing special treats for the children and giving them an annual Christmas party. The nursery sponsored several Christmas parties every year, and people commented that Sister Mary Barbara's was always the best. Older students praised her catechism classes for inspiring them.

In addition to taking care of the children, Sister Mary Barbara encouraged the sisters to help other poor people in the neighborhood. People came to the De Paul Settlement, as they did to secular settlements, for help with many different kinds of problems. The main difference was that the sisters would encourage Catholics who appealed for aid to perform religious duties such as marrying in the church, having their children baptized, attending Mass, going to confession, and taking Communion. To the credit of Sister Mary Barbara, if a lapsed Catholic refused, she taught the sisters to help the person just the same. In addition, she visited the poor in their homes, and several children were named "Barbara" in gratitude.[42]

Some of the sisters did a better job of balancing their dual commitment to self-discipline and child care than others. Sister Maria de Refugio Maes is one success story. She was very popular with the children. She was nearly twenty-nine when she came to the De Paul Settlement to supervise the nursery in 1918. She came from a farming family in New Mexico, and before joining the Daughters of Charity she had been a hatmaker. Her former trade must have stood her in good stead in maintaining the sisters' elaborate headgear. Children were naturally drawn to Sister Maria, in part because she was a tiny person and very affectionate, greeting them each morning with a hug and a kiss, and sending them off every evening the same way. Another sister remembered Sister Maria as having "a calm, soothing, quiet manner and an ever-present smile." She was fluent in both English and Spanish. While Spanish-speaking children are not mentioned in the early years of the De Paul Settlement, Sister Maria's language skills undoubtedly came in handy in 1935, when she was transferred to Catholic Social Center. Also in Chicago, this other Daughters of Charity settlement house had many Mexican and Puerto Rican neighbors.[43]

Sister Adela Koenigsmark had more difficulty balancing discipline and her work with young children. Apparently, she was as stern as Sister Maria was affectionate. Sister Adela was born in rural Illinois, the daughter of a miller, and entered the Daughters of Charity at the age of thirty-nine. The De Paul Settlement was her first posting, late in 1923, and she was put in charge of a group of children in the day-care center. Sister Adela's duties consisted of supervising the children at play, taking them on daily visits to the chapel, and teaching them their prayers. She was described as "a very serious person and not talkative," even "austere." One sister recounted a story that revealed Sister Adela's particular devotion to mortification, saying: "I still remember seeing Sister Adela eat practically all the black olives on the relish dish. This distressed me for I had a particular liking for black olives. She later told me that she practiced mortification for she had a definite dislike for them. I assured her that I too had practiced mortification by being denied them."[44]

While mortification could make Sister Adela a rather stern person, faith could comfort those who became frustrated in their work. Sister Mary Barbara taught her sisters that their job was not just to look after the health and safety of the children but also to nurture their souls. A discouraged sister could have been reassured to be reminded of the vital importance of her work. Sister Mary Barbara advised: "When the children are troublesome and annoying, just remember that it is part of the price you have to pay for serving the poor." When one sister in particular went to her in frustration about a misbehaving child, Sister Mary Barbara cautioned the sister that the child had not yet been baptized, and hence "The devil still has power over this soul," advising the sister not to lose patience with the boy.[45]

The sisters maintained an almsgiving approach to charity at the De Paul Settlement: aiding those who needed help without judgment as to who was worthy or not, directing most of their judgments toward themselves. Their approach was to outlast McCabe's. McCabe's strategy for preserving the parish worked, more or less, in the short term. The flight of his better-off parishioners never reached truly alarming rates, although the university exhibited a stabilizing influence that may have been more important than sermons about the worthy poor. By 1920 McCabe was transferred from the parish, and his successor Thomas Levan was not interested in the nursery. Levan's friends noted that he would give alms to anyone who asked for help. He did not use COS language to separate the poor into worthy and unworthy, but his personal generosity did not mean a better deal for St. Vincent's poor families. Aided by the De Paul Settlement Club, the sisters were left to maintain the work without help from Levan. The work of the sisters was successful to the extent that the De Paul Settlement continues as a functioning day-care center today. In order to survive, the settlement gradually reduced its connections to the university and never became the research center McCabe had envisioned. The sisters strengthened their connection to their order, which could offer loans and moral support, as well as supervision. They continued to rely upon the settlement club and also established an auxiliary of wealthy and prominent laywomen to raise money for them. The demise of the settlement would have meant the breakup of the little community of nuns who lived there. More important, it would have created distress for the nursery families.[46]

Parish–Model Settlements and Professionalization

While McCabe's pronouncements carried weight as the official voice of the church at St. Vincent's, different groups of women in the parish achieved varying degrees of success in shaping the actual settlement work to meet their needs. The various models of womanhood promoted at St. Vincent's illustrate the complex class and gender relations in the parish. The women of the De Paul Settlement Club, primarily middle- or stable working-class, were able to use the club work to define themselves as capable, modern, and even competitive. The economically marginal day nursery mothers had less of a choice—McCabe and even the settlement club defined them as the worthy poor and then pushed them into the labor market to prove it. All the day nursery mothers could do to resist was refuse to work outside the home when they did not need to do so. Yet voluntarily or not the day nursery mothers were also the benefactors of the whole parish, and no less than the settlement club; they helped not only their own families but those even less fortunate than themselves. The De Paul example demonstrates that the labor of women, paid or unpaid, lay or religious, was crucial to the economic status and mobility of both individual families and the parish as a whole. The De Paul example suggests that needy women were giving the Catholic community a boost from below, helping improve the economic stability of the bottom ranks of the parish and provide training opportunities for a handful of Catholic social workers. Hence the more economically marginal members of the parish were actually contributing to the rising white-collar status of other parishioners.

Like the settlement club women, the day nursery supporters promoted new activities for women, without challenging the prevailing model of domesticity. Hence they provided job opportunities to mothers who were

part-time and low-paid, leaving mothers as marginal labor rather than promoting more stable and better-paid jobs. The numerous day nurseries and
settlements across the city amounted to a program of economic uplift, a
boost, for all of Catholic Chicago. The nurseries also helped further the
twentieth-century trend of increasing workforce participation on the part
of mothers.[47] Yet, in effect, a plan to encourage mothers to enter the paid
workforce was billed as a plan to help the family, certainly not a plan to encourage career satisfaction or personal growth for parish women. This was
made easier because Catholics had long been aware that economic necessity might force a mother to find paid labor. Even though nursery mothers
may have derived their primary satisfaction from mothering, perhaps some
day nursery mothers did achieve a certain satisfaction from their nursery
experience—pride in supporting their children, or even in joining the
mothers' club or doing charity work with the other nursery mothers.
Donna F. certainly used her nursery experience to shape not just her work
and her family life but her devotional practices and her leisure time as well.

McCabe used the power of his pulpit to change parish social work, transforming COS language by incorporating the doctrine of the Mystical Body. Instead of using the language as a tool of capitalist individualism, forcing the
poor into a mad scramble to compete with each other to get any job, no matter how miserable, McCabe helped create a tool for communal survival and
advancement. The parish community would help make the nursery children
better able to survive the competitive struggle. They would be fed and cared
for to strengthen their bodies, and taught religion to strengthen their souls.
As co-members of the Body of Christ, they were required to help one another—if they did not, they would fail in their religious duties.

While they did not categorize their clients as either "worthy" or "unworthy," the Daughters of Charity and their labor were indispensable to the
nursery plan. As "silent" rescuers, these women religious did not garner the
attention afforded the women of the settlement club, yet their professional
ideals had at least as much impact in shaping the nursery experience—if
not more—than any of McCabe's rhetoric. The sisters certainly encouraged
nursery mothers to attend church and fulfill their other religious obligations. Yet, rather than worrying excessively about disciplining the nursery
mothers, the sisters focused much of their energy on disciplining themselves. Decades after McCabe left the parish, after COS ideals had faded
from currency, and even after new ethnic groups had moved into the
neighborhood, the sisters were still running the nursery for the benefit of
neighboring families and their children.

Sisters were viewed by some influential clergymen as barriers to professionalization. At the De Paul Settlement, sisters, lay volunteers, and paid
staff seem to have cooperated relatively harmoniously, even if the lay volunteers did acquire some authority because of their fund-raising abilities.
Yet across the nation as a whole, some clergy viewed laywomen as natural

allies in the move to professionalize and centralize Catholic charities, to a degree circumventing the nuns and limiting their influence and authority. For the laywomen, moving into professional charity work would most likely have seemed more like benefiting from new opportunities than trying to control the sisters. Laywomen had already demonstrated their competence and pioneered settlements by founding their own institutions—following the club and proprietary models. The parish model of settlement allowed this work to be integrated into the daily life of parishes. Although De Paul University would never acquire a social work school as McCabe had envisioned, women trained elsewhere in social work and in related disciplines would become influential in Catholic charities (and non-Catholic social work) across the city.

CHAPTER SEVEN

Professional Rescuers

The Future of Catholic Settlements

In May 1921 the *New World* published a drawing of a young woman in a professional-looking suit and hat, meant to resemble the famous military recruiting poster of World War I "We Want You for the U.S. Army." In the drawing the young woman points straight at the viewer and asks: "Have you enrolled," in the Associated Catholic Charities? She goes on to explain: "I am the charity visitor. In your place I go down into the crowded tenement districts of our city and strive to relieve the suffering there. While you are working at your desk in the loop, I am out in the forgotten places—the parts where mothers hunger and babies cry for milk."[1] The illustration was meant to inspire Catholics to donate their money to the Associated Catholic Charities of Chicago (ACCC), an umbrella organization founded in 1917 to oversee the city's Catholic charities and also to coordinate fund-raising for them. It is no coincidence that the drawing had a military inspiration—World War I brought about greater coordination and centralization in Catholic charities, both in Chicago and nationwide. But perhaps the most striking aspect of the image was that it portrayed a trained social worker: the woman volunteer of the *New World* rescue stories was being transformed into a paid professional.

The change in the rescue stories reflected two new realities in American Catholic charity organizations: they were hiring professional social workers and they were becoming more centralized. Chicago's Old St. Mary's parish illustrates in microcosm what was taking place across the city and the nation. The parish started with a number of benevolent organizations, most of them created by laypeople. When the Paulist order of priests took over the parish, they centralized these organizations under the auspices of the Paulist Settlement and hired laywomen to run the new settlement, which functioned something like a parish hall, combining regular parish activities with recreational programs, social services, and outreach to needy people in the parish. Even though the Paulists now ostensibly had authority over the settlement, they continued to rely on laywomen, both professionals and volunteers, to manage its programs and daily operations and to oversee its clubs and classes. Similar to the changes at St. Mary's, Catholic charities in Chicago and the nation were brought increasingly under the auspices of centralized charity bureaus and clearinghouses and were more closely supervised by the hierarchy than ever before. The centralization of Catholic charities tended to reinforce the authority of male clergy and reduce the independence of laywomen's organizations; however, it also provided laywomen with new, professional positions in Catholic charities that had not been available before. Further, centralization could not have occurred without the labor, paid and volunteer, of laywomen of all classes. Laywomen thus provided a boost to Catholic charities in Chicago and the nation.

Professional Rescuers in Fiction

World War I fostered changes in both Catholic charities and in the fictional rescue stories. Like many other Americans, Catholics favored staying out of World War I until the United States actually entered the conflict, at which point they threw their support behind the war effort.[2] At first, stories featured laywomen volunteering to aid the war effort, which reflected the large volume of real work done for the Red Cross and other organizations by Catholic women during the war. However, with the creation of the Associated Catholic Charities in Chicago, the heroines of the rescue stories were more likely to be paid workers of the ACCC. A few of the rescue stories went so far as to discourage some forms of women's voluntarism, and even laymen were more likely than laywomen to be featured as volunteers helping the poor. The new rescue stories continued to emphasize generosity to the poor, but they also noted that professional charity workers were trained to detect and prevent fraud. Thus the new stories presented not just a different cast of characters but also a different view of charity work than the old stories. Even though rescue stories reflected the reality that new, professional jobs were opening up for women in social work, volunteer opportunities also continued to grow with the advent of new benevolent organizations. The new rescue stories tended to mask the continued volunteer efforts of Catholic laywomen.

The war provided a great surge of interest in voluntarism among women, much of which was coordinated by settlements and women's clubs. Stories portrayed volunteers knitting stockings, sewing garments, and making bandages for soldiers overseas. The stories urged women to make sacrifices on behalf of others. In a story called "She Dared!" the members of a women's club decide to spend their money on Belgian war relief instead of entertainment for themselves. In another story a group of young Camp-fire Girls gather at a settlement house and make plans to raise money to aid European war orphans. Because most of the girls are employed in factories, their adult supervisor decides they cannot give up the club dues that will pay for their badly needed vacations, so they resolve to put on a play in order to raise the money.[3]

Toward the end of the war the image of the volunteer rescuer started to be replaced in the *New World* stories with professional Catholic social workers. The ACCC was founded during the war by Archbishop George Mundelein, in order to centralize fund-raising and to coordinate operations among the existing Catholic charities in the archdiocese. A few years later the *New World* started publishing stories (often purported to be true) in which needy Catholics were rescued by "workers" from the ACCC. These "workers" were described as female but were not given names or described as characters in the same way that the earlier fictional rescuers had been— they were shown as compassionate but anonymous and standardized. In fact the few stories that described the rescuers in any detail tended to focus on men, including parish priests and lay volunteers from the Society of St. Vincent de Paul.[4]

Some of the new stories actively discouraged volunteer contact with the poor, while others encouraged amateurs to donate money to the ACCC or to volunteer for fund-raising activities. One story suggested that well-off volunteers—"Apostles of the Genteels"—should stay away from poor neighborhoods. Other articles failed to promote women's voluntarism and then complained that not enough women were volunteering. In another story a well-off woman provides for a poor family, giving a monthly check to the ACCC for their maintenance. The money is then distributed by the ACCC visitor. Another story described a poor widow: "If you had seen the look of gratitude and love and devotion which shone in her eyes as the smiling lady visitor handed her her weekly allowance . . . well it would have repaid you, one hundred-fold for your contribution to the Associated Catholic Charities." Volunteers in a Catholic settlement house would have been able to meet the widow face-to-face.[5]

These new rescue stories not only illustrate an increasingly professionalized approach to social work, they also reveal the vast disparity in resources that the ACCC could command as compared with laywomen's settlements. First, the sheer volume of ACCC stories dwarfs the number of laywomen's rescue stories. In 1923 Archbishop Mundelein declared that on one day per month all the parochial schools in the archdiocese would sponsor a "Charities Hour"; the children would be educated about the church's charity work and they would tell their parents, who would contribute money to the ACCC. The children also wrote stories, dozens of which were published in the *New World,* easily dwarfing the number of earlier rescue stories. With professionalization, the new ACCC stories reflected an increased preoccupation with "scientific" charity methods to reduce dependency and fraud. Yet they also insisted that Catholic charity work was superior to mere "scientific" methods because it was motivated by faith.[6]

Even though the new rescue stories deemphasized voluntarism, women's actual volunteer activities continued—in fact new organizations arose to make use of women's volunteer labor. The professional rescue stories also failed to reveal the extent to which settlement work had an impact upon the church, including its parish ministry, as the existence of settlements encouraged parishes to do more to meet the physical and social needs of their parishioners. However, the rescue stories did reveal certain important truths behind the changes in Catholic charities, including the emergence of new professional opportunities for laywomen. The stories suggest the degree to which laymen and priests were successful in recapturing the leadership positions in charity that laywomen enjoyed briefly in the heyday of the settlements. Laymen's charities, especially the Society of St. Vincent de Paul, became more important with the consolidation of Catholic charities, while priests had the power and resources to sustain various works that laypeople could not command. Changes at the Paulist Settlement in Old St. Mary's parish illustrate the advantages priests had in maintaining charity work.

Emergence of the Paulist Settlement

Located at the south end of the Loop (Chicago's central business district), Old St. Mary's Church served a diverse population that included business people and travelers, as well as impoverished residents from nearby boardinghouses. The boundaries of the parish overlapped Chicago's First Ward, a notorious vice district. By the early twentieth century a number of lay people had founded charities in the parish to serve this mixed population. In a move that resembled the creation of the ACCC, these lay-founded charities were later consolidated and taken over by St. Mary's priests, forming the basis for the Paulist Settlement. In many ways the new institution demonstrated the degree to which settlements had begun to influence parish work; it offered religious education but also provided for the bodily needs of neighbors much like a Protestant institutional church. The settlement came to function like a cross between a social service institution and a parish hall, housing recreational activities for existing parishioners and conducting outreach to bring new people into the church. The Paulist order specialized in urban ministries and outreach, and the settlement model was so perfectly suited to this work that they opened a settlement in New York as well as in Chicago. They were instrumental in fostering centralization in Catholic charities nationwide. After the Paulist priests consolidated St. Mary's lay charities in the settlement house, they shaped the settlement programs to reflect their own priorities. Yet laywomen continued to play an important role in the settlement, so they were able to maintain a number of the programs they cared about, including girls' work and day care.

St Mary's parish had always served a diverse congregation, and by 1903 when the Paulists took over the parish it was one of the most pluralistic—and most challenging to minister to—in the entire city. Founded in 1833 Old St. Mary's was the first Catholic parish in Chicago, and the church even served as the city's Roman Catholic cathedral from 1845 to 1859. The church's earliest clientele included German, French, and Irish immigrants. Archbishop Quigley asked the Paulists to take over St. Mary's because of their reputation as experts in urban ministry. At that time the parish boundaries extended from the Chicago River on the north and west to Lake Michigan on the east, and to Twelfth Street on the south. By 1906 the fathers estimated that the parish served twenty-five or thirty families, and a floating population of between three and twenty thousand people. Starting in the 1880s a number of single transient Italian men began to move into the South Loop, and by 1898 the area west of Plymouth Court to the south bank of the river between Harrison and Twelfth streets held over a thousand Italians.[7]

The Paulist order was particularly suited to the task of running Old St. Mary's. They already operated St. Paul's, a similar parish in downtown Manhattan, and they had a long history of social service work. Founded by the convert Isaac Hecker in 1858, the Congregation of Missionary Priests of St. Paul the Apostle aimed to convert all of the United States to Catholicism, so they had a long history of outreach to non-Catholics. St. Mary's central location gave the Paulists an ideal opportunity to represent the Roman Catholic Church to a wider audience. As in New York they tried to make their church and services beautiful, so that passers-by who came in would leave with a favorable impression. Their services had a reputation for good music; at St. Mary's they even founded a chorus of boys and men that reportedly inspired the Bing Crosby film *Going My Way*. The order had a press in New York, printing books, magazines, and pamphlets aimed at outreach. As a result of their efforts, the fathers at St. Mary's reported a steadily increasing rate of conversions, reaching as many as 133 people in a single year.[8]

Charity was part of the Paulists' strategy of outreach: their aim was both to aid the needy and to bring people into church. Soon after their arrival they founded several parish charities, including a home for working boys and a mission for homeless men. Both institutions had substantial lay involvement. Ironically, the first charity founded by the Paulists after their arrival at St. Mary's was one of the few that did not last long enough to merge with the Paulist Settlement, the St. Vincent de Paul Home for Working Boys. Our Lady of Victory Mission for Homeless Men was founded by a layman, but it was taken over by the Paulists in 1909. The Victory Mission, in particular, aimed to win converts and bring lapsed Catholics back into the fold.[9]

While the boys' home ultimately folded, the parish's lay charities were more successful. One of the cornerstones of the Paulist Settlement, the Paulist Day Nursery, was established in 1907 at 481 Wabash Avenue by a group of laywomen. The women were members of the Ladies' Aid Society, an auxiliary to the Society of St. Vincent de Paul. Like other day nurseries, the Paulist Day Nursery helped mothers who had to work because of poverty, or because of the sickness and death of a breadwinner. The women of the Ladies Aid Society also heard stories of "hasty, ill-advised marriages. . . . Stories of desertion, or still worse the story of a refined, intelligent woman who has been obliged to invoke the protection of the law to compel the father of her children to leave her unmolested to care for them." With an eye toward public service, the nursery cared for Protestant and Jewish children as well as Catholics. At one point the day nursery closed briefly for lack of funds, but it opened again, because "all the charity workers of the downtown district, Catholic and Protestant, clamored for its reopening. There is no part of the city where . . . mothers . . . need it more urgently than the mother of this neighborhood."[10]

The priest who would ultimately consolidate all of the parish's charities under the umbrella of the settlement house, Edward T. Mallon, arrived at St. Mary's in 1909. Born in San Francisco in 1880, he had been baptized at Old St. Mary's Paulist Church in San Francisco and educated at the College of the Christian Brothers in Oakland, where he received a master's degree and a gold medal in math. He then went east to the Paulist Novitiate in Washington, D.C., and was ordained in 1904. Just twenty-four years old when he arrived in Chicago, Mallon had the necessary energy to address the "desperate needs and elusive resources of the heart of Chicago."[11]

He served as the editor of the parish newspaper for fifteen years, so Mallon illustrates the degree to which priests had a public voice that lay people did not. The parish newspaper credited a Sunday school founded by Mallon as the origin of the Paulist Settlement, whereas in fact laywomen had founded the day nursery two years before he arrived in the parish. The Sunday school was aimed primarily at the children of neighborhood Italians and soon grew to serve "three hundred children of all sizes, age and color [sic] who lived in or near the loop." The Sunday school had two sodalities to encourage the frequent reception of Communion; for girls there was the Junior Sodality of the Immaculate Conception (later renamed the Children of Mary), and boys could join the Crusaders. Catechism classes were taught by two Mercy nuns, with the assistance of several young female volunteers.

In the newspaper Mallon neglected to mention the existing charity work performed by parish women and suggested that many of their other pursuits were frivolous, saying that Sunday school work had saved the volunteers from "tango teas, dog parades and cat shows."[12]

Through the Sunday school, Mallon demonstrated his commitment to working with parish boys. The John Berchmans Sanctuary Society used friendly competition and incentives to build a corps of altar boys for the church. The altar boys had to be between the ages of ten and eighteen years, and most of them were Italian. Two examples of altar boys who competed for leadership of the Sunday school are Henry Tierno and Vincent Bentivenga. In 1914 they both made the Sunday school's honor roll. By 1916 Bentivenga had become the secretary of the altar boys, and Tierno the treasurer. In November 1916 a party was held for Bentivenga because he had served the greatest number of masses during the month; not to be outdone Tierno won this prize the following month. In addition to banquets, the altar boys also played baseball, football, and tennis. In February 1917 one of the boys' parents served them all dinner, while "Several members of the professional stage entertained the boys, who showed their appreciation by singing . . . .Italian folk songs."[13]

In 1909 the parish took its first step toward consolidating its charities. The lay charities were experiencing financial difficulties, and the St. Mary's priests formed the Paulist Relief Society. Similar to the ACCC, the relief society was an umbrella organization that raised money for parish charities. To generate additional revenues, the new society recruited members from outside of St. Mary's parish because the parish itself had so few families, and it appealed for help to former parishioners who had moved away. It also sponsored an annual Fourth of July picnic in Palos Park, Illinois, with ball games, races, music, dancing, sideshows, bowling, military drills, and even special trains to transport patrons between the city and the picnic grounds.[14]

The new Paulist Relief Society worked better for some of the parish charities than others: the boys' home soon closed, the Victory Mission continued to experience financial difficulties, but the nursery prospered. Despite fund-raising efforts, by 1916 the Victory Mission's operations still showed a deficit of nearly $1,900 during the year, while the nursery actually ran a surplus of over $200. By 1911 the nursery had moved into a new location at 919 Wabash Avenue, acquiring a large playground, an indoor playroom, bathing facilities for the children, and a modern laundry for their clothes. The nursery matron, Miss Mary Maus, hoped to install linoleum floors, considered more sanitary than wood, at a cost of $150. The nursery prospered in part because it actively recruited volunteers, including mothers whose own children had outgrown the nursery or "been transplanted to a Higher Nursery." The matron also gathered a group of volunteers to sew for the children.[15]

The Paulists' next step was to establish a settlement house. Founded in May 1915, it was located at 1122 South Wabash Avenue. The settlement would house existing parish organizations such as the Sunday school and day nursery, along with a number of new services. Mallon himself started a number of the programs that later merged with the settlement, including boys' and girls' sodalities, an athletic club for young men, and a girls' sewing club. The settlement was also intended to be a more effective form of outreach to the poor than the more common forms of parish recreation such as "euchres, concerts and suppers," which served primarily as "amusements for people who live rather comfortably."[16]

The Paulists' goals in founding the settlement included teaching discipline and abstinence from self-indulgence, as well as providing wholesome recreation to keep young parishioners away from bad influences. Using a metaphor derived from athletics, they explained to their parishioners: "The Church is the gymnasium of spirituality, the priest is the director, and Jesus Christ is the model after whose perfections you are striving. Overcome temptations, sin, and spiritual sloth, and you will build up a perfect character." Once a person indulged in sensual pleasures, however, he found himself on a slippery slope downward. Wholesome recreation, on the other hand, could bolster parishioners' virtue. Paraphrasing Jane Addams's argument in *The Spirit of Youth and the City Streets*, Mallon noted in the *Calendar* that "the best sociologists have come to the conclusion . . . that you have to give the boy and girl their pleasures in good surroundings else they will seek it [*sic*] in evil." The Paulists' vision of desirable behavior was gendered: they hoped to reduce crime and juvenile delinquency among the boys and prevent pregnancy and early marriage among the girls.[17]

Mallon had a particular interest in providing recreational activities for boys and young men. He founded the Paulist Athletic Club, which disappeared about 1915, probably absorbed into the settlement. The club was an organization for young men over eighteen; it had a clubhouse at 804 South Wabash Avenue with rooms for games, a library, and tables for billiards and pool. It had showers, a bowling alley, pool tables, and a dance hall for social events. The club sponsored baseball, basketball, golf, and bowling teams, which played in Catholic Leagues. In 1912 the club added opportunities for boxing and wrestling. It was highly popular at first but after several years had trouble retaining membership, even with reductions in dues. In its heyday the club had members both high and low. The club's president was Miles Devine Jr., the son of Miles Devine Sr., president of the Cook County Democratic Club. Yet dues were kept low, fifty cents a month, so that young men of modest means could join.[18]

Mallon argued in the parish newspaper in 1915 that young boys needed attention, noting that the neighborhood girls were chaperoned but that "somehow or other that foolish theoretical notion that a boy can take care of himself yet prevails." As a result the boys "fight against one another in united gangs with stones and sticks . . . , they gamble and play dice for money; they visit the pool room and saloon." Reaching out to "weak-willed" and "obstinate" boys, the settlement would offer recreation to keep them from the streets. The settlement had an athletic club for boys, which included baseball and other outdoor sports during the summer. During the winter the boys could play games in the settlement's gymnasium or its bowling alley. Along with recreation, the Paulists hoped to instill self-discipline, teaching that "labor is life's first law" and "patient endurance of our daily sufferings" would build character.[19]

The Paulist fathers used the settlement to reach out to neighborhood people who were unknown to them, enabling them both to educate the unchurched and protect themselves from "professional beggars." The settlement offered many varieties of religious education. The Sunday school instructed between 300 and 350 children and sponsored an annual Christmas party, which served between two and three hundred children each year. On Thursday evenings at eight o'clock, the Catholic Instruction League offered additional religious education. The kindergarten aimed to provide a Catholic influence to very small children. In addition the settlement formed a committee of volunteers to visit the poor in their homes.[20]

Like Chicago's other Catholic settlement workers, the Paulists viewed Italians as the Catholic population most in need of outreach. Mallon believed that the immigrants were mostly "uncultivated and simple," and poorly educated in their religion. He further explained in the *Calendar* that the Italians lacked priests who could minister to them in their native dialects, and that they moved frequently so that the church often lost track of them. He emphasized turning the Italians into good citizens and protecting them from radical influences. In 1918 he printed an article by a Franciscan priest who noted the dangers of American liberty. No longer bound by family tradition and universal custom, "the poor immigrants . . . soon imagine they are under no restraint and obligation whatever and may do just as they please."[21]

The settlement offered job training because Mallon believed that "from the highest to the lowest rank of wage-earners it is skilled labor that pays and that is infinitely easier in the end than untrained service, which is of necessity as laborious as it is valueless." The Paulist Settlement shop took orders for plain and fancy sewing, trained parish women to fill the orders, and paid them for their work. The domestic science department taught an evening class on Thursdays that could have been useful to train both housewives and domestic servants, especially Italian girls, who could not have learned at home to cook the kinds of foods American employers would want to eat. The settlement offered training in typesetting for boys, and instruction in typewriting for both boys and girls.[22]

The settlement also sponsored a playground and a department of sanitation and hygiene to promote healthy recreation and prevent disease. In 1915 the parish newspaper noted:

Under the direction of Miss Ann Brannack the Department of Sanitation and Hygiene has resulted in much good. Both by lectures and practical demonstration Miss Brannack has given many of our loop children a love for that best of all inventions—soap—and that most necessary of necessary things—water.

In addition the parish newspaper advertised the playground as a preventative for tuberculosis and a healthy alternative to "the tenement dark room and unclean hallway where children usually play." In addition, the playground had other attractions for the children; even though the settlement was located very near Grant Park, the children could not cross Michigan Avenue to play there. Besides, Grant Park had no play equipment, whereas the Paulist Settlement playground had swings, seesaws, a sandbox, and a giant slide.[23]

The settlement offered other recreation programs for both boys and girls, including a Club and Lodge Room, which provided a quiet place for children to study. The department of industrial arts featured crafts such as basket-weaving, and games and dancing classes were offered to both boys and girls. The settlement was able to provide the children with special benefits because of its location in the Loop and the connections of the Paulists. A volunteer from the Art Institute taught art classes, and in 1917 the children saw a puppet show performed by Mary Mason of the Toy Theatre.[24]

Films were the settlement's most popular coeducational feature, and the parish newspaper bragged that "The Paulist Settlement is one of the first social centers in Chicago to install a moving picture machine." A 1916 article in the parish newspaper described the film audience as made up of primarily mothers and children. Typical movies included, "The Goose that Laid the Golden Egg," "The Boy Who Took His Father's Place," and a film of Indians riding across the plains, which the children described as "such a lot of vacant lots." Because the films were silent, volunteers would play the piano, and the settlement children would often sing along if the songs had words. The parish newspaper noted that the audience was enthusiastic about the Paulist films, even though they could have been attending State Street films with titles like "He Loved Another" or, if they were boys, loitering in the pool rooms on Clark Street.[25]

The Paulist Settlement also offered opportunities to participate in live theater, sponsoring the Paulist Players, the Benson Club, and the Junior Dramatic Club. Mallon himself supervised the settlement's theater groups. The Benson Club was a theater group founded by Father Thomas F. Burke, pastor of Old St. Mary's Church, and was named after a Catholic writer, Monsignor Robert Hugh Benson. Members of the club included prominent Catholics as well as a group of young women who lived at a nearby YWCA. In addition to putting on plays, Benson Club members staged dramatic readings and musical presentations for one another, as well as holding social events. Another of the Paulist Settlement theater groups, the Paulist

Players, mixed Catholics, non-Catholics, amateurs, and even professional actors. The group started in May 1916 and appears to have been a group for young actors. One cast member, James Yourell, had significant professional acting experience, even though he was only sixteen years old. The Paulist Players cooperated with other amateur theater companies in the city and also staged plays on religious themes by Catholic playwrights.[26]

The Paulist Settlement combined regular parish activities like sodalities and the Sunday school with its social service work. Some of its activities, such as athletics, films, or theater, could have appealed to both better-off parishioners and those with fewer resources, hence the settlement could offer something to the more stable families of St. Mary's as well as attracting newcomers and bringing them into the parish. As priests the Paulists had the authority to define the work of both the settlement and the parish, focusing their attention on providing wholesome recreation, promoting spiritual discipline, and encouraging conversions. Especially after the lay charities were consolidated under the auspices of the Paulist Relief Society and the settlement, the Paulists consolidated their position as the official voice of St. Mary's charities. Mallon's role as editor of the parish newspaper made him literally into the voice of the Paulist Settlement. Yet, even though the Paulists were officially in charge of the settlement, the institutions could not have functioned without laywomen, including both professional social workers and volunteers, and even though the Paulists could emphasize work with boys, laywomen made sure that girls' activities were not neglected in the settlement programs.

Laywomen, Agency, and a Boost from Below

Combining St. Mary's parish charities in the settlement may have diminished the autonomy that lay people gained by running their own organizations, yet the settlement still tended to rely heavily on the labor of lay people, particularly laywomen. Like the ACCC, the settlement provided both professional jobs and opportunities for voluntarism. As the pastors of St. Mary's and the people who controlled the parish newspaper, the Paulists could take credit for the settlement and serve as its official voice. Yet they hired laywomen to direct it and actively recruited women parishioners as volunteers. Some laypeople involved with the settlement were wealthy and prominent, but others were not. Young working women served in both volunteer and paid capacities, including many women that Protestants would have viewed as charity recipients themselves. Despite the Paulists' authority over the settlement, working there still allowed a great deal of agency for these young women. Young working women used the settlement to create recreational opportunities for themselves and to provide such benefits for others. Further, the involvement of many women in running the settlement helped mitigate the Paulists' primary focus on boys and ensured that attention was paid to recreation and other opportunities for girls. The labor of women was indispensable to the settlement, providing a substantial boost to the parish as a whole.

Laypeople assisted the settlement in various ways from the very beginning, and two lay-founded charities—the day nursery and kindergarten— were incorporated into the settlement. Other laypeople helped the settlement by gathering money and supplies. Some of them must have had considerable means: one well-wisher donated a Persian rug valued at seven hundred dollars, which was raffled off to raise funds. Others donated furniture and a complete set of dishes and silverware, to be used for domestic science classes and the monthly breakfast served to the Sunday school children. Donors furnished a piano, and even a film projector. Prominent laypeople lent their names and prestige to the institution, which would also have helped fund-raising efforts. For example, in November 1917, Judge Edward Osgood Brown accepted the honorary title of president of the settlement.[27]

The Paulist fathers were eager to harness the labor of lay volunteers, and to subordinate them to their own authority. An article in the parish newspaper noted that priests were aware of the social needs of the poor but were often too busy saying Mass, hearing confession, and attending the sick to be able to do much more. The author neglected to mention that laypeople had run many charities themselves. Instead he emphasized that laypeople needed "direction and inspiration [from priests] to make them very effective auxiliaries."[28] While laypeople had always needed priestly authority to establish charities, they were being increasingly subordinated to priestly authority in running those organizations. The author further conceived of the settlement as a meeting place for volunteers and a clearinghouse for all parish charity work. Notably, even the Paulists' ability to recruit female volunteers was enhanced by their status as priests, because female parishioners provided a ready labor pool.

The settlement recruited volunteers from all over the city, including people whom Protestants probably would have considered charity recipients themselves. One group of volunteers was comprised of twenty-five young Catholic women who lived near the church at the YWCA. Unfortunately, none of these young women is identified by name in the parish publications. Some of them may have been art students, who tended to cluster at the Y, although others were probably young working women. For St. Mary's these young women were a valuable source of volunteers who demonstrated their agency by helping others.[29]

The parish newspaper identified quite a few of the settlement's other volunteers, and twenty-two can be identified in city directories. None of these lived within the parish boundaries. Nine lived on the South Side, three on the Southwest, two on the North, one on the Near North, and two on the West Side. Five cannot be accounted for. Residing outside the parish, at least six of the volunteers worked in the Loop, which may account for their interest in St. Mary's parish. In addition the six teachers among the volunteers may also have worked in the Loop. They could have worked at the Jones School, the Haven School, or St. Peter's School, all located near the settlement.[30]

The majority of the volunteers (twelve) were single women working in white-collar occupations; most were from lower-middle-class or working-class families. Of these single women, six were teachers, four were clerks, one was a private secretary, and one was a newspaper correspondent. Four others appeared in the directory with no occupation listed; four more were married women. Only one was a man, who also volunteered with the Our Lady of Victory Mission and worked as an assistant cashier in the Loop. Most of the unmarried volunteers lived at home, either with parents or at least with siblings. These families bolstered their economic security by sending more than one breadwinner into the workforce—eight families had at least two adult family members working. The volunteers' female relatives were concentrated in white-collar occupations, but their brothers and fathers were mostly in skilled blue-collar jobs. The men were waiters, printers, butchers, electricians, and foremen. A few of the male relatives had higher-level occupations, such as Helen Cragin's father, who owned the Cragin Garbage Crematory. Nellie Galvin's brother Daniel was secretary of the United Brotherhood of Carpenters and Joiners, which came in handy when the settlement decided to build a playground.[31]

Old St. Mary's was only about five blocks north of a major lodging area for single women, or "women adrift," who could both benefit from parish activities and volunteer to help run them. These were undoubtedly some of the young women who used the Athletic Association's bowling alley, danced at its dances, and blackened their faces for its minstrel shows. Others sang in the choir or embroidered the priests' vestments and altar linen. The settlement opened a branch of the Chicago Public Library, with a paid librarian. The parish newspaper particularly encouraged young women who worked in the Loop to patronize the facility during their lunch hour. Even the Paulists sometimes recognized the contributions made by young working women:

> God Bless the girl who works! . . . She is not too proud to earn her own living, nor is she ashamed to be found at her daily task. . . . Lift up your hat to her, young man, as she passes by. Her hand may be stained with dish-washing, sweeping, factory grease, or printer's ink, but it is an honest hand, a helping hand. It is a hand that stays misfortune from many a home. . . . All honor to the brave toiler! God bless and protect the girl who works!

These young working women were vital not only to their own families' survival but also to the work of St. Mary's and the settlement.[32]

The Paulist fathers might have extolled the virtues of young working women, but they were not overly thrilled at young women's participation in Athletic Association activities. Only young men could become members of the association, but in 1912 association members allowed a group of twenty-five young women to use the bowling alley one night a week. The Paulist fathers accepted the girls' enthusiasm for bowling but reminded them, in the article "Excellent Advice," that sweeping floors and making beds could be excellent forms of exercise. The women later started a physical culture department at the Paulist Settlement, which offered basketball, calisthenics, and gymnastics.[33]

Most of the volunteers worked during the day, so most clubs and classes met in the late afternoon or evening. The major programs that needed to be staffed during the day were the kindergarten and playground. One kindergarten supervisor, Mrs. Royston Crane, was married to a traveling salesman and was able to offer her services for free. Other kindergarten and playground leaders worked at the settlement full-time. One kindergarten supervisor, Lee Joyce, resided at the settlement for a time. During the summer of 1918 Mary Kabat of Madison, Wisconsin, served as resident superintendent of both the settlement and the playground.[34]

Volunteers were also needed for Tag Day, a fund-raising event sponsored by the Chicago Children's Benefit League. Every year for one day volunteers from children's charities around Chicago would fill the streets of the city, giving "tags" to passers-by in exchange for a financial donation. The taggers included middle-class and wealthy women, in addition to working-class women who lived in the parish. Organizations were allowed to have one hundred volunteers on the street at any given time; St. Mary's recruited a total of two hundred. The parish newspaper noted that volunteers of various classes had participated in Tag Day. Every year Tag Day netted between two and four thousand dollars, which went to the day nursery.[35]

While volunteers remained crucial to the settlement, many of the staff had professional experience or training in social work. The settlement's first resident, Catherine Doran, had been affiliated with the Eli Bates Settlement on Chicago's North Side. The settlement's director for 1917 and 1918, Helen Montegriffo, had previous experience in New York at St. Rose's (Catholic) Settlement and in Chicago at the United Charities. Mrs. Royston Crane was a trained kindergarten teacher, and Marion McDonough, kindergarten director in 1916, was a graduate of the University of Chicago. Settlement workers continued to pursue professional training even after they were hired: in October 1916, the president and the founder of the playground attended the Conference of Catholic Charities held at Catholic University in Washington, D.C. The significant numbers of teachers among the volunteers also raised the level of training of the settlement workers.[36]

The story of one of the Paulist Settlement's staff members, Lee Joyce, illustrates the Paulists' heavy reliance on women staff. Formerly the director of the settlement's kindergarten, Joyce stepped in as "resident" (in effect, resident director) when the previous resident fell ill. Unlike the directors of most non-Catholic settlements, Joyce was paid for her work, receiving the modest sum of twenty-five dollars per month plus board and lodging. In a 1925 article, the *New World* extolled Joyce's virtues in taming the rowdy males of the neighborhood, claiming she had transformed the local group of tough boys, known as the "Torpedo Gang," into model citizens through her kindness and patience.[37]

In accordance with the Paulists' ambivalent attitude toward women's recreation, Mallon began with an extremely limited vision of settlement work for girls. Even before the settlement opened, he called for volunteers to donate items for the boys' club, including "checker boards and checkers, punching bags, baseball suits, refreshments on their meeting nights, book cases and books, small tables for playing games, and an upright piano." For the girls' club he requested "materials for sewing, needles, etc." Mallon well understood that the neighborhood's boys needed challenging and diverse amusements to keep them out of trouble, yet he seems to have believed that the girls mostly needed training in domestic tasks and chaperoning to ensure their chastity.[38]

Fortunately for St. Mary's girls, the women who ran most of the settlement's activities had a broader vision of girls' activities. The settlement did offer sewing and cooking classes, but volunteers also started a branch of the Campfire Girls, which became one of the settlement's most successful activities. One of the women who ran St. Mary's Campfire Girls program, Ruth Russell, was a clerk who worked in the Loop. The other, Ethel Brannack, did not have a profession listed in the city directory, but she appears to have been the sister of the newspaper correspondent Ann Brannack. The Loop Campfire Girls went hiking, had beach parties, and went swimming in Lake Michigan. In May 1917 they held a "Penny Social" in order to raise enough money to go camping in Michigan during the summer.[39]

The Paulist Settlement highlights the gendered relations of power between priests and laywomen during this era: laywomen were expected to defer to the authority of priests, and to allow the priests to take center stage as leaders of the settlement even when it was actually the women who were running the institution. Nevertheless, working for the Paulists gave the women access to resources and networks of important people that no autonomous laywomen's organization could. Most important, the Paulist Settlement demonstrates that, even in a parish-model institution, laywomen were still providing the community with a substantial boost from below. Similar to nuns, professional lay social workers labored for small wages to provide services to parishioners and the settlement's neighbors. Volunteers demonstrated that even women who lived at the YWCA, and hence were viewed by Protestants as young women themselves in need, could perform countless hours of free labor to benefit the parish's children. Professionals and volunteers alike made sure that recreational opportunities remained available to women and girls, despite the lack of interest from the Paulists in girls' activities. As Catholic charities became professionalized in Chicago and across the nation, laywomen would find more and more that their settlements were drawn under the umbrellas of centralizing Catholic institutions and were subordinated to the authority of the clergy. Yet with centralization, laywomen also benefited from increasing numbers of paid professional jobs within Catholic charities, while volunteer opportunities also remained. Because they continued to be active in professional social work and volunteering, laywomen were able to continue to shape Catholic charities, even though they were increasingly under direct clerical supervision.

Laywomen's Settlements and Nationwide Professionalization

With the advent of World War I, as Catholic settlement houses across Chicago saw an increase in voluntarism in war-related activities, the Paulist Settlement participated in this larger trend as it began to provide entertainment for soldiers passing through the Loop. While the settlements bustled with activity, centralizing Catholic charities agencies such as the ACCC and the National Catholic Welfare Council sprouted and grew to encompass many of the settlements' activities and sometimes even took them over. Even though the centralizing agencies could reduce their autonomy, laywomen participated actively in establishing settlements and also promoted social work education under Catholic auspices. Through organizations like the CWL, laywomen had, in fact, pioneered centralization. Some priests even viewed them as allies against certain religious orders who were resisting centralization and the resulting loss of autonomy. In turn laywomen joined the new centralized organizations in a subordinate position to men, but they gained professional jobs within the church that they would not have attained otherwise.

The women of the Paulist Settlement provided hospitality to servicemen who passed through the Loop on their way to various postings, a work that was later taken over by St. Mary's priests with funding from the National Catholic War Council (NCWC). Between June 1918 and January 1919, the women served over thirty-three hundred Sunday breakfasts to the servicemen. In addition, between fifty and seventy-five soldiers and sailors per week were invited to enjoy wholesome entertainment on Saturday night, although the records do not reveal how many attended. Reflecting the centralization taking place in Catholic charities across the board, the laywomen's breakfasts and entertainments were incorporated into a more ambitious program by St. Mary's pastor. In January 1919, Father Burke opened the new Columbus Hotel, and the breakfast and entertainment programs were transferred there.[40]

Other Catholic settlements in Chicago also experienced an upsurge in women's voluntarism for the war effort. CWL members did Liberty Loan work and organized two units of Red Cross volunteers. Members also engaged in Red Cross work in their respective parishes. Almost the entire CWL membership purchased Liberty Bonds, and the league also did food conservation work. They furnished a mass tent, altar linens, and other devotional articles to the Great Lakes Naval Station and provided hospitality and entertainment for soldiers. Yet the league also noted that the war was making it very difficult to get enough donations to finance their other programs. Volunteers at Casa Maria Center, a proprietary settlement run by Rebecca Gallery of Chicago's prominent Onahan family, did Red Cross work, sewed for Belgian relief, grew vegetable gardens, and sold war bonds. The war may even have spurred more conservative Catholic women into voluntarism. The *New World* urged Catholic women not to wait for the formation of a Catholic Red Cross, arguing that the pressing national emergency should override their concerns about cooperating with a non-Catholic organization.[41]

The ACCC provided financial aid to individual charities, but also a degree of supervision. The new organization, established during the war by Archbishop George Mundelein, was created in part to raise funds for families missing a breadwinner because of the war. The new organization was meant to consolidate the many fund-raising appeals made each year by the city's various Catholic charities into one large drive, in part to reduce inconvenience to donors by allowing them to make one large donation per year instead of many small ones. Like a Catholic community chest, the ACCC could also provide a more stable source of income to individual charities. Yet, like a community chest, the ACCC also reduced the independence of individual Catholic charities and increased the power of central authorities. It functioned in part as a charities clearinghouse, and ACCC visitors investigated new cases for its member agencies.[42]

Laywomen spent considerable time and care promoting the church's new centralizing organizations. Indeed, laywomen can be viewed as pioneers of centralization in their own right. In 1916 Father John J. Burke of St. Mary's Paulist priests spoke at a meeting of the CWL, telling the members: "You are powerful because you are federated. Nine hundred and fourteen women have sunk their individual differences to obtain large benefits by acting as one body." Female settlement leaders were notably absent from the board of the new ACCC, but some of their husbands were on it, including William Amberg and David F. Bremner, and laywomen did organize Chicago women to raise money for the organization. Examples include settlement and CWL leaders such as Rebecca Gallery of Casa Maria, and CWL leaders Mary Burns, Rose Trainor, and Mrs. William Zeh. Since 1913 women had been able to join a newly formed women's auxiliary to the Society of St. Vincent de Paul. Because the society was so closely aligned with the ACCC, joining most likely enabled them to do volunteer work there. Administrative positions were reserved for men, but women may have participated in some casework.[43]

As the centralization in Catholic charities spread across the country, Chicago women were also involved in the creation of the National Catholic War Council, and the permanent organization that grew out of it, the National Catholic Welfare Conference (which used the same acronym as its parent organization, NCWC).[44] Margaret Long, head of the probation department of the juvenile court and member of the CWL Protectorate, organized recreational, reconstruction, and housing activities for the National Catholic War Council. Leonora Meder was a delegate from Illinois to the convention that chose the officers and directors of the National Conference of Catholic Women, created by the National Catholic Welfare Council. In 1920 a unit of the National Council of Catholic Women was established in Chicago under the leadership of Mrs. Edward I. Cudahy, a member of the prominent meatpacking family.[45]

Catholic women allied themselves with liberal clergy in promoting both higher education for women and professional social work training under Catholic auspices. When the Reverend Frederic Siedenburg was establishing the Loyola School of Social Work, Leonora Meder supported the formation of the school; and Mary Amberg provided training for Loyola social work students at Madonna Center. At about the same time, Francis McCabe was beginning his failed attempt to create such a school at De Paul University. Catholic women also enthusiastically supported the formation of Rosary College, an undergraduate institution for women.[46]

The Paulists were at the center of the movement for professionalization and centralization of Catholic charities, and for Catholic social work education. A conference held at the Paulist Settlement in 1917 emphasized the need for Catholic charities to promote professional standards of organization. Speakers included Mary Amberg's old friend Frederic Siedenburg, and even Francis McCabe of St. Vincent's Parish and the De Paul Center. The main address of the conference was delivered by the Reverend William J. Kerby, who taught at Catholic University and who became highly influential in the National Conference of Catholic Charities. John J. Burke, a Paulist, served as chairman of the committee on special war activities of the National Catholic War Council and later became the executive secretary of the National Catholic Welfare Council. He was also one of the founders of the National Service School for Women, a social work school at Catholic University in Washington, D.C. The Paulists strongly supported the formation of Rosary College. In January 1920, the Reverend Edward J. Mullaly of St. Mary's Church spoke at a fund-raising event for the college, lauding the institution as a giant step forward for Catholic women and predicting that "women would occupy seats in the Senate and even fill the presidential chair. 'You smile at that as you smiled at nationwide prohibition, five years ago. . . . Women—Just be prepared and ready to take places as leaders in the new era.'"[47]

Some clergymen viewed laywomen as natural allies in the process of centralization of Catholic charities, whereas some religious orders of nuns—reluctant to cede authority over the institutions they had built at great cost of money and labor—resisted some of the steps taken to centralize Catholic charities, including revealing information about their clients and their work. When the National Conference of Catholic Charities attempted to compile a nationwide directory of Catholic charities, William Kerby of Catholic University claimed accusingly: "Some sisterhoods have stood in the way of this work. They have been backward, even suspicious in answering necessary inquiries. They are near-sighted; they cannot see the great, far-away good that will come . . . not only to themselves, but to the church they are pledged to serve." Kerby referred specifically to nuns' reluctance to answer questions for a centralized directory of Catholic charities. Further, even though some nuns cooperated in the centralization and professionalization of Catholic charities, laywomen represented a largely untapped pool of labor to which the hierarchy turned when it needed all the charity workers it could get.[48]

Laywomen's organizations had less money and clout than the religious orders and were more likely to need the resources offered by the new centralizing agencies. They had more to gain from participating in the establishment of the new agencies. From the point of view of nuns, the National Catholic Welfare Council and the ACCC competed for authority with the religious orders, which were already centralized. Nuns controlled vast networks of hospitals and parochial schools, in addition to day nurseries and settlement houses. Laywomen had less to lose; while the amount of settlement work done by Catholic laywomen was substantial, it could never equal the sheer number of institutions established by women religious. Laywomen's settlements may have lost some of their autonomy with centralization, but the women gained new career opportunities that enabled them to serve the poor without joining religious orders. They also won recognition of their expertise, first developed in the settlements, from the leading clergymen in Catholic charities. Laywomen's involvement with non-Catholic reformers and their work in city and county social services may have helped them see the benefits of centralization before others in the Catholic community did. Finally, even as laywomen's settlements were eclipsed by more innovative agencies, a number of them continued to exist and serve their neighborhood constituencies as they had always done.

Professionals and Volunteers

In September 1918 Father Mallon of the Paulist Settlement was promoted to the position of rector of St. Lawrence's Church in Minneapolis, and with his departure the settlement began to play a less prominent role in the parish. Ultimately, the settlement building was taken over as headquarters of the Catholic Youth Organization (CYO), which promoted a settlement-like program aiming to reform street youth, especially boys, through athletics.[49] The CYO was founded by Bishop Frederic Siedenburg of Chicago and grew to have a nationwide scope, which further illustrates the growing trend toward centralization in Catholic charities. Even though centralization tended to solidify the authority of clergymen, the process still afforded Catholic laywomen professional positions within the church that they never would have had before. Like settlement work, centralization would not have been possible without the labor, paid and volunteer, of laywomen of all classes. Professionalization and centralization gave laywomen a boost within the church, but they also provided a boost to Catholic charities through their hard work.

Parish-model settlements like the one at St. Mary's reveal how Catholic settlements and day nurseries did not merely die out; a number of them survived centralization intact, while others were absorbed into church structures. Parish settlements highlight gendered power differentials within the church because, as a member of an influential order of priests, Mallon had access to important people, to funding, to volunteers, and to moral authority that laywomen could never hope to equal. Parish-model settlements did not give women the same autonomy as club-model or proprietary-model settlements, yet they did continue to provide volunteer opportunities for female parishioners and a source of jobs for professional Catholic social workers. The work of volunteers—ranging from some of Chicago's most prominent Catholic women to young single working women from a nearby lodging-house district—illustrates the continuing settlement pattern of cross-class cooperation for the advancement of the entire Catholic community.

Even as professional Catholic social workers became part of Catholic charities, voluntarism continued to play an important role. Scholars have noted that the professionalization of social work drastically reduced opportunities for volunteers to work directly with "clients," yet Catholic charities do not entirely fit this pattern. Centralized agencies such as the ACCC continued to use volunteers, and new organizations such as Big Brothers and Big Sisters that emerged in the 1920s fostered contact between volunteers and clients. Volunteering as big sisters would have enabled laywomen to continue to pursue their work with young girls, even if centralized organizations such as the CYO may have slighted girls in their emphasis upon boys' sports such as boxing.[50] Volunteer work also continued within parishes, especially as parishes like St. John's, Sacred Heart, and Our Lady of Mount Carmel adopted settlement-like recreation programs to meet the physical needs of parishioners.[51] Settlement work thus influenced regular parish ministry, even as the settlements themselves were eclipsed by new charities and centralized agencies.

Catholic Settlements

Church and State

In March 1925 the *New World* published an article extolling the virtues of the resident director of the Paulist Settlement, Lee Joyce. Noting that she received a modest salary for her efforts, the paper commented: "There are many welfare workers like her, giving their all, to be found in Chicago and elsewhere, but the settlement boards cannot locate them because it is the consensus of the Board opinion that welfare workers are wealthy and take up the work for a hobby."[1] Professionalization in Catholic charities provided additional career opportunities to many of the same women whose assistance had been indispensable to the settlements all along. While the standard narrative posits settlement workers as young women from middle-class families, eager for meaningful work to do outside their homes, Joyce and her kind represent something different. They were working girls, graduates of parochial high schools, blue-collar daughters taking tentative steps into white-collar employment. Organized by more prominent Catholic women, the labor of such working girls along with that of day nursery mothers made it possible for Catholic settlements to promote the increased provision of social services by both church and state.

In addition to providing economic support for poor families and recreational facilities in underserved neighborhoods, the working girls and nursery mothers also gave a boost to Chicago's more prominent laywomen, making it possible for them to achieve positions in Catholic settlements and day nurseries, and ultimately as government officials on the school board and in the Department of Public Welfare. These leaders sometimes cooperated with non-Catholic women reformers on shared projects like traveling libraries and summer vacation schools, but in the neighborhoods, Catholic settlements often meant competition for influence over immigrant populations. Protestant missions, nonsectarian institutions, aldermen, and priests all crowded into the same neighborhoods and struggled to win the loyalties of newly arriving populations, especially the Italians. Catholic settlements enabled the church to compete by providing social services and recreation, but they had the unexpected effect of making it possible for settlement women to challenge the authority of neighborhood priests. Ultimately, for the settlement women, success in the neighborhoods also meant more involvement with the state, as they began to mediate between their neighbors and the city's emerging juvenile court system.

In addition to fostering Catholic women's involvement in government, settlement work also helped Catholics adjust to the vast cultural changes taking place during the late nineteenth and early twentieth centuries. The rescue stories used domestic and religious imagery to reassure Catholics concerned about women's new roles outside the home, about the upward mobility of old immigrants, and about the arrival of large numbers of new immigrants. Settlement work provided several opportunities for the upwardly mobile to embody more directly a new class status, by serving in a genteel occupation that kept one connected to the working-class Catholic community, by sponsoring charity balls that would enable one to display one's best finery, by allowing the wealthy directors of the proprietary settlements to play the lady of the manor in their neighborhoods. Club-model and proprietary settlements afforded laywomen more autonomy than parish-model ones, and they also provided more opportunities to embody a new class status, through the CWL charity ball or the financial support of a settlement house.

Even as some settlement women strove to promote Victorian social and sexual mores among their neighbors, they were forced to confront the realities of an increasingly aggressive, sexualized, and heterosocial popular culture, as well as an emerging regulatory state. Although they began with conservative intentions, their actions in fact represented a compromise, allowing their neighbors some access to the new amusements while chaperoning them to mitigate any potential ill effects. In addition to showing "clean" films and theater productions, the Catholic settlements sponsored heterosocial recreation, from dances to libraries, that enabled young women and men to mix, sometimes over the objections of their immigrant parents. The settlements promoted increased leisure activities for girls, who had been viewed earlier as primarily laborers in the home. Settlements could also provide a few Catholic women with the privacy and separation from family that were necessary for them to establish "Boston Marriages" with each other. Yet while the settlements enabled a handful of prominent Catholic women to explore new forms of relationships, they also participated in the juvenile court's policing of their neighbors' sexuality, sometimes shielding their neighbors and sometimes aiding the court to control them.

By the 1920s and 1930s, new organizations arose to meet some of the needs that Catholic settlements had been created to fill. Centralization reduced the autonomy of lay-run institutions, while professionalization created more jobs that drew laywomen into the orbit of the new centralized Catholic charities. Individual parishes began to do more settlement work. Immigration restriction reduced the numbers of new immigrants just as several agencies were created to work among the Italians. Rome created a bureau to look after the Italians in 1921, and in 1923 a social work school opened in Milan to train Italian social workers to care for them as well. In addition several Italian religious orders came to Chicago to minister to them. The CWL nurseries survived until at least 1939, and the league itself until 1954; however, it began to lose its innovative character with the deaths of a number of the first generation of officials, settlement house volunteers, and longtime members. During the 1930s several more organizations rose to prominence and took over the innovative role once performed by settlements: the CYO took up youth work, while the Catholic Worker emerged as both a social service provider and a strong advocate for the poor.[2]

Yet the Catholic settlements left a legacy that continued to have an impact throughout the twentieth century. Catholic settlements had competed with Protestants, nonsectarian charities, and ethnic leaders to establish poor and immigrant Catholics as a clientele, thus giving the church added leverage in the 1930s when the ACCC became a branch of the federal government and was able to administer the distribution of federal relief funds to the city's poor Catholics.[3] It is possible that laywomen were also among the volunteers who helped distribute money from the Federal Emergency Relief Administration to needy Catholics, and laywomen certainly participated in the centralization that made possible the ACCC's role in the New Deal. Through their earlier work in government, laywomen had already helped expand the role of the state in social service provision, and they had worked to convince reluctant Catholics to accept state participation in a task handled traditionally by the church. Because the need was so great, many of the Catholic day nurseries remained open during the depression, yet the New Deal ultimately reduced support for day care and the labor of mothers by promoting largely paternalist measures designed to provide benefits to families through male breadwinners.

After the 1930s Catholic settlements continued to have an impact upon the church and the city. Madonna Center remained open until the deaths of Mary Amberg and Marie Plamondon in the 1960s. The De Paul Center and Marillac House, both run by the Daughters of Charity, survive into the present day and serve new populations of city residents. Marillac House changed with its neighborhood and began to minister primarily to African Americans, later playing an active role during the Civil Rights Movement. Within the church, the recreation programs developed by the settlements continued in individual parishes, while the labors of laywomen in helping promote First Holy Communion, Confirmation, and the more frequent reception of the Eucharist among Italians had increased the likelihood that more Italian Catholics would conform to Irish Catholic standards of piety.[4]

Chicago's Catholic settlements and day nurseries were unique, both because of the liberal and labor-oriented nature of many of the midwestern clergy and because of the city's great importance as a center of non-Catholic social work. Yet Catholic settlements were established in major cities from New York to Los Angeles. If we add to this tally settlements that never really outgrew their status as day nurseries, researchers will undoubtedly find a much more widespread interest among Catholic women for settlement work than has been previously supposed. While the liberalism of the church in Chicago may have afforded Catholic laywomen unique opportunities to craft their own institutions, even in conservative Boston benevolent work afforded laywomen meaningful work to do outside their homes. Studying Catholics not just as members of the working class or ethnics but as members of a powerful religious community will reveal how they profoundly shaped American urban life over the course of the nineteenth and twentieth centuries.

Appendix

Catholic Day Nurseries, Settlement Houses, and Churches Doing Settlement Work, 1892–1930

Even though professionalization meant a decline in the autonomy of laywomen's settlements, their pioneering work caught on and spread to parishes across the city.

Year Founded	Institution	Activities	Founder/Director	Parish
1892	St. Peter's Day Nursery	Nursery, kindergarten, visiting nurses	Miss Forschner	St. Peter
1893	All Saints Day Nursery	Nursery	Catholic Woman's League (CWL)	
1893	St. Anne's Day Nursery and Kindergarten	Nursery	CWL	
1893	St. Elizabeth's Settlement	Settlement work	CWL	
1898	Guardian Angel Center (later renamed Madonna Center)	Catechism, clubs, and classes	Agnes Amberg	Guardian Angel (Ital.)
1904	St. Elizabeth's Day Nursery	free dispensary, night school, sewing school, sterilized milk station	Rev. Andrew Spetz, Sisters of the Third Order of St. Francis	St. Stanislaus Kostka (Pol.)
1905	St. Mary's Settlement (formerly All Saints Day Nursery)	Nursery, settlement work	CWL	

Year Founded	Institution	Activities	Founder/ Director	Parish
1910	St. Mary and St. Agnes Day Nursery and Settlement	Nursery, settlement work	Mrs. M. Hardin	
ca. 1911	Day Nursery	Nursery, small-scale settlement work		St. Philip Benizi (Ital.)
1912	Guardian Angel Day Nursery (Pol.)	Nursery	Felician Sisters, Rev. Louis Brudinski, Rev. Stanley Cholewinski, Rev. Frank Karadasz	St. John of God, St. Joseph's, and Sacred Heart
1913	Day Nursery	Nursery	Holy Family Nuns	St. Adalbert (Pol.)
1913	St. Juliana	Nursery	CWL	
ca. 1913		Small-scale settlement work	Sisters of St. Mary of Divine Providence	Santa Maria Incoronata (Ital.)
1914	Casa Maria	Citizenship, classes, community garden	Rebecca Gallery	
ca. 1914	Catholic Social Center	Nursery, kindergarten, kitchengarten, mothers' club	Daughters of Charity of St. Vincent de Paul	
1914	De Paul Settlement and Day Nursery	Nursery, friendly visiting, sewing classes	Rev. Francis McCabe, Daughters of Charity, De Paul Settlement Club	St. Vincent
1915	Paulist Fathers' Settlement	Nursery, catechism, clubs, movies, sports	Rev. Francis Mallon, various paid directors	Old St. Mary's
ca. 1917	Settlement and Nursery	Nursery, classes in Italian	Rev. Giacomo Gambera	Santa Maria Addolorata (Ital.)
1921	Madonna Center (outgrowth of Guardian Angel Center)	Clubs and classes, summer outings, medical care, gymnasium	Mary Amberg, Marie Plamondon	

Year Founded	Institution	Activities	Founder/ Director	Parish
ca.1920s	Orchid Club Social Center	Open to whole neighborhood, including German, Irish, and Jewish youths	Rev. Angelo Della Vecchia, C.P.P.S.	Our Lady of Mount Carmel
unknown	St. John's Community Center	unknown	unknown	St. John
unknown	Settlement and Day Nursery	unknown	unknown	St. Patrick
unknown	West End Catholic Women's Club Settlement	unknown	unknown	

Sources: Tenth Annual Announcement, 21–26; Koenig, *Caritas Christi Urget Nos,* 2:853–54, 981–85; Men and Women's Committee, Committee on Special War Activities, folder 2, box 13, series 10, NCWC, ACUA; Amberg, *Madonna Center,* 64; David A. Badillo, "Catholic Church and the Making of the Mexican-American Parish Communities in the Midwest," in Dolan and Hinojosa, *Mexican Americans,* 277; Walsh, "Catholic Church in Chicago," 128–55.

Abbreviations Used in Text and Notes

ACUA	Archives Catholic University of America
AWA	Agnes Ward Amberg
Buck Papers	Robert M. Buck Papers, Chicago Historical Society
COS	Charity Organization Society
CTF	Chicago Teachers' Federation
CWL	Chicago Woman's League
DPCC	De Paul Center Collection, Daughters of Charity of St. Vincent de Paul Archives, Evansville, Indiana
DPSC	De Paul Settlement Club, DPCC
DRMA	St. Vincent's Church Records and Biographical Files, DeAndreis-Rosati Memorial Archives of the Congregation of the Mission (Vincentian Fathers), St. Mary's of the Barrens, Perryville, Missouri
FLPS	Foreign Language Press Survey, Special Collections, Regenstein Library, University of Chicago, Illinois
MAA	Mary Agnes Amberg
MCR	Madonna Center Records, Department of Special Collections and University Archives, Marquette University, Milwaukee, Wisconsin
MP	Marie Plamondon
NCWC	National Catholic War Council, ACUA
PAR	Parish Annual Reports, Joseph Cardinal Bernardin Archives, Archdiocese of Chicago, Illinois
PPSJ	Reverend Paul M. Ponziglione, S.J., Collection, Missouri Province V Biographical Files, Midwest Jesuit Archives, St. Louis, Missouri
SMC	*St. Mary Calendar*
VW	*Vincentian Weekly*
WAA	William A. Amberg

Notes

Introduction—A Hull House and a Church

1. Mary Agnes Amberg, *Madonna Center: Pioneer Catholic Social Settlement* (Chicago: Loyola University Press, 1976), 123; Report of the Head Resident Read at the Annual Meeting of the Governing Members, Oct. 12, 1922 (Madonna Center Records, Department of Special Collections and University Archives, Marquette University, Milwaukee, Wisconsin; hereafter MCR) 2:6 (quote); Jane Addams, *Twenty Years at Hull-House with Autobiographical Notes* (New York: Macmillan, 1910).

2. In his classic work on settlements, Allen Davis argues that secularism was the hallmark of the settlement movement in the United States, whereas English settlements were largely church based. He mentions religious settlements only to dismiss them as "missions," saying they contributed little to social reform. Allen F. Davis, *Spearheads for Reform: The Social Settlements and the Progressive Movement, 1890–1914* (New York: Oxford University Press, 1967), 14–16, 27–29. More recently, other scholars have viewed Catholic settlements as pioneers in professionalization for Catholic charities, as members of transatlantic networks of Catholic reformers, as missions created by the American church for "new" immigrants, even as agents of industrial discipline for workers. See Deirdre M. Moloney, *American Catholic Lay Groups and Transatlantic Social Reform in the Progressive Era* (Chapel Hill: University of North Carolina Press, 2002), 141–66; Michael E. Engh, "Mary Julia Workman: The Catholic Conscience of Los Angeles," *California History* 72.1 (1993): 2–19; Margaret Mary McGuinness, "Response to Reform: An Historical Interpretation of the Catholic Settlement Movement, 1897–1915" (Ph.D. diss., Union Theological Seminary, 1985), and "Body and Soul: Catholic Social Settlements and Immigration," *U.S. Catholic Historian* 13.3–4 (Summer 1995): 63–75; Ruth Hutchinson Crocker, *Social Work and Social Order: The Settlement Movement in Two Industrial Cities, 1889–1930* (Urbana: University of Illinois Press, 1992), 164–81.

3. Leo XIII, *Rerum Novarum*, in *The Papal Encyclicals*, ed. Claudia Carlen (Raleigh, N.C.: McGrath, 1981), 247.

4. Scholars have begun to explore the idea that the boundaries between classes are fluid, noting mobility between working class and middle class and cooperation between members of these classes during the Progressive Era. Chicago's Catholic community provides an excellent example of such fluid boundaries, since Catholics were an upwardly mobile population, and prominent Catholics derived their authority from leading the working class. See Robert D. Johnston, *The Radical Middle Class: Populist Democracy and the Question of Capitalism in Progressive Era Portland, Oregon* (Princeton, N.J.: Princeton University Press, 2003), 99; Andrew Wender Cohen, "Obstacles to History? Modernization and the Lower Middle Class in Chicago, 1900–1940," in Burton J. Bledstein and Robert D. Johnston, eds., *The Middling Sorts: Explorations in the History of the American Middle Class* (New York: Routledge, 2001), 189–200. On the development

of the Catholic middle class at the turn of the century, see Timothy J. Meagher, *Inventing Irish America: Generation, Class, and Ethnic Identity in a New England City, 1880–1928* (Notre Dame, Ind.: University of Notre Dame Press, 2001).

5. The scholarly literature on women's agency has often looked for signs of female empowerment in activities that might result in injury or exploitation, such as negotiating sexual relationships or taking family members to court to stop domestic violence. In contrast, voluntarism was a less dangerous way for young women to express themselves, even within a male-dominated church. See Mary Odem, *Delinquent Daughters: Protecting and Policing Adolescent Female Sexuality in the United States, 1885–1920* (Chapel Hill: University of North Carolina Press, 1995); Linda Gordon, *Heroes of Their Own Lives: The Politics and History of Family Violence, Boston, 1880–1960* (New York: Viking, 1988).

6. Amberg, *Madonna Center,* 60.

7. Melanie Gustafson, *Women and the Republican Party, 1854–1924* (Urbana: University of Illinois Press, 2001), 94. Scholarship on women's involvement in party politics is expanding rapidly, although it tends to focus on Republican women more than Democrats. Rebecca Edwards, *Angels in the Machinery: Gender in American Party Politics from the Civil War to the Progressive Era* (New York: Oxford University Press, 1997). The literature on maternalism and women's relationship to the state is also mushrooming. The works most relevant to Catholic settlements are Susan Pedersen, "Catholicism, Feminism, and the Politics of the Family during the late Third Republic," in *Mothers of a New World: Maternalist Politics and the Origins of Welfare States,* ed. Seth Koven and Sonya Michel (New York: Routledge, 1993), 246–76; Sonya Michel, *Children's Interests/Mothers' Rights: The Shaping of America's Child Care Policy* (New Haven: Yale University Press, 1999); Theda Skocpol, *Protecting Soldiers and Mothers: The Political Origins of Social Policy in the United States* (Cambridge, Mass.: Belknap Press, 1992); and Maureen Fitzgerald, *Habits of Compassion: Irish Catholic Nuns and the Origins of New York City's Welfare System, 1830–1920* (Urbana: University of Illinois Press, 2006).

8. Maureen Flanagan, *Seeing with Their Hearts: Chicago Women and the Vision of the Good City, 1871–1933* (Princeton, N.J.: Princeton University Press, 2002), 6.

9. Kathy Peiss, *Cheap Amusements: Working Women and Leisure in Turn-of-the-Century New York* (Philadelphia: Temple University Press, 1986); Patricia Murolo, *The Common Ground of Womanhood: Class, Gender, and Working Girls' Clubs, 1884–1928* (Urbana: University of Illinois Press, 1997).

10. Paula Kane, *Separatism and Subculture: Boston Catholicism, 1900–1920* (Chapel Hill: University of North Carolina Press, 1994), 200–201, 219, 248–49, 251.

11. Faith Davis Ruffins, "'Lifting as We Climb': Black Women and the Preservation of African American History and Culture," *Gender and History* 6.3 (1994): 376–96; Evelyn Brooks Higginbotham, *Righteous Discontent: The Women's Movement in the Black Baptist Church* (Cambridge: Harvard University Press, 1993); Glenda Elizabeth Gilmore, *Gender and Jim Crow: Women and the Politics of White Supremacy in North Carolina, 1896–1920* (Chapel Hill: University of North Carolina Press, 1996), 149.

12. Davis, *Spearheads for Reform,* 30–31, 43–45, 151–62; Addams, *Twenty Years,* 167–75.

13. Allen F. Davis, *American Heroine: The Life and Legend of Jane Addams* (London: Oxford University Press, 1973), 87; Mary J. Oates, *The Catholic Philanthropic Tradition in America* (Bloomington: Indiana University Press, 1995); Fitzgerald, *Habits of Compassion,* 201.

14. Stephen J. Shaw, *The Catholic Parish as a Way-Station of Ethnicity and Americanization: Chicago's Germans and Italians, 1903–1939* (Brooklyn, N.Y.: Carlson, 1991), 2–5.

15. Aaron I. Abell, *American Catholicism and Social Action: A Search for Social Justice, 1865–1950* (Notre Dame, Ind.: University of Notre Dame Press, 1963), 98–114; Dorothy M. Brown and Elizabeth McKeown, *The Poor Belong to Us: Catholic Charities and American Welfare* (Cambridge, Mass.: Harvard University Press, 1997); Fitzgerald, *Habits of Compassion;* Christopher J. Kauffman, *Faith and Fraternalism: The History of the*

Knights of Columbus, 1882–1982 (New York: Harper and Row, 1982); Philip Gleason, *The Conservative Reformers: German-American Catholics and the Social Order* (Notre Dame, Ind.: University of Notre Dame Press, 1968).

16. Kane, *Separatism and Subculture,* 206; Shaw, *Catholic Parish,* 9; John Patrick Walsh, "The Catholic Church in Chicago and Problems of an Urban Society: 1893–1915" (Ph.D. diss., University of Chicago, 1948), 235; Charles Shanabruch, *Chicago's Catholics: The Evolution of an American Identity* (Notre Dame, Ind.: University of Notre Dame Press, 1981), 1–30, 54–77; Lawrence J. McCaffrey et al., eds., *The Irish in Chicago* (Urbana: University of Illinois Press, 1987), 7.

17. Moloney, *American Catholic Lay Groups,* 141–66; Engh, "Mary Julia Workman"; McGuinness, "Response to Reform"; Crocker, *Social Work,* 164–81.

18. Walsh, "Catholic Church in Chicago," 147–49, 176–80; Mel Piehl, *Breaking Bread: The Catholic Worker and the Origins of Catholic Radicalism in America* (Philadelphia: Temple University Press, 1982); Peter D'Agostino, "Missionaries in Babylon: The Adaptation of Italian Priests to Chicago's Church, 1870–1940," 2 vols. (Ph.D. diss., University of Chicago, 1993); Edward R. Kantowicz, "Polish Chicago: Survival through Solidarity," in *Ethnic Chicago: A Multicultural Portrait,* ed. Melvin G. Holli and Peter D'A. Jones (Grand Rapids, Mich.: William B. Eerdmans, 1995): 173–98.

19. Robyn Muncy, *Creating a Female Dominion in American Reform, 1890–1935* (New York: Oxford University Press, 1991); Flanagan, *Seeing with Their Hearts;* Thomas R. Pegram, *Partisans and Progressives: Private Interest and Public Policy in Illinois, 1870–1922* (Urbana: University of Illinois Press, 1992).

1—Laywomen to the Rescue

1. Jeanne Madeline Weimann, *The Fair Women: The Story of the Woman's Building, World's Columbian Exposition, Chicago 1893* (Chicago: Academy Chicago, 1981), 70 (quote); T. J. Boisseau, "White Queens at the Chicago World's Fair, 1893: New Womanhood in the Service of Class, Race, and Nation," *Gender and History* 12 (Apr. 2000): 66–69; Rev. James J. McGovern, DD, ed., *The Life and Letters of Eliza Allen Starr* (Chicago: Lakeside Press, 1905), 425–27; *New World* articles "The Isabella Statue," 4 Mar. 1893, Eliza Allen Starr, "Statue of Queen Isabella," 24 Feb. 1894, and "Eliza Allen Starr," 21 Apr. 1894; Hubert Howe Bancroft, *The Book of the Fair* (Chicago: Bancroft, 1893), 835–38, 844–47, 856–63, 881–90.

2. Abell, *American Catholicism,* 98–114; Mary Jane Burns, "Twenty-Five Years of the Catholic Woman's League of Chicago," *Catholic Charities Review* 2 (Dec. 1918): 308–10; Walsh, "Catholic Church in Chicago," 128–30; "An Organization of Catholic Ladies," *New World,* 10 June 1893; Kane, *Separatism and Subculture,* 214; "Woman's League Alters Name," *Chicago Daily Tribune,* 26 Apr. 1903.

3. Lawrence J. McCaffrey, "The Irish-American Dimension," in McCaffrey et al., *Irish in Chicago,* 1–21; Flanagan, *Seeing with Their Hearts,* 68, 210; *New World* articles "Vacation Schools," 1 July 1899, P. J. O'Keeffe, "Margaret Sullivan Dead," 2 Jan. 1904, "The Death of Mrs. Margaret F. Sullivan," 2 Jan. 1904, "Mrs. Sullivan's Funeral," 2 Jan. 1904, and "Chicago's Great Catholic Writer," 9 Jan. 1904.

4. David O'Brien, *Public Catholicism* (New York: Macmillan, 1989), 91; *New World* articles "Some Prominent Chicagoans," 19 Dec. 1903, and "Death Takes John P. Hopkins, Noted Catholic Once Mayor of Chicago," 18 Oct. 1918; *Tenth Annual Announcement of the Catholic Woman's League, 1903–1904* (Chicago: Catholic Woman's League, 1904), 81, 78; Mary J. Herrick, *The Chicago Schools: A Social and Political History* (London: Sage, 1971), 137.

5. "Death Takes John P. Hopkins, Noted Catholic Once Mayor of Chicago," *New World,* 18 Oct. 1918; *Tenth Annual Announcement,* 81.

6. McCaffrey, "Irish-American Dimension"; Ellen Skerrett, "The Catholic Dimension," in McCaffrey et al., *Irish in Chicago,* 37–39.

7. Twelfth Manuscript Census.

8. Thomas M. Mulkerins, *Holy Family Parish Chicago: Priests and People* (Chicago: Holy Family Press, 1923), 737; Skerrett, "Catholic Dimension," 37–39.

9. *New World* articles "Eliza Allen Starr," 21 Apr. 1894, "Miss Starr's Masterpiece," 18 Jan. 1896, "The Holy Father," 30 May 1896, "Miss Starr Honored," 24 Mar. 1900, and "Miss Starr's Greatest Book," 23 May 1900; Eliza Allen Starr, *Poems by Eliza Allen Starr* (Philadelphia: McGrath, 1867); Horowitz, *Culture and the City,* 32; Anne C. Rose, "Some Private Roads to Rome: The Role of Families in American Victorian Conversions to Catholicism," *Catholic Historical Review* (Jan. 1999): 52; McGovern, *Eliza Allen Starr,* 13–19.

10. Kane, *Separatism and Subculture,* 180–96; Flanagan, *Seeing with Their Hearts,* 35, 43, 75, 216; Edith Ogden Harrison, *"Strange to Say": Recollections of Persons and Events in New Orleans and Chicago* (Chicago: A. Kroch and Son, 1949), 69–72, 78, 96–99; *New World* articles "Eliza Allen Starr," 21 Apr. 1894, "Woman Philanthropist near Death," 12 Dec. 1908, and "Noted Woman Passes Away," 21 Aug. 1909; Davis, *Spearheads for Reform,* 29.

11. *Chicago Blue Book of Selected Names* (Chicago: Chicago Directory Company, 1902), 15–26; *New World* articles Zi Pré, "Beneficiaries of the Ball," 24 Dec. 1904, and Helen Hughes, "Nellie McShane, Convert," 24 July 1909.

12. *Tenth Annual Announcement; Chicago Blue Book of Selected Names, 1903; Lakeside Annual Directory of the City of Chicago* (Chicago: Chicago Directory Company, 1903); "Resigns from Biscuit," *Chicago Record-Herald,* 21 July 1905.

13. Pegram, *Partisans and Progressives,* 121–48; Herrick, *Chicago Schools,* 93–144; Skerrett, "Catholic Dimension," 37–39; Janet Nolan, *Servants of the Poor: Teachers and Mobility in Ireland and Irish America* (Notre Dame, Ind.: University of Notre Dame Press, 2004).

14. Kane, *Separatism and Subculture,* 211.

15. Of the nineteen rescue stories mentioned below, twelve were written by women, two were written by men (one of them a priest), and five either are not attributed or have an author whose gender cannot be determined. It is probable that some of the unattributed stories were written by women, especially since fiction writing was a popular outlet for women's talents at the time. The one novel cited here was written by a woman. The stories written by women are Mary Lupton, "The Little Wanderer," 11 July 1903, [Mrs.] S. M. O'Malley, "Queer Friends," 12 Sept. 1903, Marie Rouselle, "The Mission," 7 Aug. 1909, Mary F. Nixon-Roulet, "The Community Club," 17 Dec. 1915, Louise Louis, "Rose Castelmond's Career," 13, 20 July 1917, and Alice G. Hayde, "The Pity of It," 28 Jan. 1921, as well as two stories by Rae Dickerson and five by Maria Da Venezia. The novel is Kathleen Norris, *The Story of Julia Page* (New York: Grosset and Dunlap, 1915). One of the stories written by a man was Watson Hyde, "Giovanni, Socialist," 20 Jan. 1912. The second was serialized from 5 Sept. 1924 to 6 Mar. 1925. The two installments that discuss Catholic settlement work are Francis McDonnell (a.k.a. Rev. C. F. Donovan), "The Left Hander? Experiences of a Modern 'Child of Mary,'" 16, 23 Jan. 1925. See also Joseph H. Meier, "Catholic Author's Identity Revealed," 8 May 1925. The five stories whose authors cannot be identified by gender include "A Client of 'Good St. Anne'," 29 July 1899, "The Boy Who Went to Sewing School," 21 Aug. 1902, M. E. Mannix, "Little Bartolo," 6 Nov. 1909, "Old White Dresses," 7 May 1915, and "A Woman's Point of View," 8 July 1921. See also Peggy Pascoe, *Relations of Rescue: The Search for Female Moral Authority in the American West, 1874–1939* (New York: Oxford University Press, 1990), and "Catholic Literators of Chicago," *New World,* 26 Aug. 1905.

16. Mary Amberg, "The Settlement-House Signorina," manuscript, n.d., MCR 2:5. See also Norris, *Julia Page;* and *New World* articles "Catholic Woman's National League," 22 Feb. 1902, untitled editorial, 14 Nov. 1903, "Catholic Literators of Chicago," 26 Aug.

1905, and William Stetsin Merrill, "Fiction by Catholic Authors in the Chicago Public Library," 14 July 1906.

17. *New World* articles "The Boy Who Went to Sewing School," 21 Aug. 1902, and "Old White Dresses," 7 May 1915.

18. Colleen McDannell, "'The Devil Was the First Protestant': Gender and Intolerance in Irish Catholic Fiction," *U.S. Catholic Historian* 8 (1989): 51–65; Penny Edgell Becker, "'Rational Amusement and Sound Instruction': Constructing the True Catholic Woman in the *Ave Maria*, 1865–1889," *Religion and American Culture* 8.1 (Winter 1998): 55–90; Kathleen Sprows Cummings, "'Not the New Woman?': Irish American Women and the Creation of a Usable Past, 1890–1900," *U.S. Catholic Historian* 19.1 (Winter 2001): 37–52. See also Karen Kennelly, "Ideals of American Catholic Womanhood," in *American Catholic Women: An Historical Exploration*, ed. Karen Kennelly (New York: Macmillan, 1989); James J. Kenneally, *The History of American Catholic Women* (New York: Crossroad, 1990); Samuel J. Thomas, "Catholic Journalists and the Ideal Woman in Late Victorian America," *International Journal of Women's Studies* 4.1 (1991): 89–100.

19. Laura Hapke, *Tales of the Working Girl: Wage-Earning Women in American Literature, 1890–1925* (New York: Twayne Publishers, 1992), 45–67, 70; Susan Hill Lindley, "Gender and the Social Gospel Novel," in *Gender and the Social Gospel*, ed. Wendy J. Deichman Edwards and Carolyn De Swarte Gifford (Urbana: University of Illinois Press, 2003), 187; Sherri Broder, *Tramps, Unfit Mothers, and Neglected Children: Negotiating Family in Nineteenth-Century Philadelphia* (Philadelphia: University of Pennsylvania Press, 2002).

20. Meagher, *Inventing Irish America;* "A Client of 'Good St. Anne,'" *New World*, 29 July 1899.

21. "Old White Dresses," *New World*, 7 May 1915.

22. Addams, *Twenty Years*, 113–28; "A Client of 'Good St. Anne,'" *New World*, 29 July 1899.

23. Hapke, *Tales of the Working Girl*, 23–43, 48–66; Murolo, *Common Ground of Womanhood*, 38–40.

24. Charles Merriam, *Chicago: A More Intimate View of Urban Politics* (New York: Macmillan, 1929), 133 (statistics); *New World* articles "A Client of 'Good St. Anne,'" 29 July 1899, and "The Boy Who Went to Sewing School," 21 Aug. 1902.

25. *New World* articles Mary F. Nixon-Roulet, "The Community Club," 17 Dec. 1915, "The Boy Who Went to Sewing School," 21 Aug. 1902, and "Tenth of an Orphan," 9 Mar. 1917.

26. Louise Louis, "Rose Castelmond's Career," *New World*, 13, 20 July 1917.

27. Rae Dickerson "The Christmas King," *New World*, 17 Dec. 1915; Douglas Bukowski, *Big Bill Thompson, Chicago, and the Politics of Image* (Urbana: University of Illinois Press, 1998), 47–48; Hapke, *Tales of the Working Girl*, 107–25.

28. Norris, *Julia Page*, 13.

29. Ibid., 122–47.

30. *New World* articles "A Woman's Point of View," 8 July 1921, and Francis McDonnell, "The Left Hander? Experiences of a Modern 'Child of Mary,'" 23 Jan. 1925.

31. Robert Orsi, *The Madonna of 115th Street: Faith and Community in Italian Harlem, 1880–1950* (New Haven: Yale University Press, 1985), 61–63.

32. Marie Rouselle, "The Mission," *New World*, 7 Aug. 1909. See also Fitzgerald, *Habits of Compassion*, 95–96; Koven and Michel, *Mothers of a New World*, 4–5; Estelle Freedman, *Maternal Justice: Miriam Van Waters and the Female Reform Tradition* (Chicago: University of Chicago Press, 1996), 100; Elizabeth Rose, *A Mother's Job: A History of Day Care, 1890–1999* (New York: Oxford University Press, 1999), 16.

33. *New World* articles M. E. Mannix, "Little Bartolo," 6 Nov. 1909, [Mrs.] S. M. O'Malley, "Queer Friends," 12 Sept. 1903, and Mary Lupton, "The Little Wanderer," 11 July 1903.

34. Rae Dickerson, "The Rosaries," *New World,* 19 Mar. 1915.

35. David R. Roediger, *Working toward Whiteness: How America's Immigrants Became White* (New York: Basic Books, 2005); Thomas A. Guglielmo, *White on Arrival: Italians, Race, Color, and Power in Chicago, 1890–1945* (New York: Oxford University Press, 2003); Shannon Jackson, *Lines of Activity: Performance, Historiography, Hull-House Domesticity* (Ann Arbor: University of Michigan Press, 2001), 54; A. J. Richards, *Italian Americans: The Racializing of an Ethnic Identity* (New York: New York University Press, 1999); D'Agostino, "Missionaries in Babylon"; *New World* articles Watson Hyde, "Giovanni, Socialist," 20 Jan. 1912, M. E. Mannix, "Little Bartolo," 6 Nov. 1909, and [Mrs.] S. M. O'Malley, "Queer Friends," 12 Sept. 1903.

36. *New World* articles "Stories Here at Home," 5 Aug. 1905, "Catholic Literators of Chicago," 26 Aug. 1905, and Maria Da Venezia, "How Tonio Saved Bambino," 15 July 1905.

37. Maria Da Venezia, "In the Heart of Little Italy," *New World,* 5 Aug. 1905, 23 Sept. 1906.

38. Mary Jo Bona, *Claiming a Tradition: Italian American Women Writers* (Carbondale: Southern Illinois University Press, 1999).

39. Maria Da Venezia, "In the Heart of Little Italy: The Triumph of Queen Marpessa," *New World,* 9 Sept. 1905.

40. Ibid., 5 Aug., 9 Sept. 1905.

41. Ibid., 9 Sept. 1905.

42. "A.P.Aism in Chicago Public Schools," *New World,* 20 Jan. 1906; John Higham, *Strangers in the Land: Patterns of American Nativism, 1860–1925* (New Brunswick, N.J.: Rutgers University Press, 1988), 80–87.

43. *New World* articles "How About Our Men?" 5 Dec. 1908 (quote), and "A Word with Our Catholic Societies," 19 Oct. 1912.

44. George E. Moran, comp., *Moran's Dictionary of Chicago and Its Vicinity* (Chicago: George E. Moran, 1895), 48–49, 119, 214, 255; Sister M. Sevina Pahorezki, OSF, "The Social and Political Activities of William James Onahan" (Ph.D. diss., Catholic University of America, 1942), 42–44; *New World* articles "The Columbus Club," 6 May 1893, 21 Apr. 1894, 25 Jan. 1896, "Veragua Honored," 13 May 1893, "Edward E. S. Eagle," 28 Apr. 1894, "Catholic Chicago," 7 Sept. 1895, and "Some Characteristics of the Nineteenth Century," 4 Apr. 1896.

45. Helen Lefkowitz Horowitz, *Culture and the City: Cultural Philanthropy in Chicago from the 1880s to 1917* (Lexington: University Press of Kentucky, 1976), 45–48; "An Organization of Catholic Ladies," *New World,* 10 June 1895; "Resigns from Biscuit," *Chicago Record-Herald,* 21 July 1905; Pahorezki, "William James Onahan," 42–44.

46. *New World* articles "Catholic Woman's League," 8 Dec. 1900 (quote), "Catholic Culture for Women," 15 Apr. 1899, "The Catholic Woman's National League," 28 Apr. 1900, and "Religion, Literature and Art," 22 Oct. 1898.

47. Florence Gilmore, "What Eileen Said," *New World,* 5 Mar. 1900.

48. *New World* articles "Catholic Woman's National League," 22 Feb. 1902, untitled editorial, 14 Nov. 1903, "Catholic Literators of Chicago," 26 Aug. 1905, and William Stetsin Merrill, "Fiction by Catholic Authors in the Chicago Public Library," 14 July 1906.

49. *New World* articles "Catholic Woman's National League," 22 Feb. 1902, "Catholic Woman's League Entertains Artists," 22 Jan. 1910, "Little Ones Learn about Art," 4 May 1912, "Children's Culture Club Meets," 2 Nov. 1912, and "Made President of Culture Club," 29 Mar. 1913.

50. *New World* articles "Catholic Charity Ball Report," 26 Jan. 1894, and "The Charity Ball," 21 Jan. 1899; Amberg, *Madonna Center,* 59–61.

51. Leo XIII, "Rerum Novarum," 241–61.

52. *New World* articles "The Charity Ball," 8 Dec. 1900 (quotes), "Automobile Raffle," 24 Dec. 1904, "Another Charity Ball Game," 23 Sept. 1907, "Catholic Womens [sic] League," 14 Jan. 1911, and "The League Ball Realizes $3,000," 25 Feb. 1911.

53. Meagher, *Inventing Irish America*, 172–78.

54. Fitzgerald, *Habits of Compassion*, 91; David Roediger, *The Wages of Whiteness: Race and the Making of the American Working Class* (London: Verso, 1991); Noel Ignatiev, *How the Irish Became White* (New York: Routledge, 1995). "A Shameful Insult to the Race," *New World*, 7 Mar. 1908 (quotes).

55. Maureen Murphy, "Bridget and Biddy: Images of the Irish Servant Girl in *Puck* Cartoons, 1880–1890," in *New Perspectives on the Irish Diaspora*, ed. Charles Fanning (Carbondale, Il.: Southern Illinois University Press, 2000), 152–75; *New World* articles "A.P.Aism in Chicago's Public Schools," 20 Jan. 1906 (quote), and "Whitewashing Hyde Park High School," 3 Feb. 1906; Dale T. Knobel, *Paddy and the Republic: Ethnicity and Nationality in Antebellum America* (Middletown, Conn.: Wesleyan University Press, 1986), 16.

56. "The League Ball Realizes $3,000," *New World*, 25 Feb. 1911.

57. "Says Age Lacks Piety," *Chicago Record-Herald*, 26 Nov. 1904 (quote); "Catholics Have Social Prestige," *New World*, 9 Mar. 1912.

58. Helen Hughes, "Nellie McShane, Convert," *New World*, 24 July 1909.

59. Zi Pré, "Beneficiaries of the Ball," *New World*, 24 Dec. 1904. In other sources, Dunne referred to himself as Zi Pré; see Edmund M. Dunne, *Memoirs of Zi Pré* (St. Louis: B. Herder, 1914).

60. "Says Age Lacks Piety," *Chicago Record-Herald*, 26 Nov. 1904.

61. *New World* articles "The Modern Arena," 19 June 1909, "Arrange Lecture for St. Mary's Settlement," 18 Jan. 1913, and "Catholic Woman's League," 18 Jan. 1913.

2—Settlements and the State

1. "Puts Religion in Politics," *Chicago Daily Tribune*, 16 Feb. 1908; *New World* articles "William Jennings Bryan to Lecture for Catholic Charity," 8 Feb. 1908, "A Notable Lecture," 15 Feb. 1908, "Bryan on Religion," 29 Feb. 1908, and "Lecture Netted $4,000," 21 Mar. 1908.

2. "Women and Catholic Education," *New World*, 9 July 1910.

3. *New World* articles "A Nursery Picnic," 10 Sept. 1892, "St. Peter's Day Nursery and Kindergarten," 24 Dec. 1892, "The Day Nursery," 21 Jan. 1893, "St. Elizabeth's Day Nursery," 26 Aug. 1893, "St. Peter's Day Nursery," 17 June 1893, "St. Peter's Day Nursery and Kindergarten," 26 Aug. 1893, "Notes," 25 Nov. 1893, "Santa Claus at the Day Nursery," 13 Jan. 1894, and "St. Peter's Day Nursery," 9 June 1894.

4. *New World* articles "St. Anne's Day Nursery," 22 Dec. 1894, "Catholic Woman's National League," 20 Oct. 1900, "The Charity Ball," 1 Dec. 1900, "Catholic Woman's League," 11 Feb. 1905, "South Side Catholic Settlement," 28 Sept. 1907, and "Catholic Woman's League," 7 Mar. 1908.

5. Territorial parishes (a Catholic term) included all Catholics living within certain areas as members. Ethnic parishes, on the other hand, were established for people from different ethnic groups. In practice, territorial parishes were often composed primarily of Irish Americans.

6. Emily D. Cahan, *Past Caring: A History of U.S. Preschool Care and Education for the Poor, 1820–1965* (New York: National Center for Children in Poverty, Columbia University, 1989), 12–14; Geraldine Youcha, *Minding the Children: Child Care in America from Colonial Times to the Present* (Cambridge, Mass.: Da Capo Press, 1995), 133–51; Sonya Michel, "The Limits of Maternalism: Policies toward American Wage-Earning Mothers during the Progressive Era," in Koven and Michel, *Mothers of a New World*, 284; Michel, *Children's Interests/Mothers' Rights*, 14–15, 19; Rose, *Mother's Job*, 5, 9.

7. Addams, *Twenty Years*, 101–4, 167–75; Davis, *Spearheads for Reform*, 44–45; "Grand Ball by Chicago's Catholic Women," *New World*, 21 Apr. 1906 (quote).

8. Skocpol, *Protecting Soldiers and Mothers,* 424–79; Molly Ladd Taylor, *Mother Work: Women, Child Welfare, and the State, 1890–1930* (Urbana: University of Illinois Press, 1994); Koven and Michel, *Mothers of a New World;* Addams, *Twenty Years,* 169; Minute Book, Holy Name Conference, 1 Mar. 1915, Records of St. Vincent de Paul Society, Bernardin Archives.

9. *New World* articles "Grand Ball by Chicago's Catholic Women," 21 Apr. 1906 (quote), "Charity and Children," 24 Feb. [1894], untitled, 14 Jan. 1899, and "A Worthy Lay Charity," 23 Apr. 1904; Michel, "Limits of Maternalism," 279; Rose, *Mother's Job,* 5, 9.

10. *New World* articles "A Chicago Day Nursery," 12 Sept. 1903, and "Catholic Charity Ball," 27 Jan. 1900; Maureen Fitzgerald, "Charity, Poverty, and Child Welfare," *Harvard Divinity Bulletin* 25.4 (1996): 12–17; Fitzgerald, *Habits of Compassion;* Brown and McKeown, *Poor Belong to Us,* 4–5; Brown and McKeown, "Saving New York's Children," *U.S. Catholic Historian* 13 (Summer 1995): 77–95; Kenneth Cmiel, *A Home of Another Kind: One Chicago Orphanage and the Tangle of Child Welfare* (Chicago: University of Chicago Press, 1995).

11. Information in the last two paragraphs is taken from Walsh, "Catholic Church in Chicago," 134, and *New World* articles "Charity and Children," 24 Feb. 1894, "St. Anne's Day Nursery," 22 Dec. 1894, "The Charity Ball," 14 Jan. 1899, untitled, 14 Jan. 1899, "Day Nursery Officers Elected," 5 June 1914, and "Work of St. Mary's Settlement," 31 July 1914.

12. Leo XIII, *Rerum Novarum,* 248; *New World* articles "A Chicago Day Nursery," 12 Sept. 1903 (quotes), and "The Charity Ball," 1 Dec. 1900 (banking); Kathleen D. McCarthy, *Noblesse Oblige: Charity and Cultural Philanthropy in Chicago, 1849–1929* (Chicago: University of Chicago Press, 1982), 106–7.

13. *New World* articles "St. Elizabeth's Day Nursery," 26 Aug. 1893, and "Charity and Children," 24 Feb. [1894].

14. *New World* articles "To Observe Arbor Day," 19 Apr. 1913 (quote), "St. Elizabeth's Day Nursery," 26 Aug. 1893, "Work of St. Mary's Settlement," 31 July 1914, "A Worthy Lay Charity," 23 Apr. 1904 (quote).

15. *New World* articles "Child Training at Home: Settling Children's Disputes," 8 Apr. 1921, Gertrude L. Coursen, "Careers for Women: The Kindergartner," 22 Feb. 1924, Rae Dickerson, "The Year's at the Spring," 2 Apr. 1915, and untitled, 14 Jan. 1899.

16. *New World* articles "Catholic Woman's League," 7 Jan. 1899 (quote), untitled, 14 Jan. 1899, Mary F. Nixon-Roulet, "The Community Club," 17 Dec. 1915, and "Charity and Children," 24 Feb. [1894].

17. *Tenth Annual Announcement,* 21–24.

18. Michel, *Children's Interests/Mothers' Rights,* 53–56; Ann Taylor Allen, "Gardens of Children, Gardens of God: Kindergartens and Day-Care Centers in Nineteenth-Century Germany," *Journal of Social History* 19.3 (1986): 436–49.

19. *New World* articles "Charity and Children," 24 Feb. 1894, "St. Anne's Day Nursery," 22 Dec. 1894, and Rae Dickerson, "The Year's at the Spring," 2 Apr. 1915.

20. "St. Anne's Day Nursery," *New World,* 22 Dec. 1894.

21. Rose, *Mother's Job,* 102–3.

22. Rose A. Trainor to Agnes Nestor, 14 Feb. 1907, and Nestor to Hon. Robert M. Buck, 29 Sept. 1915, both in Agnes Nestor Papers, Chicago Historical Society, Chicago, Illinois.

23. *New World* articles "Catholic Woman's National League," 20 Oct. 1900, "Catholic Woman's League," 11 Feb. 1905, "South Side Catholic Settlement," 28 Sept. 1907, "Catholic Woman's League," 7 Mar. 1908, untitled, 4 Apr. 1908, and untitled, 29 Jan. 1918.

24. "Catholic Women Hold Reception," *Chicago Daily Tribune,* 3 May 1908; Flanagan, *Seeing with Their Hearts,* 68, 210; *New World* articles "Vacation Schools," 15 Apr., 1 July 1899 (quote).

25. Shanabruch, *Chicago's Catholics,* 147. Quotations are from *New World* articles "Topics of the Hour," 16 May 1908 ("freaks"), Michael Barrykay, "A Talk on Women's Clubs," 13 May 1908 ("theories"), "Feminine Uplifters," 29 Sept. 1906 ("Amazons"). See also *New World* articles "The Woman Reformer," 15 June 1901, "The Club Woman," 3 May 1902, "Good Milk during Summer," 14 June 1902, "The Story of an Old Maid," 28 June 1902, "Is Hull House All?" 17 Oct. 1903, "Christ among the Lowly," 1 Oct. 1904, E. L. Scharf, "The Child-Slaves of America," 28 Jan. 1905, "Religion versus Anarchy," 7 Mar. 1908, Mary K. Neill, "Are Social Settlements a Menace?" 25 Apr. 1908, Honor Walsh, "The Woman and the Devil," 30 Sept. 1908, "Catholic Social Settlement Organized," 12 Dec. 1908, "Social Settlements Not Highest Toil," 13 Feb. 1909. "Crops or Kids," 12 Jan. 1917, and "Mother Welfare," 12 Jan. 1917.

26. *New World* articles "The Catholic Woman's National League," 28 Apr. 1900 (quote), "Charity and Children," 24 Feb. [1894], "St. Anne's Day Nursery," 23 Dec. 1894, and Rae Dickerson, "The Year's at the Spring," 2 Apr. 1915; Rose, *Mother's Job,* 33.

27. Skerrett, "Catholic Dimension," 42; William T. Stead *If Christ Came to Chicago* (New York: Clarion Books, 1964), 265–67; Bukowski, *Big Bill Thompson,* 17, 44; John F. McClymer, "Of 'Morning Glories' and 'Fine Old Oaks': John Purroy Mitchel, Al Smith, and Reform as an Expression of Irish-American Aspiration," in *The New York Irish,* ed. Ronald H. Bayor and Timothy J. Meagher (Baltimore: Johns Hopkins University Press, 1996), 374–94; Daniel T. Rodgers, "In Search of Progressivism," *Reviews in American History* Vol.10, No. 4 (Dec. 1982): 113-32; J. Joseph Huthmacher, "Urban Liberalism and the Age of Reform," *Mississippi Valley Historical Review* 49.2 (1962): 231–41; Pegram, *Partisans and Progressives,* 87–148.

28. Michael Katz, *In the Shadow of the Poorhouse: A Social History of Welfare in America* (New York: Basic Books, 1986), 58–84.

29. *Chicago Daily Tribune* articles "Will Open Playroom in Juvenile Court Today," 14 May 1913, "Policewomen Go on Duty Today," 5 Aug. 1913, "New City Chief of Public Welfare," 12 May 1914; "Catholic Woman Social Worker," *New World,* 30 Aug. 1913 (quote).

30. *New World* articles "Philanthropists Explain Work," 9 Mar. 1912, "Catholic Woman Social Worker," 30 Aug. 1913, "City Undertakes Social Work," 8 May 1914, "Civic Office for Catholic Woman," 15 May 1914; "New City Chief of Public Welfare," *Chicago Tribune,* 12 May 1914; untitled article, *The Survey* 23 (Aug. 1914): 533.

31. *New World* articles "Catholic Women in Reform Work," 27 Nov. 1909 ("Reform"), "Topics of the Hour," 16 May 1908 (freaks), "An Organization of Catholic Ladies," 10 June 1893.

32. *New World* articles "What Our Catholic Women Are Doing," 23 Sept. 1911, "Philanthropists Explain Work," 9 Mar. 1912, and "Protectorate Saves Girls," 13 Mar. 1914.

33. Susan Glenn, *Daughters of the Shtetl: Life and Labor in the Immigrant Generation* (Ithaca: Cornell University Press, 1990), 52–53; *New World* articles "Help to Save Our Girls," 3 June 1911, and "Protectorate Saves Girls," 13 Mar. 1914.

34. Suellen Hoy, "Caring for Chicago's Women and Girls: The Sisters of the Good Shepherd, 1859–1911," *Journal of Urban History* 23 (Fall 1997): 260–94: Sharon E. Wood, *The Freedom of the Streets: Work, Citizenship, and Sexuality in a Gilded Age City* (Chapel Hill: University of North Carolina Press, 2005), 186–212; NCWC Questionnaire—Catholic Woman's League of Chicago, June–July 1918, box 13, series 10, NCWC.

35. Leo XIII, *Rerum Novarum,* 246, 250, 252; *New World* articles "Gives Protection to Girls," 1 Apr. 1911, "Help to Save Our Girls," 3 June 1911, "The Catholic Woman's League Protectorate," 10 June 1911, untitled, 23 Sept. 1911, "Annual Report of the Catholic Woman's League Protectorate," 8 June 1912, "Protectorate Saves Girls," 13 Mar. 1914, "Papal Blessing for the Protectorate," 29 June 1912; NCWC Questionnaire—Catholic Woman's League of Chicago, June–July 1918, box 13, series 10, NCWC.

36. Walsh, "Catholic Church in Chicago," 151–54.

37. *New World* articles "Philanthropists Explain Work," 9 Mar. 1912, "Annual Report of the Catholic Woman's League Protectorate," 8 June 1912, "Funds Needed for the Protectorate," 20 July 1912 (quote).

38. *New World* articles "Help to Save Our Girls," 3 June 1911 (quote), and "Philanthropists Explain Work," 9 Mar. 1912.

39. Merriam, *Chicago,* 141.

40. Joan K. Smith, *Ella Flagg Young: Portrait of a Leader* (Ames, Iowa: Education Studies Press, 1976), 150–53; "Lecture by Mr. P. J. O'Keefe," *New World,* 17 Oct. 1908.

41. Charles Fanning, Ellen Skerrett, and John Corrigan, *Nineteenth-Century Chicago Irish: A Social and Political Portrait,* Insights Series 7 (Urbana: Center for Urban Policy, Loyola University of Chicago, 1980), 29; Herrick, *Chicago Schools,* 121–22; "Board Votes on Mrs. Young Today," *Chicago Daily Tribune,* 30 July 1913; "Some Prominent Chicagoans," *New World,* 19 Dec. 1903; *Tenth Annual Announcement,* 95; Smith, *Ella Flagg Young,* 170–73.

42. *New World* articles "Pastors Speak Out," *New World,* 17 Dec. 1898 (element), "Topics of the Hour," 22 Apr. 1905 (parsons), and "Reformers Who Need Reforming," 3 Sept. 1910; "Gov. Elect and Mrs. Dunne Lead March at Ball of Catholic Woman's League," *Chicago Daily Tribune,* 23 Nov. 1912.

43. Paul Michael Green, "The Chicago Democratic Party, 1840–1920: From Factionalism to Political Organization" (Ph.D. diss., University of Chicago, 1975), 38–52, 74.

44. Ibid., 38, 46; "Abandon the Ball," *New World,* 11 Dec. 1909.

45. *Tenth Annual Announcement,* 80–81; Green, "Chicago Democratic Party," 75–76.

46. Green, "Chicago Democratic Party"; Pegram, *Partisans and Progressives,* 132; Elizabeth Cady Stanton et al., eds., *History of Woman Suffrage,* repr. (Salem, N.H.: Ayer, 1985), 3:560–93.

47. "Mrs. Florence P. Vosbrink Re-elected Head of the Catholic Woman's League," *Chicago Record-Herald,* 27 Apr. 1908; Herrick, *Chicago Schools,* 121; Merriam, *Chicago,* 185–89 (189).

48. Herrick, *Chicago Schools,* 121–22 (quote), 137; *Tenth Annual Announcement,* 78, 80; Nolan, *Servants of the Poor,* 88–102.

49. *Chicago Daily Tribune* articles "Schools Miss Their Goal," 5 May 1907, "Catholic Women Count Vote," 25 Apr. 1909, "Trouble at Club 'Playday'," 9 May 1909, and "Catholic Women at Peace," 29 May 1909; *New World* articles "Only Woman on Board of Education," 27 July 1911, "Catholic Woman on Board of Education," 3 July 1913, "Banquet to New Board of Education Appointee," 16 Aug. 1913, "Asks Four Women on School Board," 10 May 1914, and "Prepare for Charities Conference," 7 Aug. 1914.

50. "Stenographic Transcript of Meeting of the Board of Education," 27 June 1916 (both quotes), and "Efficient Chicago Teachers Dropped from the Service on June 27, 1916," Buck Papers.

51. "Summary of the News in the *Sunday Record-Herald* of Apr. 26, 1908," *Chicago Record-Herald,* 27 Apr. 1908; letters to Alderman Buck from "One who can ill afford to reveal her identity," 13 July 1916 (quote), from Emma Sichels, 27 June 1916, and from RTN, 8 July 1916, all in Buck Papers.

52. Herrick, *Chicago Schools,* 128, 131–37, 142.

53. *New World* articles untitled, 15 May 1914, "City Undertakes Social Work," 18 May 1914, "Chicago Has One Playground for 50,000 Children," 14 May 1915; Leonora Z. Meder, *First Semi-Annual Report of the Department of Public Welfare* (Chicago: Western Newspaper Union, 1915).

54. Leo XIII, *Rerum Novarum,* 241–61; Abell, *American Catholicism,* 23–80.

55. Leo XIII, *Rerum Novarum,* 115, 245–47, 250–53.

56. *New World* articles by Leonora Z. Meder, "Finding Work for the City's Unemployed," 5 Mar., "Unemployment: A Problem that City Must Handle," 16 Apr., "Immi-

grant Girls Robbed When Seeking Employment," 28 May, "Stray Thoughts on Unemployment," 4 June, and "How John Got a Job and Lost It Again," 13 June 1915.

57. Koven and Michel, *Mothers of a New World,* 4.

58. Leonora Z. Meder, "The Utilization of Municipal Agencies in Relief Work," in *Third Biennial Meeting of the National Conference of Catholic Charities* (Washington, D.C.: Catholic University of America, 1914), 277. See also *New World* articles "New State Law Designed to Aid Foreign Mothers," 9 July 1913, and "Civic Aid in Private Charity," 25 Sept. 1914; Skocpol, *Protecting Soldiers and Mothers;* Pedersen, "Catholicism, Feminism, and the Politics of the Family," 248; Michel, "Limits of Maternalism," 279.

59. *New World* articles by Leonora Z. Meder, "Unemployment: A Problem that City Must Handle," 16 Apr. 1915 (quote), and "Stray Thoughts on Unemployment," 4 June 1915.

60. Meder, "Unemployment: A Problem that City Must Handle," *New World,* 16 Apr. 1915 (quotes); Leonora Z. Meder, "'Urbs in Horto' Solves Problem of Unemployed," *New World,* 23 April 1915; Olivier Zunz, *The Changing Face of Inequality: Urbanization, Industrial Development, and Immigrants in Detroit, 1880–1920* (Chicago: University of Chicago Press, 1982), 269–70.

61. Lori D. Ginzberg, "Pernicious Heresies: Female Citizenship and Sexual Respectability in the Nineteenth Century," in *Women and the Unstable State in Nineteenth-Century America,* ed. Allison M. Parker and Stephanie Cole (College Station: Texas A&M University Press, 2000); Leonora Z. Meder, "Immigrant Girls Robbed When Seeking Employment," *New World,* 28 May 1915 (quotes).

62. *New World* articles "Sociologists Speak to South Side Woman's Club," *New World,* 4 Dec. 1914, and by Leonora Z. Meder, "Treatment that Women Receive in Police Cells," 7 May, "Chicago Has One Playground for 50,000 Children," 14 May, "Women We Lock in the House of Correction," 11 June, and "Abolition of the Morals Court Is Very Necessary," 25 June 1915.

63. See Kathryn Kish Sklar, *Florence Kelly and the Nation's Work: The Rise of Women's Political Culture, 1830–1900* (New Haven: Yale University Press, 1995); *New World* articles "Catholic Women to Aid Children," 11 Dec. 1914, and "Child Labor Conference Meets at Washington," 8 Jan. 1915.

64. Meder, "Municipal Agencies in Relief Work," 274; Leo XIII, *Rerum Novarum,* 247.

65. Meder, "Municipal Agencies in Relief Work," 273 (quote), and "Discussion," in *Third Biennial,* 273–85.

66. Ibid., 278–81, 283–84 (281, 284).

67. *Chicago Daily Tribune* articles "News Summary," 3 Feb. 1922, "Catholic Daughters Honor Attorney Leonora Meder," 31 Oct. 1927, "Mrs. Leonora Meder again Heads Business Women," 24 May 1935, and "Daughters of Confederacy Meet," 4 June 1935.

68. Chicago Department of Welfare, Annual Report, 1915; "Politics Pays for Her," *New World,* 21 May 1915; Flanagan, *Seeing with Their Hearts,* 142.

69. "City Undertakes Social Work," *New World,* 8 May 1914.

3—Sacred Space and Worldly Authority

1. "The Teachers of the Italian Mission Sunday School," Jan. 1903, MCR 3:1 (quote); Amberg, *Madonna Center,* 36–38, 85, 41–45; D'Agostino, "Missionaries in Babylon," vol. 1.

2. John T. McGreevy, *Parish Boundaries: The Catholic Encounter with Race in the Twentieth-Century Urban North* (Chicago: University of Chicago Press, 1996).

3. Mulkerins, *Holy Family Parish,* 20–22, 502, 740, 878; Evelyn M. Kitagawa and Karl E. Taeuber, eds., *Local Community Fact Book, Chicago Metropolitan Area, 1960* (Chicago: University of Chicago, 1963), 70; Reports of the Parish of the Holy Family,

Dec. 31, 1890, 1898, 1915, and 1920, Parish Annual Reports, Joseph Cardinal Bernardin Archives, Archdiocese of Chicago, Illinois (hereafter PAR).

4. Mulkerins, *Holy Family Parish,* 250; Dunne, *Memoirs of Zi Pré,* 78–79 (quote); Harry C. Koenig, STD, *A History of the Parishes of the Archdiocese of Chicago* (Chicago: Archdiocese of Chicago, 1980), 2:363, 382–83.

5. Merriam, *Chicago,* 141.

6. Ellen Skerrett, "The Irish of Chicago's Hull House Neighborhood," in *New Perspectives on the Irish Diaspora,* ed. Charles Fanning (Carbondale: Southern Illinois University Press, 2000): 189–222.

7. Mulkerins, *Holy Family Parish,* 10–11, 106–7; Report of the Parish of the Holy Family, Dec. 31, 1890, PAR.

8. Mulkerins, *Holy Family Parish,* xi-xxii, 13, 26, 28–32.

9. Ibid., 103–4, 129, 134–35, 721, 820, 875, 893.

10. Amberg, *Madonna Center,* 73 (quote), 56, 76.

11. J. De. Gigord, "Translation of 'The Life of Agnes Ward Amberg' as Appears in 'Un Centenaire, Enfants de Marie du Sacré Coeur'" (Paris, 1932), MCR 1:1.

12. "William A. Amberg—Inventor and Town Builder" *Milwaukee Catholic Citizen,* 23 Sept. [1911]; "William A. Amberg, Jury Commissioner who Introduced System to the Work of Selecting Talesmen for Cook County Courts. Appointed because of Experience and Peculiar Fitness," ca. 1907, unidentified newspaper, MCR 1:2; "Inaugural Address of William A. Amberg, Esq., President of the Columbus Club," 12 Jan. 1892, MCR 1:2.

13. Amberg, *Madonna Center,* 23–27. Quotation is from J. De. Gigord, "Translation of 'The Life of Agnes Ward Amberg' as Appears in 'Un Centenaire, Enfants de Marie du Sacré Coeur'" (Paris, 1932), MCR 1:1. See also "The Agnes Ward Amberg Club," Kansas City, Missouri, Dec. 1919; Clipping from unidentified newspaper in Rochester, N.Y., about Agnes Amberg's reading circle, 15 Jan. 1895; "In a Happy Reunion. Alumnae of the Sacred Heart Meet," unidentified newspaper, 20 Jan. 1898; Clipping from unidentified newspaper, 15 Jan. 1895, all in MCR 1:1. "Annual High Mass of the Christ-Child Society," *New World,* 1 Jan. 1909; Kenneally, *American Catholic Women,* 100.

14. Kitagawa and Taeuber, *Local Community Fact Book,* 70, 76; Mulkerins, *Holy Family Parish,* 723–25.

15. *Bon-Ton Directory* (Chicago: Harris & Morrow, 1879–1880), 15; *Elite Directory and Club List of Chicago* (Chicago: Elite Publishing, 1885), 5; *Chicago Blue Book of Selected Names of Chicago and Suburban Towns* (Chicago: Chicago Directory Company, 1894), 478; *Chicago Blue Book of Selected Names of Chicago and Suburban Towns 1910* (Chicago: Chicago Directory Company, 1910), 506; Mulkerins, *Holy Family Parish,* 941–42.

16. Amberg, *Madonna Center,* 10–11, 24, 40–41, 75.

17. D'Agostino, "Missionaries in Babylon," 1:121; Ponziglione to Rev. John [Frieden], 19 Apr. 1892 (quote), Reverend Paul M. Ponziglione, S.J., Collection, Missouri Province V Biographical Files, Midwest Jesuit Archives, St. Louis, Missouri (hereafter PPSJ).

18. Amberg, *Madonna Center,* 41; Ponziglione to Rev. John Frieden, 19 Apr. 1892, PPSJ.

19. Amberg, *Madonna Center,* 42–43; Mulkerins, *Holy Family Parish,* 366–67.

20. Ponziglione to Frieden, 19 Apr. 1892, PPSJ.

21. Amberg, *Madonna Center,* 36 (quote), 42–43; Mulkerins, *Holy Family Parish,* 367.

22. Mulkerins, *Holy Family Parish,* 366–67; Shaw, *Catholic Parish,* 101–12; Moloney, *American Catholic Lay Groups,* 142; Amberg, *Madonna Center,* 40–41.

23. Amberg, *Madonna Center,* 41, 42 (quote), 120; Mulkerins, *Holy Family Parish,* 595, 839–41, 961.

24. Amberg, *Madonna Center,* 44–45.

25. "Activities of the Children of Mary," n.d., MCR 1:1; Amberg, *Madonna Center,* 46.

26. Amberg, *Madonna Center,* 47, 52–54, 67 (52); Reports of the Parish of Holy Guardian Angel, Dec. 31, 1899, 1902, and 1905, PAR.

27. Mulkerins, *Holy Family Parish,* 224, 880–81, 931.

28. Shanabruch, *Chicago's Catholics,* 51–52. See also Michael McTighe, *A Measure of Success: Protestants and the Public Culture in Antebellum Cleveland* (Albany: State University of New York Press, 1994).

29. D'Agostino, "Missionaries in Babylon," 1:121; Amberg, *Madonna Center,* 46–50.

30. Amberg, *Madonna Center,* 52.

31. Ibid., 48, 66.

32. Addams, *Twenty Years,* 91 (quote); Eleanor J. Stebner, *The Women of Hull House: A Study in Spirituality, Vocation, and Friendship* (New York: State University of New York Press, 1997).

33. Amberg, *Madonna Center,* (quotes 83, 190), 134.

34. D'Agostino, "Missionaries in Babylon," 1:125–26; Shaw *Catholic Parish,* 53, 159–60 n. 99; Humbert S. Nelli, "The Role of the 'Colonial' Press in the Italian-American Community of Chicago, 1886–1921" (Ph.D. diss., University of Chicago, 1965), 38; Philip Cannistraro and Gerald Meyer, eds., *The Lost World of Italian-American Radicalism* (Westport, Conn.: Praeger, 2003).

35. "Evening Schools and the Irish Priests' Activities," *La Tribuna Italiana,* Foreign Language Press Survey, Special Collections, Regenstein Library, University of Chicago, Illinois (hereafter FLPS).

36. Dunne, *Memoirs of Zi Pré,* 22–27; Amberg, *Madonna Center,* 48, 55–56; Report of the Parish of Holy Guardian Angel, Dec. 31, 1899, PAR; "The Teachers of the Italian Mission Sunday School," Jan. 1903, in General Correspondence, 1903–1916, MCR 3:1.

37. Shaw, *Catholic Parish,* 102; Report of the Parish of Holy Guardian Angel, Dec. 31, 1905, PAR; Amberg, *Madonna Center,* 48, 55.

38. Amberg, *Madonna Center,* 47.

39. Dunne, *Memoirs of Zi Pré,* 50–53; "In Regard to Parochial Schools," *La Tribuna Italiana,* 9 Sept. 1906 (quote), FLPS; Rivka Lissak, *Pluralism and Progressives: Hull House and the New Immigrants, 1890–1919* (Chicago: University of Chicago Press, 1989), 98–99; *L'Italia* articles "Catholic Schools, not Governmental Schools," 1 Oct. 1892, and "The Italian School of the Church of the Guardian Angel," 3 Oct. 1910, both in FLPS.

40. D'Agostino, "Missionaries in Babylon," 1:16–18, 2:328.

41. Giovanni E. Schiavo, *The Italians in Chicago: A Study in Americanization* (Chicago: Italian-American, 1928), 184; Nelli, "'Colonial' Press," 39.

42. Shanabruch, *Chicago's Catholics,* 132–39; Rudolph J. Vecoli, "Prelates and Peasants: Italian Immigrants and the Catholic Church," in *The Other Catholics,* ed. Keith R. Dyrud, Michael Novak, and Rudolph J. Vecoli (New York: Arno Press, 1978), 226; McGuinness, "Response to Reform," 162–66.

43. Addams, *Twenty Years,* 424–25; Lissak, *Pluralism and Progressives,* 97–98.

44. Quotations are from *La Parola dei Socialisti* articles "The Giordano Bruno Club," 10 May 1913, and "Unemployment in Chicago," 16 Jan. 1915; see also *La Parola del Popolo* articles "The House of the People," 20 Oct. 1923, and "For the Erection of the 'House of the People' in Chicago," 2 June 1923, all in FLPS.

45. *La Parola dei Socialisti,* articles "Bruno Club to Hold Festival," 5 Mar. 1908, "Vaudeville Theatre," 20 June 1908 (quote), "Olivia Dramatic Company to Give Presentations," 4 July 1908, and "At the Hull House Theatre," *L'Avanti,* 15 Dec. 1918 (quote), all in FLPS; Shannon Jackson, *Lines of Activity: Performance, Historiography, Hull-House Domesticity* (Ann Arbor: University of Michigan Press, 2001), 212–36.

46. Schiavo, *Italians in Chicago,* 79, 107; Family B, 1908–1917, MCR 4:1; [Agnes Amberg (hereafter AWA)] to [Miss Montegriffo], n.d., MCR 3:1; "The Activities of the Garibaldi Institute," *Vita Nuova,* June 1927, FLPS.

47. Carolyn De Swarte Gifford, ed., *The American Deaconess Movement in the Early Twentieth Century* (New York: Garland, 1987), 144–45 (quote); Rose, *Mother's Job,* 41.

48. Dunne, *Memoirs of Zi Pré,* 5, 84, 86.

49. Madge Anderson, "What Garibaldi Institute Has Meant to Me," *Vita Nuova,*

Oct. 1929, FLPS.

50. Amberg, *Madonna Center,* 39, 83.

51. Dunne, *Memoirs of Zi Pré,* 3, 6–7, 11 (6).

52. Ibid., foreword, 28, 37, 40, 47–48 (ii).

53. Ibid., 29, 37, 38. See also Shaw, *Catholic Parish,* 55–56; Orsi, *Madonna of 115th Street.*

54. Daniel A. Lord, SJ, "A Catholic Social Center," *Queen's Work* 1 (Oct. 1914): 285–90 (287); James R. Barrett and David Roediger, "Inbetween Peoples: Race, Nationality, and the 'New Immigrant' Working Class," *Journal of American Ethnic History* 16.3 (Spring 1997): 7–9.

55. Leslie Woodcock Tentler, *Seasons of Grace: A History of the Catholic Archdiocese of Detroit* (Detroit: Wayne State University Press, 1990), 171.

56. James Owen to [unreadable], 18 Dec. 1916, MCR 3:1; Tentler, *Seasons of Grace,* 189–96.

57. Tentler, *Seasons of Grace,* 171; AWA to Brother Liguori, 14 May 1912, 20 May 1913, 12 May 1914, Brother Liguori to AWA, 16 May 1912, 26 May 1913, AWA to Brother Justus Res, 23 May 1916, all in MCR 3:1; Amberg, *Madonna Center,* 67.

58. Amberg, *Madonna Center,* 50.

59. Ibid., 37, 139; [Mary Agnes Amberg (henceforth MAA)] to Mother McLaughlin, 2 Feb. 1921, MCR 3:1; Donna R. Gabaccia, *From Sicily to Elizabeth Street: Housing and Social Change among Italian Immigrants, 1880–1930* (Albany: State University of New York Press, 1984), xv–xvi, 4, 100–116.

60. Dunne, *Memoirs of Zi Pré,* 17, 16.

61. Orsi, *Madonna of 115th Street.*

62. Maria Da Venezia, "In the Heart of Little Italy," *New World,* 23 Sept. 1906; "Sicilians Close Church Feast," *Chicago Daily Tribune,* 19 Aug. 1901, FLPS.

63. Harvey Zorbaugh, *The Gold Coast and the Slum: A Sociological Study of Chicago's Near North Side* (Chicago: University of Chicago Press, [1929]), 174; "Parade by Court Order," *Chicago Chronicle,* 24 July 1905, FLPS.

64. Dunne, *Memoirs of Zi Pré,* 17–18; Tentler, *Seasons of Grace,* 185–86; Amberg, *Madonna Center,* 85.

65. "The Procession," *La Tribuna Italiana,* 13 Aug. 1907, FLPS; Amberg, *Madonna Center,* 85.

66. *La Tribuna Italiana* articles "The Procession," 13 Aug. 1907 (quote), and "Three Italian Families Were Starving while $800 Hung on the Robe of the Blessed Virgin at the Solemn Festival of Melrose Park," 12 Aug. 1905, both in FLPS.

67. "Sicilians Celebrate the Assumption of the Virgin," *Chicago Daily Tribune,* 16 Aug. 1901, FLPS; Dunne, *Memoirs of Zi Pré,* 2; Shaw, *Catholic Parish,* 101–5.

68. Orsi, *Madonna of 115th Street.*

69. Reports of the Parish of Holy Guardian Angel, Dec. 31, 1899, 1902, 1905, 1910, PAR; Amberg, *Madonna Center,* 66–67.

70. Nelli, "'Colonial' Press," 181–98; Shaw, *Catholic Parish,* 140; Lizabeth Cohen, *Making a New Deal: Industrial Workers in Chicago, 1919–1939* (Cambridge: Cambridge University Press, 1990), 83–97.

71. Nelli, "'Colonial' Press," 2, 45; Schiavo, *Italians in Chicago,* 104 (quote).

72. Daphne Spain, *Gendered Spaces* (Chapel Hill: University of North Carolina Press, 1992).

73. Amberg, *Madonna Center,* 57, 64; *New World* articles "Harvest Party for Day Nursery," 13 Oct. 1913, and "Suffrage Meeting of Two Italian Parishes," 20 Mar. 1914. On the Onahans, see Pahorezki, "William James Onahan." On Casa Maria, see *Chicago Tribune* articles "Woman Deserts Society to Aid Little Italians," 21 Mar. 1915, "Casa Marie [sic] Center Children Prepare for Gardening," 11 June 1919, and "Social Center Will Be Made Home for Girls," 5 June 1921.

4—Leisure Culture and Boston Marriage

1. Mary Amberg, "The Settlement-House Signorina," manuscript, n.d., MCR 2:5. The story may date from about 1922. See also Pat to Mary, 10 Feb. 1922, MCR 3:1.

2. Barbara Welter, "The Feminization of American Religion, 1800–1860," in Barbara Walter, *Dimity Convictions* (Athens: Ohio University Press, 1976); Tentler, *Seasons of Grace,* 204–11; Amberg, *Madonna Center,* 66–67.

3. Amberg, *Madonna Center,* 70, 90–96; William Amberg (henceforth WAA) to MAA, 22 Aug. 1917, MCR 3:1; "Mission Christmas Letter, 1912, model no. 4," MCR 3:1.

4. John P. Rousmaniere, "Cultural Hybrid in the Slums: The College Woman and the Settlement House, 1889–1894," *American Quarterly* 22 (Spring 1970): 45–66; Graham Taylor, *Chicago Commons through Forty Years* (Chicago: Chicago Commons Association, 1936), 4; Amberg, *Madonna Center,* 10–11, 24, 40–41, 75, 95.

5. Amberg, *Madonna Center,* 80–81 (quote), 78, 82–85.

6. MAA to Marie Plamondon (hereafter MP), 3 Oct. 1924, MCR 3:2; Albert, from Girard, Ill., to MAA, 29 June [1917], and Victor, Peter, and Frank to Miss Jordan, 9 Jan. 1914, both in MCR 3:1.

7. Frances McElroy to MAA, 27 July 1914 (quote), to Margaret McKenna, 21 June 1923, to MAA, 26 Aug. 1920, Notes (author unidentified, probably MAA), ca. 1914, all in MCR 3:1; Frances McElroy to "Dear Lady," 13 Aug. 1926, MCR 3:2.

8. [AWA] to Mr. Bogan, n.d., MCR 3:1; "Evening Schools and the Irish Priests' Activities," *La Tribuna Italiana,* 14 Jan. 1905, FLPS. See also Louise Odencrantz, *Italian Women in Industry: A Study of Conditions in New York City* (New York: Russell Sage Foundation, 1919), 35–36. Amberg, *Madonna Center,* 67, 135–38; letters to MAA from D. Bremner, 30 May 1915, Peter De Salvo, 2 Dec. 1914, J. A., 15 Nov. 1918, Mary Prindeville, 30 Sept. 1917, Notes (author unidentified, probably MAA), ca. 1914, all in MCR 3:1.

9. Gail Bederman, *Manliness and Civilization: A Cultural History of Gender and Race in the United States, 1880–1917* (Chicago: University of Chicago Press, 1995); Allen Warren, "Popular Manliness: Baden-Powell, Scouting, and the Development of Manly Character," in *Manliness and Morality: Middle-Class Masculinity in Britain and America, 1800–1940,* ed. J. A. Mangan and James Walvin (New York: St. Martin's Press, 1987), 199; Marie McGuire to MP, 11 Mar., and MP to Marie McGuire, 14 Mar. 1923. MCR 3:2.

10. James T. Farrell, *Studs Lonigan* (New York: Modern Library, 1932); Lord, "Catholic Social Center"; J. Don Kearins to MAA, 6 Mar. 1921, "Invitation, Opening of the Young Men's Club Room at Guardian Angels' Center," 16 Mar. 1916, and Jas. D. Kearins to MAA, 12 June 1916, all in MCR 3:1.

11. Boy Scouts of America, "Suggestions Regarding the Formation of Roman Catholic Troops," May 1914, MAA to Joseph M. Cudahy, 27 June 1917, Chester B. Spires to MAA, 25 May 1915, Sydney A. Teller to Head Resident, 9 Mar. 1916, all in MCR 3:1; David Macleod, "Act Your Age: Boyhood, Adolescence, and the Rise of the Boy Scouts of America," *Journal of Social History* 16.2 (Winter 1982): 3–20; Warren, "Popular Manliness."

12. Frank to MAA, 15 Jan. 1917, MCR 3:1.

13. Miriam Cohen, *Workshop to Office: Two Generations of Italian Women in New York City, 1900–1950* (Ithaca: Cornell University Press, 1992), 37–59; Residents of Hull-House, *Hull-House Maps and Papers* (New York: Thomas Y. Crowell & Co., [1895]), 54–57. See also Odencrantz, *Italian Women in Industry,* 169; Virginia Yans-McLaughlin, *Family and Community: Italian Immigrants in Buffalo, 1880–1930* (Ithaca: Cornell University Press, 1971); Gabaccia, *From Sicily to Elizabeth Street;* Judith E. Smith, *Family Connections: A History of Italian and Jewish Immigrant Lives in Providence, Rhode Island, 1900–1940* (Albany: State University of New York Press, 1985).

14. MAA to Mr. N. C. Hurley, 10 Dec. 1916, MAA to Archbishop George Mundelein, DD, 29 June 1921, and WAA to MAA, 29 July 1917, all in MCR 3:1. Maxine Seller, "The Education of the Immigrant Woman: 1900–1935," *Journal of Urban History* 4.3 (May 1978):

307–30; Elizabeth Ewen, *Immigrant Women in the Land of Dollars: Life and Culture on the Lower East Side, 1890–1925* (New York: Monthly Review Press, 1985), 76–91.

15. Lord, "Catholic Social Center," 289–90.

16. Amberg, *Madonna Center,* 132–33, 138; Cohen, *Workshop to Office,* 102–3; Philomena and John C., 1921–1929, MCR 4; Alessandro Mastrovalerio, "The Italian Colony in Chicago," in Residents, *Hull-House Maps and Papers,* 136–37; [Mary or Agnes Amberg] manuscript pages, ca. 1914, MAA to Archbishop George Mundelein, 29 June 1921, "The Teachers of the Italian Mission Sunday School," Jan. 1903, and MAA to Mrs. William S. Monroe, 15 Nov. 1927, all in MCR 3:1.

17. J. A. to MAA, 15 Nov. 1918 (quote), [Sorority President] to Miss Powers, 30 Jan. 1920, President to Frances & Shirley McElroy, ca. Jan. 1920, and The Sorority to Archbishop George Mundelein, 3 June 1917, all in MCR 3:1. See also Peiss, *Cheap Amusements;* Murolo, *Common Ground of Womanhood;* Anne Meis Knupfer, *Toward a Tenderer Humanity and a Nobler Womanhood: African American Women's Clubs in Turn-of-the-Century Chicago* (New York: New York University Press, 1996).

18. Unsigned to MAA, 26 July 1914, MCR 3:1.

19. Amberg, *Madonna Center,* 100–104; [AWA] to Miss Williams, 12 Feb. 1913, Guardian Angel Settlement Board of Directors to Archbishop George Mundelein, May 1917, MAA to Mundelein, 28 July 1916, WAA to MAA, 29 July 1917, Annual Report of the Head Resident, Sept. 1918 to Sept. 1919, all in MCR 3:1.

20. WAA to MAA, 29 July 1917, F. X. Breen to MAA, 14 Dec. 1918, Louis Foquarette to MAA, 5 Aug. 1917, Francis X. Breen, SJ, to "Dear Friend" form letter, 11 Mar. 1918, all in MCR 3:1. See also Shanabruch, *Chicago's Catholics,* 171; Tentler, *Seasons of Grace,* 211.

21. "Red Cross File," n.d., and President of "The Sorority" to Miss Marian Hallinan, 30 Jan. 1920, MCR 3:1; Amberg, *Madonna Center,* 99; "Charles A. Gardiner," typescript of article from *New World,* n.d., MCR 2:5.

22. Amberg, *Madonna Center,* 111–17; Obituary of Agnes Amberg, 16 Nov. 1919, *Herald-Examiner,* and untitled article on William Amberg, *Milwaukee Catholic Citizen,* both in MCR 1:1.

23. Mary Middleton, "Madonna Center Unit Honors Miss Plamondon," unidentified newspaper, 4 June 1963, Welfare Council of Metropolitan Chicago, Chicago Historical Society, 369:4; Amberg, *Madonna Center,* 91; "My dear Heiress," 6 Oct. 1924, and MP to Mr. Francis Peabody, 12 Sept. 1921, both in MCR 3:1.

24. Amberg, *Madonna Center,* 98–99; Middleton, "Madonna Center Unit Honors Miss Plamondon"; "Mass Wednesday for Settlement's Miss Plamondon," *Chicago's American,* 15 May 1967; MP to Mr. Francis Peabody, 12 Sept. 1921, MCR 3:1.

25. John Cavanaugh to MP, 22 June 1924, MCR 3:2; Amberg, *Madonna Center,* 112–13. See also Mina Carson, *Settlement Folk: Social Thought and the American Settlement Movement, 1885–1930* (Chicago: University of Chicago Press, 1990), 157; Eugene Lies to MP, 18 June 1920, and L. E. [Bernard] to MAA, 16 Dec. 1920, MCR 3:1.

26. Rev. John A. McCarthy, "To Whom It May Concern," 19 Feb. 1921, M. Evelyn Carroll to MAA, 27 Apr. 1920, and Florence E. Neill to [MAA], 14 Oct. 1920, all in MCR 3:1; Amberg, *Madonna Center,* 150.

27. Elizabeth Israels Perry, "From Achievement to Happiness: Girl Scouting in Middle Tennessee, 1910s–1960s," *Journal of Women's History* 5.2 (Fall 1993): 76–77; Lynda M. Sturdevant, "Girl Scouting in Stillwater, Oklahoma: A Case Study in Local History," *Chronicles of Oklahoma* 57.1 (Spring 1979): 34–48.

28. "Guardian Angels Explanation of Father Breen's Change of Office Quarters," n.d., MCR 3:1.

29. "Some of the late sayings of Father Breen within the last month in Mr. Marzano's Office and other places," ca. 1922, MCR 2:5; "From the sermon given by Father Breen S.J. in Guardian Angels Church, Apr. 10th, 1921," and untitled typescript, 3 Apr. 1921, both in MCR 3:1.

30. Spain, *Gendered Spaces;* Amberg, *Madonna Center,* 149; untitled typescript, 3 Apr. 1921 (quote), MAA to MP, 20, 23 Feb. 1922, and typescript relating to the incident with Father Breen, 10 Apr. 1921, all in MCR 3:1.

31. Louis Foquarette to MAA, 5 Aug. 1917 (quote), MCR 3:1; Margaret Prang, "'The Girl God Would Have Me Be': The Canadian Girls in Training, 1915–1939," *Canadian Historical Review* 66 (June 1985): 159; Peter M. H. Wynhoven, "Opportunities of Girl Scout Leaders," *Catholic Charities Review* 10 (Jan. 1927), 22–25 (24); Peiss, *Cheap Amusements,* 69–70; Cohen, *Workshop to Office,* 69; MAA to MP, 23, 20 Feb. 1922, MCR 3:1; Ruth Craven, "The Orsinis' New Visitor," *Catholic Charities Review* 11 (May 1928): 158–62; Perry, "From Achievement to Happiness," 77–80.

32. Odencrantz, *Italian Women in Industry,* 203. See also Cohen, *Workshop to Office,* 105–13; Rose Laub Coser et al., *Women of Courage: Jewish and Italian Immigrant Women in New York* (Westport, Conn.: Greenwood Press, 1999), 41–42; Orsi, *Madonna of 115th Street.*

33. "List of Those Receiving Diplomas for Red Cross Course in Home Hygiene and Care of the Sick," n.d., ca. Apr. 1921, [MAA or MP] to Miss Collins, American Red Cross, 19 Apr. 1921, Chairman, Red Cross Activities, form letter, 19 Apr. 1921, and untitled typescript, 10 Apr. 1921, all in MCR 3:1.

34. MAA to MP, 23 Feb., 3 May (quote) 1922, and "Guardian Angels Explanation of Father Breen's Change of Office Quarters," n.d., all in MCR 3:1; "Italy of Today: Lectures by Countess Lisi Cipriani," ca. 1924, William J. Bogan to MAA, 1 Dec. 1924, and MAA to William J. Bogan, 5 Dec. 1924, MCR 3:2.

35. Alice Conway to MAA, 15 June 1921, [MAA] to MP, 4 Sept. 1924, MAA to MP, 16 Sept. 1924, John P. McGoorty to Rev. Frederic Siedenburg, SJ, 1 Nov. 1915, fund-raising letter, Dec. 1915, all in MCR 3:1.

36. MAA to MP, 3 May 1922, MCR 3:1.

37. Shaw, *Catholic Parish,* 106, 138. For the term *Boston Marriage* see John D'Emilio and Estelle Freedman, *Intimate Matters: A History of Sexuality in America* (New York: Harper and Row, 1988), 192.

38. Amberg, *Madonna Center,* 118–19; untitled clipping, *Milwaukee Catholic Citizen,* 23 Sept. [1911], MCR 1:1; Delta Sigma Gamma Girls to the boss and the chief, 14 June 1923, MCR 3:1; MAA to MP, 24 July 1925, MCR 3:2; "Mass Wednesday for Settlement's Miss Plamondon," *Chicago's American,* 15 May 1967.

39. Amberg, *Madonna Center,* 118–19, 129–30, 139–42; MAA to Most Rev. George Mundelein, DD, 29 June 1921, MCR 3:1; MAA to MP, 28 Oct. 1924, and MP to "Dear Babes," 16 Apr. 1924, MCR 3:2.

40. Kathryn Kish Sklar, "Hull House in the 1890s: A Community of Women Reformers," *Signs* 10 (Winter 1985): 658–77; Stebner, *Women of Hull House;* Carroll Smith-Rosenberg, "The Female World of Love and Ritual: Relations between Women in Nineteenth-Century America," *Signs* 1.1 (Autumn 1975): 4; Mary Jo Deegan, "'Dear Love, Dear Love': Female Pragmatism and the Chicago Female World of Love and Ritual," *Gender and Society* 10.5 (Oct. 1996): 597.

41. Antoinette and Nick B., MCR 4:1. See also Rev. A. J. Kelly, *Why Be Pure?* (New York: Paulist Press, 1942); *The New Sunday School Companion, Containing the Baltimore Catechism* (New York: Benziger Brothers, 1898), 72.

42. Freedman, *Maternal Justice;* George Chauncey, *Gay New York: Gender, Urban Culture, and the Making of the Gay Male World, 1890–1940* (New York: Basic Books, 1994), 72–76.

43. [MP] to MAA, ca. Sept. 1924, [MP] to Father Agnew, 19 Mar. 1921, MCR 3:1; Amberg, *Madonna Center,* 80; MAA to MP, 20 Feb. 1922, MCR 3:2.

44. MP to MAA, 27 Sept., MAA to MP, 28 Oct., 11 Nov. 1924, all in MCR 3:2.

45. MP to MAA, 13 Oct. (telegram), MAA to MP, 8 Nov. (resignation), MP to MAA, 27 Sept. 1924, MCR 3:2.

46. [MAA] to MP, 18 July 1925, MCR 3:2 (Marie dear); MAA to MP, 20, 23 Feb. 1922, MCR 3:1; MP to Thomas Cusack, 31 Oct. 1925, MCR 3:2.

47. MAA to MP, 23 July 1925 (Mr. Moore), [MAA] to Mr. D. F. Bremner, 15 Nov. 1923, MP to Thomas Cusack Co., 11 Mar. 1924, MP to Thomas Cusack, 31 Oct. 1925, "Old Faithful" to "My Dear," 30 Oct. 1925 (heartbroken), all in MCR 3:2.

48. Shaw, *Catholic Parish,* 111; Joseph A. Luther, SC, to MAA, 2 Mar. 1931, MCR 3:3; Reverend Charles Fani to MAA, 25 Oct. 1914, MCR 3:1; MAA to MP, 27 Sept., 28 Oct. 1924, MCR 3:2.

49. [MAA to MP], 14 Feb. 1922, MCR 3:1; Ruth Rosen, *The Lost Sisterhood: Prostitution in America, 1900–1918* (Baltimore: Johns Hopkins University Press, 1982), 140–42.

50. Ann Cox to MAA, 20 Mar. 1924, and untitled list of club activities, n.d., both in MCR 3:2; untitled typescript regarding children's activities, n.d., MCR 2:1.

51. Madeline and John D., 1923–1935, Josephine and Philip M., 1925, MCR 4; Lord, "Catholic Social Center," 287; Gordon, *Heroes of Their Own Lives.*

52. Mrs. Jane Howe-Kennedy to MAA, 7 May 1923, MCR 3:2.

53. Amberg, *Madonna Center,* 163; permission slip from Mrs. S., 30 July 1926, MCR 2:1; letters to MAA and MP, all dated 4 July 1925, from Margaret B., Anna P., Charlotte P., Mary P. (quote), Gertrude G., and Florence Wagner, all in MCR 3:2.

54. Amberg, *Madonna Center,* 132; Agnes Ward Amberg Communion Guild to MAA, 19 Jan. 1924, MAA to Agnes Ward Amberg Club, 24 Jan. 1924, Mr. Phil Byrne, Director of the Comrades [to MAA], 7 Dec. 1923, untitled list of club activities, n.d., all in MCR 3:2.

55. Cohen, *Workshop to Office;* form letter about the Business Girls' Club, 17 Jan. 1924, form letter about Club for Young Married Women, 17 Jan. 1924, untitled list of club activities, n.d., MCR 3:2.

56. Amberg, *Madonna Center,* 163; [MAA] to Joe P., 25 May 1925, MCR 2:1.

57. Applications for membership to the Frata Club from Angelo M. and James S., n.d., MCR 2:1.

58. Boys of the NCC Club to "Mike," 13 Oct. 1923 (quote), Francis A. Mentone to MAA and MP, 25 Apr. 1923, Nic-Con Camping Club to MAA, 6 Mar. 1923, MAA to Nic-Con Camping Club, 8 Mar. 1923, MCR 3:2; Constitution and By Laws, Nic-Con Camping Club, n.d., MCR 2:5.

59. F. Family, 1921–1922, MCR 4:2; Joe P., 1923–1930, MCR 4:3; MP to Rev. John Cavanaugh, 14 July 1924, MCR 3:2; Amberg, *Madonna Center,* 162–63; A. Family, 1933–1935, MCR 4:1.

60. Interview with Mrs. Anthony Serritella, quoted in Shaw, *Catholic Parish,* 127 (quote); D'Emilio and Freedman, *Intimate Matters,* 195–96; Ann Cox to MAA, 20 Mar. 1924, MCR 3:2.

61. Paula Fass, *The Damned and the Beautiful: American Youth in the 1920s* (New York: Oxford University Press, 1977); Ewen, *Immigrant Women,* 208–24; Cohen, *Workshop to Office,* 72–73; Rose L., 1927–1932, MCR 4; "Jordy" to "My Dear" [MAA], 14 Sept. 1923, and "Frank" to MP, 15 Sept. 23, MCR 3:2; Amberg, *Madonna Center,* 156–58.

62. Pascoe, *Relations of Rescue;* Odem, *Delinquent Daughters;* Muncy, *Creating a Female Dominion,* xv.

63. D'Emilio and Freedman, *Intimate Matters,* 194–201, 233–35; Anna R. March to MAA, 12 Mar. 1920, and Minnie M. to MAA, 14 Nov. 1921 (quote), MCR 3:1.

64. Elizabeth J. Clapp, *Mothers of All Children: Women Reformers and the Rise of the Juvenile Courts in Progressive Era America* (University Park: Pennsylvania State University Press, 1998); Michael Willrich, *City of Courts: Socializing Justice in Progressive Era Chicago* (New York: Cambridge University Press, 2003); Rose Alexander, *The "Girl Problem": Female Sexual Delinquency in New York, 1900–1930* (Ithaca: Cornell University Press, 1995); Kathy

Peiss, "'Charity Girls' and City Pleasures: Historical Notes on Working-Class Sexuality, 1880–1920," in *Unequal Sisters: A Multi-Cultural Reader in U.S. Women's History*, ed. Ellen Carol DuBois and Vicki L. Ruiz (New York: Routledge, 1990), 157–66.

65. Carmella to [MP], 15 Oct. 1920, 18 Jan. 1921, both in MCR 3:1. See also Tentler, *Seasons of Grace*, 171–72; Odem, *Delinquent Daughters*, 179; Mary M. Bartelme to MP, 4 Feb. 1921, MCR 3:1.

66. Hoy, "Chicago's Women and Girls," 260–94.

67. Anna and Ferdinand E., 1929–1936, MCR 4:2.

68. D'A. Family, 1921–1934, Lena and Jasper C., 1929–1932, MCR 4:1.

69. Odem, *Delinquent Daughters*, 115, 143–45; Katharine Flood to MAA, 27 Sept. 1923, MCR 4:1; MAA to Katharine Flood, 15 Nov. 1923, MCR 3:1; Leona and Joseph M., 1929–1931, MCR 4:3; Enlow and Frank B., 1925–1932, MCR 4:1; Mary and Frank S., 1920–1927, MCR 4:3.

70. Margaret and Ralph C., 1930–1939, Lena and Jasper C., 1929–1932, Mary and Frank C., 1915–1934, Mary and Tony C., 1924–1928, Theresa and Joe C., 1919–1928, all in MCR 4:1.

71. D'Emilio and Freedman, *Intimate Matters*, 109–11, 207, 211–12, 224–25; Amberg, *Madonna Center*, 129–30, 139–42; Richard White, *Remembering Ahanagran: Storytelling in a Family's Past* (New York: Hill and Wang, 1998), 201.

72. Antoinette and Nick B., 1929–1934, MCR 4:1.

73. Christina and George B., 1916–1927, Madeline and Louis C., 1926–1937, Rosie and Tony A., 1922, Raphello A., 1920–1924, Bridget and Tony B., 1921–1924, all in MCR 4:1.

74. Adeline A., 1925, MCR 4:1; John M. to Mary Amberg, 27 Jan. 1915, MCR 3:1.

75. Rose P., 1923–1933, MCR 4:3.

76. Mary B., 1927–1928, MCR 4:1. See also Lawrence and Philomena A., 1929–1940, MCR 4:1.

77. Josie and Nick C., 1925–1933, James C., 1925–1929, Lucy and Amillio C., 1916–1931, Angelina and Joe B., 1920–1923, all in MCR 4:1; S. P. to MAA, 24 Mar. 1917, MCR 3:1.

78. Adeline A., 1925, MCR 4:1; Josie and Sam C., 1917–1928, MCR 4:1; N. family, 1918, MCR 4:3; Mary and Pasquale S., 1922–1930, MCR 4:3; Lizzie and Jack C., 1927–1934, MCR 4:1; B. Family, 1908–1917, MCR 4:1; Katie and John H., 1923–1935, MCR 4:2; Mary and [Christ] S., 1922–1926, MCR 4:3; [Dora] and Vito G., 1920–1927, MCR 4:2.

79. Raphello A., 1920–1924, Katie A., 1920–1930, Mary A., 1920–1925, Mary and Carl B., 1914–1928, Rose and Sam B., 1926–1927, Bridget and Tony A., 1921–1924, Mary and James B., 1919–1923, Constantine and Anna B., 1927, Theresa and Patsy C., 1921–1924, all in MCR 4:1.

80. Josie and Nick C., 1925–1933, Julia and Felix C., 1919–1925, Beatress and Nick B., 1922–1932, Mary and Sam C., 1928–1935, all in MCR 4:1.

81. Philomena and Lawrence A., 1929–1940, also Madeline and Fiora B., 1914–1923, both in MCR 4:1.

82. Mary and Edward B., n.d., MCR 4:1; Carmella A., 1922–1933, MCR 4:1; Antoinette and Dominic T., 1929–1934, MCR 4:4; Josie and Nick C., 1925–1933, MCR 4:1; Rose C., 1935–1936, MCR 4:1; Ernesta and Michael D., 1930–1941, MCR 4:1; Mrs. L., n.d., MCR 4:2; Amberg, *Madonna Center*, 133–34.

83. MAA to MP, 3 Oct. 1924, MCR 3:2; Katherine and John H., 1923–1935, MCR 4:2; Mary and [Christ] S., 1922–1926, MCR 4:3; and Nick D., 1926, MCR 4:1.

84. Mary Amberg, "The Settlement-House Signorina," manuscript, n.d., MCR 2:5; [MP] to "Dearest Arthur," 16 Nov. 1920, MCR 3:1; John Cavanaugh to MP, 22 June 1924, MCR 3:2 (quote).

5—Aspiring Politicians

1. Quotation is from "Dedication of Day Nursery," 10 May 1923, Scrapbook 1923–1929, Daughters of Charity of St. Vincent de Paul Archives, De Paul Center Collection, Evansville, Indiana (hereafter DPCC); untitled article, *New World,* 21 Feb. 1911.

2. "Dedication of De Paul Day Nursery," 10 May 1923, Scrapbook 1923–1929, DPCC.

3. Vivien Palmer, "Study of the Development of Chicago's Northside" (quote), manuscript, n.d., Chicago Historical Society, Illinois; Kitagawa and Taeuber, *Local Community Fact Book,* 28–29.

4. Koenig, *Parishes,* 2:961–63; Kitagawa and Taeuber, *Local Community Fact Book,* 28–29.

5. Koenig, *Parishes,* 2:961–63.

6. Kitagawa and Taeuber, *Local Community Fact Book,* 28 (quote); "Advertise in the Vincentian Weekly," *Vincentian Weekly* (hereafter *VW*), 17 Nov. 1912.

7. Rev. Patrick Mullins, CM, "The Voice of De Paul, 1910–1920," typescript, Scrapbook 1915–1922, DPCC; *VW* articles "The College Theatre," 11 Sept. 1910, and "Wiley's College Theatre," 28 Sept. 1913.

8. Koenig, *Parishes,* 2:963; *VW* articles "De Paul High School," 25 Sept. 1910, "Farewell Banquet to Seniors of De Paul High School," 30 Apr. 1911, and "High School Notes," 8 June 1913.

9. *VW* articles "De Paul High School," 25 Sept. 1910 (quote), "Chicago Telephone Company," 14 May 1911, "High School Notes," 24 Sept. 1911, 15 Feb. 1914.

10. *VW* articles "High School Notes," 3, 24 (quote) Sept., 1911, 4 May 1913; Kane, *Separatism and Subculture,* 203.

11. *VW* articles "Farewell Banquet to Seniors of De Paul High School," 14 May 1911, and "Sweetness of Temper," 22 Sept. 1912.

12. Mrs. Jane Howe-Kennedy to MAA, 7 May 1923, MCR 3:2.

13. "Servites in Little Italy," *New World,* 29 Mar. 1913; DPSC minutes, June, July 1915, DPCC; "De Paul Settlement Club," *VW,* 3 Oct. 1915.

14. "The Last Shall Be First," *VW,* 28 Dec. 1913. See also Oates, *Catholic Philanthropic Tradition,* 12; Colleen McDannell, "Going to the Ladies' Fair: Irish Catholics in New York City, 1870–1900," in Bayor and Meagher, *New York Irish.*

15. *VW* articles "An Act of Charity Rewarded," 22 Jan. 1911, "Making Others Thankful," 3 Dec. 1911, "Her Christmas Gift," 17 Dec. 1911, and "Bringing Happiness to Others," 17 Mar. 1918.

16. *VW* articles untitled, 2 Oct. 1910, and "Bazaar Notes," 9 Oct. 1910.

17. "Bazaar Notes," *VW,* 18 Sept. 1910 (quote); Rev. Patrick Mullins, CM, "The Voice of De Paul, 1910–1920," typescript, Scrapbook 1915–1922, DPCC; "Bazaar Notes," *VW,* 9 Oct. 1910 (quote).

18. *VW* articles "Bazaar Notes," 25 Sept. 1910, "Choir Notes," 25 Sept., 2 Oct. 1910, untitled, 2 Oct. 1910, "High School Notes," 30 Oct. 1910, "Central District," 20 Nov. 1910, and "Young Men's Catholic Club," 3 May 1914.

19. *VW* articles "Bazaar Notes," 27 Nov. 1910, and "Central District," 20 Nov. 1910.

20. "De Paul Settlement Club," *VW,* 19 Jan. 1916. See also *VW* articles "Bazaar Notes," 18, 25 Sept. 1910, "The Last Shall Be First," 28 Dec. 1913.

21. McGuinness, "Response to Reform," 116–30; Davis, *Spearheads for Reform,* 30–31.

22. Harry Koenig, ed., *Caritas Christi Urget Nos: A History of the Offices, Agencies, and Institutions of the Archdiocese of Chicago,* vol. 11 (Chicago: Archdiocese of Chicago, 1981), 981; overview of Nestor's work on the Women in Industry Committee of the Council of National Defense, folders 6–7, box 1, Agnes Nestor Papers, Chicago Historical Society, Chicago, Illinois.

23. DPSC minutes, June, July, 20, 27 Sept., Nov. 1915, 14 Aug. 1916; *VW* articles "De Paul Settlement Club," 21 Jan. 1917, Untitled, 28 Jan. 1917, "De Paul Settlement Club," 12 Dec. 1915 (quote), and "De Paul Settlement Auxiliary," 12 Dec. 1915; DPSC minutes, 23 Apr., 9 July 1917.

24. *VW* articles "Congratulations," 1 Mar. 1914, "Veronica Walsh," 6 Sept. 1914, "Pastor's Column," 4, 11 Oct. 1914, "Entertainment and Lecture," 21 Feb. 1915, "De Paul Settlement Club," 17, 24 Feb., 3, 10, 17 Mar., 30 June 21 July 1918, and "Attention Men and Women Voters," 24 Oct. 1920. The following entries in the Settlement Club minutes note that Father McCabe delivered special talks on matters of charity: Settlement Club minutes, 21 Sept. 1914, 12 Apr., 23 Aug. 1915, 12 Nov. 1917, 9, 22 Sept. 1918, 19 Oct. 1914. See also Jeffrey P. Moran, "'Modernism Gone Mad': Sex Education Comes to Chicago, 1913," *Journal of American History* 82.2 (Sept. 1996): 481–513; Shanabruch, *Chicago's Catholics*, 139; Gustafson, *Women and the Republican Party*, 61–74; Patricia Lamoureux, "Irish Catholic Women and the Labor Movement," *U.S. Catholic Historian* 16 (Summer 1998): 24–44; Flanagan, *Seeing with Their Hearts*, 177–80.

25. *VW* articles "De Paul Settlement Club," 30 Jan. 1916, and "Pastor's Column," 27 Sept. 1914; DPSC minutes, 30 Nov. 1914, 2 Feb. 1916.

26. "A Tribute," *VW*, 7 June 1914; "Altar Society," *VW*, 4 Oct. 1914.

27. Oates, *Catholic Philanthropic Tradition*, 82.

28. Mrs. Burke and Sister Servant both quoted from Sister Catherine Welch to Sister Mary Barbara, assistant, Marillac Seminary, Normandy, Missouri, 25 Nov. 1928, Scrapbook 1923–1929, DPCC; "Beginnings of De Paul Settlement and Day Nursery," typescript, n.d., 18, DPCC; *VW* articles "De Paul Settlement Club," 14 Nov. 1915, 21 Nov. 1914, and "Charity Workers," 24 Oct. 1911.

29. Minute Book, De Paul University Settlement Club, 1914–1919, and Feast of the Immaculate Conception of Our Blessed Mother, Dec. 8 1915, guest book, both in DPCC; *The Lakeside Business Directory of Chicago* (Chicago: Chicago Directory Company, 1914–1919).

30. "Pastor's Column," *VW*, 4 Oct. 1914; Sister Catherine Welch to Sister Mary Barbara, assistant, Marillac Seminary, Normandy, Missouri, 25 Nov. 1928 (quote), "Dedication of Day Nursery," 10 May 1923, both in Scrapbook 1923–1929, DPCC; DPSC minutes, 17 Aug. 1914; *VW* articles "University Notes," 9 Oct. 1910, "The Hundred Dollar Club," 2 Apr. 1911, "Important Meeting," 20 Sept. 1914, and "De Paul Settlement Club," 17 Feb. 1918.

31. "Fashionable Churches," *VW*, 29 Sept. 1912; Rev. Patrick Mullins, CM, "The Voice of De Paul, 1910–1920," typescript, Scrapbook 1915–1922, DPCC; James O'Donnell Bennett, "What the Preacher Is Like: Francis Xavier McCabe," *Chicago Daily Tribune*, 16 Mar. 1914; DPSC minutes, 2 Feb. 1915; "Choir Notes," *Monthly Calendar*, Sept. 1902; "The Chimes of Normandy," *VW*, 28 Dec. 1913.

32. Untitled article, *VW*, 14 May 1911 (quote); DPSC minutes, 24, 31 Aug., 23 Nov. 1914, 14 Aug. 1916; "Pastor's Column," *VW*, 22 Nov. 1914; "Dedication of Day Nursery," 10 May 1923, Scrapbook 1923–1929, and "Constitution and By-Laws of the De Paul Settlement Club," n.d., Scrapbook 1915–1922, both in DPCC.

33. "De Paul Settlement Club," *VW*, 30 Apr. 1916.

34. *VW* articles "De Paul Settlement Club," 26 Nov. (potatoes), 3 Dec. 1916, 13 May (babies), 3 June, 7 Oct., 11 Nov. 1917, 28 Apr., 5 May, 30 June 1918.

35. "De Paul Settlement Club," *VW*, 10 Oct. 1915.

36. "Settlement Club," *VW*, 8 Feb. 1925; DPSC minutes, 26 Oct., 16 Nov., 21 Dec. 1914, 8, 27 Mar., 27 Sept., 11 Oct. 1915, 8 July 1918, 24 Mar., 24 Nov. 1919. The miraculous medal bore the image of Mary crushing a serpent beneath her foot, on the front, and the letter "M" combined with a cross, on the back. The images were said to have been revealed by Mary to St. Catherine Labouré, a Daughter of Charity of St. Vincent de Paul, in 1830. Mary told St. Catherine that all who wore the medal around their

necks would receive great graces. The medals are distributed by priests of the congregation of the mission, commonly known as the Vincentians. *New Catholic Encyclopedia,* vol. 10 (Washington, D.C.: Catholic University of America, 1967), 894–95.

37. *VW* articles "Knights and Ladies of America," 8 June 1913, "Sodality of the Blessed Virgin," 1 Nov. 1914, 19 Nov. 1916, "Settlement Club," 12 Jan. 1919, "Ladies of Isabella," 22 Feb. 1914, 4 Apr. 1915, "Patriotic Card Party," 27 Jan. 1918; DPSC minutes, 7 Dec. 1914, 11 June, 1 Mar., 12, 17 Apr. 1915, 22 June 1917.

38. "Pastor's Column," *VW,* 7 Nov. 1915 (quote); "Dedication of Day Nursery," 10 May 1923, Scrapbook 1923–1929, [Sister Catherine] to Sister Eugenie, Visitatrix, Marillac Seminary, Normandy, Mo, n.d., Scrapbook 1915–1922, both in DPCC; *VW* articles "Financial Report," 28 Oct. 1917, and "Report of the Ladies of Charity of St. Vincent's Parish for Season of 1916–1917," 28 Oct. 1917; Sister Andrea to Sister Virginia Kingsbury, Mater Dei Provincialate House, 8 Feb. 1973, Scrapbook 1915–1922, DPCC.

39. Untitled, *VW,* 12 Dec. 1915 (ad); "Settlement Club," *VW,* 5 Mar. 1916; De Paul Center brochure, 16 Dec. 1926, Scrapbook 1923–1929, DPCC.

40. Kate Weber, "Concert Proceeds Will Furnish New De Paul Nursery," *Chicago Tribune,* 8 Apr. 1923; Sister Andrea to Sister Virginia Kingsbury, Mater Dei Provincialate House, 8 Feb. 1973, Scrapbook 1915–1922, DPCC (quote).

41. DPSC minutes, 23 Apr., 9 July 1917; "De Paul Settlement Club," *VW,* 13 May 1917.

42. Sister Catherine Welch to Sister Visitatrix, n.d., Scrapbook 1915–1922, DPCC; DPSC minutes, 10 Sept., 12 Nov. 1917, 22 Sept. 1918. *VW* articles "De Paul Settlement Club," 9 Dec. 1917, "Service List," 6 Jan. 1918, "Patriotic Card Party," 27 Jan. 1918, "Pastor's Column," 21 Apr. 1918, "Settlement Club," 9 Nov. 1919.

43. Sister Catherine to Sister Eugenie [1922], Scrapbook 1915–1922, DPCC. See also "Settlement Club," *VW,* 11 Apr. 1920; "Dedication of Day Nursery," 10 May 1923, Scrapbook 1923–1929, DPCC; Sister Andrea to Sister Virginia Kingsbury, Mater Dei Provincialate House, 8 Feb. 1973, Scrapbook 1915–1922, DPCC; "St. Ann's Sodality," *VW,* 3 Sept. 1922; Helen Hall, *Unfinished Business in Neighborhood and Nation* (New York: MacMillan, 1971), xii.

6—Unexpected Rescuers

1. McCabe used the terms *worthy* and *deserving* interchangeably to describe poor parishioners. DPSC minutes, 30 Nov. 1914; "Parish Items," *Monthly Calendar,* Feb. 1910; "Pastor's Column," *VW,* 6 Dec. 1914 (quote).

2. "Pastor's Column," *VW,* 13 (quote), 20 Dec. 1914.

3. Carol Coburn and Martha Smith note that the term *nun* specifically refers to women in cloistered orders, but that in popular usage it often refers to any female member of a religious order. Like Coburn and Smith, I use the term *nuns* to refer to members of the Daughters of Charity even though the order is not cloistered. Other terms used here more or less interchangeably include *sisters* and *women religious.* In the latter case, the term *religious* is a noun used to identify a member of a religious community. Carol K. Coburn and Martha Smith, *Spirited Lives: How Nuns Shaped Catholic Culture and American Life, 1836–1920* (Chapel Hill: University of North Carolina Press, 1999), 228.

4. James O'Donnell Bennett, "What the Preacher Is Like," 15 Mar. 1914, *Chicago Record-Herald,* clipping (quote), and Francis McCabe, "The Opening of the Mission," both in McCabe—Notes, Scrapbooks, and Francis McCabe, "Sins of the Tongue," in McCabe's Sermon Notebook, all in III-C-McCabe, box 1, St. Vincent's Church Records and Biographical Files, DeAndreis-Rosati Memorial Archives of the Congregation of the Mission (Vincentian Fathers), St. Mary's of the Barrens, Perryville, Missouri (hereafter DRMA). James O'Donnell Bennett, "What the Preacher Is Like: Francis Xavier McCabe," *Chicago*

Daily Tribune, 16 Mar. 1914; Francis X. McCabe, "Preliminary Remarks on the Mission Work," in F. X. McCabe's Mission Notes and Instructions, III-C-McCabe, box 1, DRMA.

5. "Pastor's Column," *VW,* 4 Oct. 1914 (quote); Reports of the Parish of St. Vincent de Paul, Dec. 31, 1900 and 1910, PAR; "Pastor's Column," *VW,* 3 Jan. 1915 (quote).

6. Katz, *Shadow of the Poorhouse;* Kenneth Kusmer, "The Functions of Organized Charity in the Progressive Era: Chicago as a Case Study," *Journal of American History* 60 (Fall 1973): 657–78; Seller, "Immigrant Woman"; Lissak, *Pluralism and Progressives;* Ewen, *Immigrant Women;* Deborah Skok, "Organized Almsgiving: Scientific Charity and the Society of St. Vincent de Paul in Chicago, 1871–1918," *U.S. Catholic Historian* 16 (Fall 1998): 19–35.

7. Roy Lubove, *The Professional Altruist: The Emergence of Social Work as a Career, 1880–1930* (Cambridge, Mass.: Harvard University Press, 1965); Paul Boyer, *Urban Masses and Moral Order in America, 1820–1920* (Cambridge: Harvard University Press, 1978), 158 (quote).

8. "Dedication of Day Nursery," 10 May 1923, Scrapbook 1923–1929, DPCC. See also Lester Francis Goodchild, "The Mission of the Catholic University in the Midwest, 1842–1980" (Ph.D. diss., University of Chicago, 1986).

9. F. X. Lawlor, "Mystical Body of Christ," in *New Catholic Encyclopedia* (San Francisco: Catholic University of America, 1967), 10:167; Émile Mersch, SJ, *The Whole Christ: The Historical Development of the Doctrine of the Mystical Body in Scripture and Tradition* (Milwaukee: Bruce, 1938).

10. Francis McCabe, "Love of God and Neighbor," Sermon Notebook, untitled typescript, [Mission Notes], McCabe—Notes, Scrapbooks, and "F.X. McCabe's Mission Notes and Instructions," McCabe—Notes, Scrapbooks, all in III-C-McCabe, box 1, DRMA.

11. Untitled typescript (quote), [Mission Notes], McCabe—Notes, Scrapbooks, III-C-McCabe, box 1, DRMA; Joseph P. Chinnici, "The Eucharist, Symbol of the Church," in Joseph P. Chinnici, ed., *Living Stones: The History and Structure of Catholic Spiritual Life in the United States* (New York: MacMillan, 1989), 119–56.

12. Sister Camilla to Sister Eugenia, typescript, 15 Dec. 1915 (quote), F. X. McCabe to Sister Eugenia, typescript, 1 Dec. 1915, and "Dedication of Day Nursery," 10 May 1923, Scrapbook 1923–1929, all in DPCC; "Obituary," *VW,* 7 Sept. 1941; "De Paul Settlement Club Column," *VW,* 12 Dec. 1915; DPSC minutes, 22 Nov. 1915, DPCC.

13. "De Paul Settlement and Day Nursery, Chicago, Illinois," c. 1924, Scrapbook 1923–1929, and Sister Camilla to Sister Eugenia, 15 Dec. 1915, typescript (quote), both in DPCC.

14. Sister Camilla to Sister Eugenia, 15 Dec. 1915, typescript, and "Beginnings of De Paul Settlement and Day Nursery," n.d., both in DPCC; Michel, *Children's Interests/Mothers' Rights,* 65.

15. *VW* articles "De Paul Settlement Club," 24 Sept. 1916, and "De Paul Day Nursery," 16 Dec. 1917.

16. *VW* articles "Pastor's Column," 22 Nov. 1914, 7 Nov. 1915; "Dedication of Day Nursery," 10 May 1923 (quote), and untitled fund-raising appeal letter, 16 Dec. 1926, Scrapbook 1923–1929, DPCC; Katz, *Shadow of the Poorhouse,* 77; Cahan, *Past Caring,* 12–24.

17. "Parish Announcements," 24 Apr. 1910, box IIC (II)3, DRMA; *Monthly Calendar* articles untitled, Mar. 1901, "A Mother's Influence," May 1901, "What Sort of Man Shall I Have?" Feb. 1903, M. A. Lambing, "Total Abstinence the Remedy," Apr. 1903 (reprint from *The Tablet*); Amy Jane Leazenby, "Day Nurseries as an Agency for Child Care" (Master's thesis, University of Chicago, 1920), 31; "Financial Report," *VW,* 28 Oct. 1917. The statistics in this paragraph come from Martha May, "The Historical Problem of the Family Wage: The Ford Motor Company and the Five Dollar Day," in DuBois and Ruiz, *Unequal Sisters,* 289; John A. Ryan, *A Living Wage* (New York: MacMillan, 1920); Winifred Wandersee, *Women's Work and Family Values, 1920–1940* (Cambridge: Harvard

University Press, 1981).

18. "Ladies of Isabella," *VW,* 4 Apr. 1915 (quote); Maria Lopez, "Day Nurseries," *St. Vincent De Paul Quarterly* (Aug. 1899): 232; Weber, "Concert Proceeds."

19. "Pastor's Column," *VW,* 22 Nov. 1914; "Dedication of Day Nursery," 10 May 1923, Scrapbook 1923–1929, DPCC; *Daily News* articles "Singer Aids Little Folk," 20 Apr. 1923, and Jesse Ozias Donahue, "The Chicago Society World: Mrs. Lester Armour Plans Benefit for De Paul Settlement and Day Nursery," 6 Apr. 1923 (quote).

20. "Dedication of Day Nursery," 10 May 1923 (quote), Scrapbook 1923–1929, DPCC; "The Poor," *VW,* 4 Feb. 1917 (quote); Crocker, *Social Work,* 164–81.

21. "De Paul Settlement Club," *VW,* 12 Dec. 1915; Constance B. Stitt, "DePaul Day Nursery and Social Center: The Founding and First Five Years" (Research paper, Northeastern Illinois University, 1976), DPCC; "De Paul Day Nursery," *VW,* 16 Dec. 1917; Cahan, *Past Caring,* 19; Leazenby, "Day Nurseries," 38; "Pastor's Column," *VW,* 25 Oct. 1914; DPSC minutes, 12 Mar. 1917, DPCC; Weber, "Concert Proceeds."

22. Leazenby, "Day Nurseries," 16–17, 25–26, 38; DPSC minutes, 27 Sept. 1915; Constance B. Stitt, "DePaul Day Nursery and Social Center: The Founding and First Five Years" (Research paper, Northeastern Illinois University, 1976), DPCC; "De Paul Settlement Club," *VW,* 24 Sept. 1916. Sister Camilla to Sister Eugenia, typescript, 15 Dec. 1915, photograph of sick child in isolation, Scrapbook 1923–1929, "Day Nursery Is Moved into Old Police Station," *Chicago Evening Post,* 21 Aug. 1922, Scrapbook 1915–1922, "Beginnings of De Paul Settlement and Day Nursery," typescript, 18 Feb. 1977, 6, all in DPCC.

23. Cahan, *Past Caring,* 16 (quote); "De Paul Settlement and Day Nursery, Chicago, Illinois," DPCC; "De Paul Council No. 14, Ladies of Isabella," *VW,* 13 May 1923.

24. "Dedication of Day Nursery," 10 May 1923 (quotes), Scrapbook 1923–1929, DPCC; *VW* articles "De Paul Day Nursery," 16 Dec. 1917, "A Father's Neglect," 26 Mar. 1916, and "A Defect of America," 26 Mar. 1916; Michel, "Limits of Maternalism," 287.

25. "Pastor's Column," *VW,* 13 Dec. 1914.

26. F. X. McCabe to Sister Eugenia, typescript, 1 Dec. 1915, Sister Camilla to Sister Eugenia, typescript, 15 Dec. 1915 (quote), both in DPCC; "De Paul Settlement Club," *VW,* 9 Dec. 1917 (quote); Addams, *Twenty Years,* 167–69; "The Madonna of the Curb," *Catholic Charities Review* 5 (Apr. 1921): 127.

27. Sister Camilla to Sister Eugenia, typescript, 15 Dec. 1915, DPCC; *VW* articles "De Paul Nursery and Social Center," 12 Dec. 1915, and "De Paul Settlement Club," 21 May, 24 Sept. 1916.

28. "De Paul Nursery and Social Center," *VW,* 12 Dec. 1915; fund-raising letter, 16 Dec. 1926, Scrapbook 1923–1929, DPCC. See also Leslie Woodcock Tentler, *Wage-Earning Women: Industrial Work and Family Life in the United States, 1900–1930* (New York: Oxford University Press, 1979), 136–79; Michel, "Limits of Maternalism," 281, 303.

29. "De Paul Settlement Club," *VW,* 21 May 1916; H. E. G., "Beginnings of De Paul Settlement and Day Nursery," typescript, 25 Nov. 1963, DPCC; Tentler, *Wage-Earning Women,* 136–79; Rose, *Mother's Job,* 48.

30. Rose, *Mother's Job,* 62.

31. Hasia Diner, *Erin's Daughters in America* (Baltimore: Johns Hopkins University Press, 1984), 94.

32. Fund-raising letter, 16 Dec. 1926, in Scrapbook 1923–1929, Sister Andrea to Sister Virginia Kingsbury, 8 Feb. 1973, and "Irish Bread Treat," clipping, n.d., both in Scrapbook 1915–1922, all in DPCC; "De Paul Settlement Club," *VW,* 24 Sept. 1916. I have changed Donna F.'s name for the sake of privacy.

33. "De Paul Settlement Club," *VW,* 25 Aug. 1918; "Irish Bread Treat," clipping, n.d., and "The Way We Were, 1914–1922," partial transcript of an oral history interview of Donna F., 26 July 1977, both in Scrapbook 1915–1922, DPCC.

34. Maria Lopez, "Day Nurseries," *St. Vincent De Paul Quarterly* (Aug. 1899): 232–37 (quotes); photographs of children, Scrapbook 1923–1929, DPCC. See also Ann Taylor Allen, "Let Us Live with Our Children: Kindergarten Movements in Germany and the United States, 1840–1914," *History of Education Quarterly* 28 (Spring 1988): 23–48.

35. Diane Durante, interview with author, Chicago, 16 June 2005.

36. *VW* articles "Financial Report," 28 Oct. 1917, and "Report of the Ladies of Charity of St. Vincent's Parish for Season of 1916–1917," 28 Oct. 1917.

37. Gordon, *Heroes of Their Own Lives.*

38. Coburn and Smith, *Spirited Lives,* 1–11, 211; "Dedication of the De Paul Day Nursery," 10 May 1923, Scrapbook 1923–1929, DPCC.

39. Coburn and Smith, *Spirited Lives,* 7; "De Paul Settlement and Day Nursery, Chicago, Illinois," c. 1924, Scrapbook 1923–1929, DPCC.

40. Sisters' biographies, Daughters of Charity of St. Vincent de Paul Archives, Mater Dei Provincialate, Evansville, Indiana.

41. The information and quotations in the following several paragraphs come from *Sister Mary Barbara Regan: First Assistant of the St. Louis Province of the Daughters of Charity of St. Vincent de Paul, 1910–1930* (St. Louis: Wellington Printing Company, n.d.), 73–79, 98–107, 113–15, 118, 121, 189, 199–200.

42. "De Paul Day Nursery," *VW,* 16 Dec. 1917.

43. "Sister Mary Maes," Sisters' biographies, Daughters of Charity of St. Vincent de Paul Archives, Mater Dei Provincialate, Evansville, Indiana.

44. "Sister Adela Koenigsmark," Sisters' biographies, Daughters of Charity of St. Vincent de Paul Archives, Mater Dei Provincialate, Evansville, Indiana.

45. *Sister Mary Barbara Regan,* 118–19.

46. "Levan, Thomas F.," obituary (reprinted from *New World,* 14 Feb. 1936), and "Very Rev. Thomas F. Levan, CM, DD, PhD, a Sketch (In Memoriam),' obituary, both in personnel file Levan, Thomas F., DRMA; [Sister Catherine] to Sister Eugenie, Visitatrix, Marillac Seminary, Normandy, Mo., n.d., Scrapbook 1915–1922, DPCC; *Daily News* articles Jesse Ozias Donahue, "The Chicago Society World—Mrs. Lester Armour Plans Benefit for De Paul Settlement and Day Nursery," 6 Apr., and "Clubs and Societies," 9 Apr. 1923; *Chicago Tribune* articles "De Paul Girls to Assist Day Nursery Benefit," 18 Apr., and "Church Dignitaries Here to Honor Mundelein Today," 23 Apr. 1923.

47. Alice Kessler-Harris, *Out to Work: A History of Wage-Earning Women in the United States* (New York: Oxford University Press, 1982).

7—Professional Rescuers

1. "The Last Call," *New World,* 21 May 1921.

2. *New World* articles Rae Dickerson, "The Mother of It," 13 Apr. 1917, and Helen E. Sullivan, "The Inspiration of Isabelle: A Story of the Draft," 29 Mar. 1918.

3. *New World* articles Alice G. Hayde, "Is It All Over?" 23 May 1919, "Songs of the Red Cross Workers," 1 Mar. 1918, Helen A. Hawley, "She Dared!" 23 Mar. 1917 (reprinted from *The Continent*), and "Tenth of an Orphan," 9 Mar. 1917.

4. The move to centralize the church's social work was happening in many other cities at the same time as in Chicago. See *New World* articles "Centralization Is Need of Church's Social Endeavors," 19 Oct. 1917, "One Organization of Charities of the Archdiocese," 6 Apr. 1917, "Central Catholic Charities' Body Formed for City," 21 Dec. 1917, Press Service of the Central Verein, Central Bureau, "The Priest in the Slums," 6 Oct. 1922, "Personal Service in Charity," 22 Dec. 1922, "Little Stories of Real Life," 6 July 1923, and Mary T. Waggaman, "A Christmas Thaw," 7 Dec. 1923.

5. *New World* articles "Children's Benefit Tag Day Successful," 21 Oct. 1921, "In

the Homes of the Poor," 26 Jan. 1923 (quote), "A Chicago Lady and Her Investments," 21 Sept. 1923, and "In a Charity Worker's Day," 23 May 1924.

6. *New World* articles "Mary Jane's Experience," 22 Apr. 1921, "A Woman's Point of View," 19 Aug. 1921, "Little Stories of a Charity Visitor," 9 Sept. 1921, "Charity and Character," 30 Sept. 1921, "Seeing Ourselves," 28 Oct. 1921, "What Mary Did," 14 July 1922, "Education in Charity and Its Advantages," 12 Jan. 1923, "In the Homes of the Poor," 26 Jan. 1923, "The Charity Hour in Our Schools a Big Success," 9 Feb. 1923, "Little Journeys," 6 Apr. 1923, "In a Charity Worker's Day," 23 May 1924.

7. Koenig, *Parishes,* 1:578–88; *St. Mary Calendar* (hereafter *SMC*) untitled articles, Jan., Feb. 1905; Reports for the Parish of St. Mary's, Chicago, Illinois, Dec. 31, 1906, 1908, 1909, PAR; Humbert S. Nelli, *Italians in Chicago, 1880–1930: A Study in Ethnic Mobility* (New York: Oxford University Press, 1970), 28–29, 31.

8. *New World* articles "Praise for the Paulist Fathers," 21 Apr. 1894, and "Crusade of the Paulist Fathers," 18 Jan. 1896, "The Story of the Paulist Choristers," 9 Nov. 1912; John Farina, ed. *Essays on the Thought of Isaac Hecker* (New York: Paulist Press, 1983); Martin J. Kirk, CMF, *The Spirituality of Isaac Thomas Hecker: Reconciling the American Character and the Catholic Faith* (New York: Garland, 1988); Koenig, *Parishes,* 1:588; *SMC* articles "The Paulist Fathers," Jan. 1905, "The First Sanctuary Choir of the Middle West," Feb. 1905, "Fifty Years of the Paulists," Feb. 1910 (reprint from *The Missionary*), "Paulist Choristers Return," July 1918; Joseph McSorley, CSP, *Father Hecker and His Friends: Studies and Reminiscences* (St. Louis: B. Herder, 1952), 162–68; Reports for the Parish of St. Mary's, Chicago, Illinois, Dec. 31, 1905, 1906, 1908, 1909, PAR.

9. *SMC* articles "Monthly Confession a Necessity to Young Men," June 1905, "Save the Boy!" Jan. 1905, "A Study in Chicago Life," Aug. 1905, and "Parish Notes," Oct. 1905, "Lady of Victory Mission," Nov., Dec. 1916. See also *New World* articles "Catholic Chicago," 7 Sept. 1895, and "Some Prominent Chicagoans," 19 Dec. 1903.

10. *SMC* articles "Society Directory," Christmas 1907, "The Ladies' Aid Society," Apr. 1909, "A Day in the Nursery," July 1911 (marriages), and "The Ladies' Aid Society," Apr. 1909 (charity workers).

11. "Father Mallon's Promotion" *SMC,* Sept. 1918.

12. *SMC* articles "Our Lady of Victory Mission," Apr. 1909, Oct. 1917, and "The Sunday School," May 1914 (quotes), "Parish Notes," Dec. 1910, and "Father Mallon's Promotion," Sept. 1918.

13. "Our Altar Boys," *SMC,* Feb. 1917.

14. *Chicago Charities Directory, 1906* (Chicago: Charities Directory Association, 1905), 54; *SMC* articles "Remember the Boys," Jan. 1906, "The Boys' Home," May 1906, "Charity," May 1906, "Christmas Thanks," Christmas Day 1908, and "Parish Notes," Feb. 1909, "The Paulist Relief Society," Oct. 1909, "Ninth Annual Picnic," June 1913, and "Home Coming Day," June 1913.

15. *SMC* articles "Nursery Baby Talks," June 1911, "A Day in the Nursery," July 1911, "The Paulist Victory Mission Society," Christmas 1915, "The Lady of Victory Mission," Feb. 1917, and "Tag Day Third Week of October," Oct. 1918.

16. *SMC* articles "Parish Notes," Feb. 1915, "Settlement Rays," June 1915, "Mardi-Gras Carnival," Mar. 1916, and Father Hawks, "The Reason for a Settlement I," Nov. 1917 (quote).

17. Quotes are from *SMC* articles "The Fruits of Self-Indulgence," Christmas 1912 (Jan. 1913), "The Principle of Resistance," July 1913, and "The Remedy," May 1915. See also Jane Addams, *The Spirit of Youth and the City Streets* (Urbana: University of Illinois Press, 1972), and Father Hawks, "The Purpose of a Settlement II," *SMC,* Dec. 1917.

18. *SMC* articles about the Paulist Athletic Association, Feb., Christmas 1910, Apr., Aug., Oct., Nov., Christmas 1912, June, Nov. 1913, Dec. 1914, May 1915; also "The Minstrel Show," *SMC,* Feb. 1911; Green, "Chicago Democratic Party," 183–84, 189; Nelli, *Italians in Chicago,* 122.

19. *SMC* articles "The Fact," May 1915 (quote), "Settlement Rays," June 1915 (quotes), "Settlement Notes," Feb. 1916, Sergeant Thomas Ryan, Chicago Police Department, "The Purpose of a Settlement II," Dec. 1917 (quotes).

20. *SMC* articles Father Hawks, "The Reasons for a Settlement I," Nov. 1917 (quote), "Settlement Rays," Dec. 1916, Nov. 1917, and "How You Can Help the Settlement," Oct. 1917.

21. Cincinnati O., "The Purpose of a Settlement III," *SMC,* Feb. 1918.

22. *SMC* articles "Incompetent Women," Apr. 1915, "The Paulist Settlement Shop," May 1915, "Settlement Notes," May 1915, "Settlement Items," Apr. 1916, and "Settlement Rays," Apr. 1918.

23. *SMC* articles "Settlement Notes," Nov. 1915 (Miss Ann Brannack), "To People Who Live in Tenement Houses," Aug. 1914, "A Settlement Vista " Mar. 1917 (tenement), and "Settlement Rays," Sept. 1916.

24. *SMC* articles "A Settlement Vista," Mar. 1917, and "Paulist Settlement Rays," Apr. 1917.

25. *SMC* articles "Movies at the Paulist Settlement," May 1916 (quotes), and "Settlement Notes," June 1916.

26. *SMC* articles "Settlement Notes," May, Aug. 1916. "The Benson Club," Nov., Dec. 1916, Apr., June 1917, "Settlement Rays," Feb. 1917, "Paulist Settlement Rays," Apr. 1917, "A Paulist Settlement Notable," Apr. 1917, "Father Mallon's Promotion," Sept. 1918, and "The Benson Club, Past, Present, and Future," Dec. 1918.

27. *SMC* articles "Parish Notes," Feb. 1915, "Settlement Rays," June 1915, Nov. 1917, "Mardi-Gras Carnival," Mar. 1916. On Brown, see also "Catholic Chicago," *New World,* 7 Sept. 1895.

28. Father Hawks, "The Reasons for a Settlement I," *SMC,* Nov. 1917.

29. "The Paulist Settlement," n.d., MCR 3:1; "The Benson Club, Past, Present, and Future," *SMC,* Dec. 1918; Green, "Chicago Democratic Party," 223; Gordon, *Heroes of Their Own Lives.*

30. "Movies at the Paulist Settlement," *SMC,* May 1916. All statistics are compiled from *New World* articles "Settlement Items," Apr. 1916, "Settlement Notes," May, Sept., Nov. 1915, Feb., May, June, Aug., 1916, Mar. 1917, "Settlement Rays," Sept., Nov., Dec. 1916, Feb. 1917, "Paulist Settlement Rays," Apr. 1917, "The Benson Club," June 1917, and "Settlement Rays," Aug., Nov. 1917; *Lakeside Business Directory of Chicago* (1915–1917).

31. *SMC* articles "Settlement Rays," Sept. 1916, and "A Settlement Vista," March 1917.

32. Joanne J. Meyerowitz, *Women Adrift: Independent Wage Earners in Chicago, 1880–1930* (Chicago: University of Chicago Press, 1988), 108; *SMC* articles "The Minstrel Show," Feb. 1911, "The Athletic Association," Oct. 1912, "Athletic Club Notes," Nov. 1912, "Settlement Rays," Nov. 1917, "A Branch of the Public Library," Dec. 1917, "A Branch Library at the Settlement," Oct. 1918, "The Girl Who Works," Christmas 1912 (quote). For other advice to young women, see *SMC* articles "A Few Don'ts for Girls," Nov. 1911, "How to Be Happy though an Old Maid," Sept. 1913, and "For Men to Read," Mar. 1913.

33. *SMC* articles on the Paulist Athletic Association, Christmas 1910, Aug., Oct., Nov., Christmas 1912, and June 1913, "Excellent Advice," Feb. 1911 (reprinted from *Sacred Heart Review*), "The Benson Club, Past, Present, and Future," Dec. 1918; "The Paulist Settlement," n.d., MCR 3:1.

34. Constance Elberton, "The Torpedo Gang," *New World,* 8 March 1925; *SMC* articles "Paulist Settlement Rays," Apr. 1917, and "Settlement Rays," Feb. 1918.

35. Margaret E. Hourly, Chairman Supply Committee. Chicago Children's Benefit League, MCR 3:1; *SMC* articles "Tag Day Third Week of October," Oct. 1918, 'The Day Nursery," Nov. 1916, "The Day Nursery Safe for One More Year," Nov. 1918.

36. *SMC* articles "The Paulist Settlement Shop," May 1915, "The Blackstone Theatre Benefit," Dec. 1916, "Settlement Rays," Nov., Dec. 1916, ["Settlement Rays,"] Oct.

1917, Father Hawks, "The Reasons for a Settlement I," Nov. 1917, and "Settlement Notes," Dec. 1917; Mary Meehan to Mrs. Amberg, 3 June 1913, MCR 3:1.

37. Constance Elberton, "The 'Torpedo Gang,'" *New World,* 6 Mar. 1925.

38. *SMC* articles "The Appeal," May 1915 (quote), "The Fact," May 1915, and "Chaperoning," Sept. 1917.

39. *SMC* articles "Paulist Settlement Rays," Sept. 1916, Apr., May, Aug. 1917, "One Week at the Paulist Settlement," Apr. 1917; *Lakeside Business Directory of Chicago* (1915).

40. "The Paulist Settlement," n.d., MCR 3:1; *SMC* articles "Soldiers and Sailors, Come Be Our Guests!" Oct. 1918, and "The Soldiers and Sailors Hotel Now in Sight," Nov. 1918.

41. Report on Casa Maria Center, Men and Women's Committee, Committee on Special War Activities, folder 2, and Report on the Catholic Woman's League of Chicago, folder 7, both in box 13, series 10, NCWC; Mary Jane Burns, "The Catholic Woman's League of Chicago," *Catholic Charities Review* 2 (Feb. 1918): 53–54; *New World* articles "Your Red Cross," 30 Mar. 1917, and "Catholic Red Cross," 18 May 1917.

42. *New World* articles "One Organization of Charities of the Archdiocese," 6 Apr. 1917, "Archbishop Mundelein in Urging Centralization of Catholic Charities Says Catholics of City Are behind Government with All Resources as One Man," 13 Apr. 1917, "Centralization Is Need of Church's Social Endeavors," 19 Oct. 1917, "Central Catholic Charities' Body Formed for City," 21 Dec. 1917, "Archbishop Mundelein Tells Associated Catholic Charities to Keep Home Fires Burning," 15 Feb. 1918, and "Vast Relief Was Given in Homes by Our Charities," 6 June 1919.

43. *New World* articles "'Enthusiasm' Is 1916 Slogan for League," 5 Oct. 1915 (quote), "Will Ask Funds to Assist Poor in Their Homes," 12 Oct. 1917, "Camp Grant Man First to Give to Charity Campaign," 26 Oct. 1917, "Million Dollar Drive of Associated Catholic Charities of City Is On," 5 Apr. 1918, "First Report of Drive for Funds for Our Charities," 12 July 1918, "New Figures Are Given in Drive for Charity Fund," 16 Aug. 1918, "Women Organized for Charity Drive in Business World," 18 July 1919, and "Trades Reported Responding Well in Charity Drive," 25 July 1919; Walsh, "Catholic Church in Chicago," 83.

44. Douglas J. Slawson, *The Foundation and First Decade of the National Catholic Welfare Council* (Washington, D.C.: Catholic University Press, 1992); Lisa Hartmann-Ting, "Called to Service: The National Catholic School of Social Service and the Development of Catholic Social Work, 1900–1947" (Ph.D. diss., Brown University, 2003).

45. *New World* articles "Mrs. Margaret Long to Washington," 1 Nov. 1918, "National Catholic Women's Council Formed in Washington: Delegates from Chicago in Momentous Assembly," 12 Mar. 1920, "Catholic Women Meet: National Council Here," 30 Apr. 1920, and "Chicago Women Join Forces in National Body," 2 July 1920.

46. Amberg, *Madonna Center,* 134; Goodchild, "Catholic University in the Midwest"; *New World* articles "Women Lead in Future Catholic Women Prepare Advises Father Mullaly," 30 Jan. 1920, and "Number of Donations in Rosary College Drive Stimulates Work in First Week Reports," 27 Feb. 1920.

47. *New World* articles "Our Charities Must Be More Business-like," 26 Jan. 1917, "Catholic Woman's League," 3 Jan. 1920, "National Catholic Women's Council Formed in Washington: Delegates from Chicago in Momentous Assembly," 12 Mar. 1920, and "Honor Head of National Council Catholic Women," 23 Apr. 1920; John O'Grady, *Catholic Charities in the United States: History and Problems* (Washington, D.C.: National Conference of Catholic Charities, 1930), 300–301, 340–41; Hartmann-Ting, "Called to Service," 64–65, 93–94, 105–7; "Women Lead in Future Catholic Women Prepare Advises Father Mullaly," *New World,* 30 Jan. 1920 (quote).

48. "Our Charities Must Be More Business-like," *New World,* 26 Jan. 1917 (quote).

On tensions between nuns and laywomen involved in social work, see Hartmann-Ting, "Called to Service," 185, 189–90.

49. *SMC* articles "Father Mallon's Promotion," Sept. 1918, "Paulist Day Nursery," May 1926, and "Paulist Settlement," May 1926; Nelli, *Italians in Chicago,* 204.

50. Lubove, *Professional Altruist; New World* articles "Auxiliary of the Good Shepherd Home to Organize to Do Big Sister Work," 16 Feb. 1917, "Personal Service Is Important Welfare Factor, Says Hurley," 11 July 1919, "Here's Model Report for You Big Brothers," 8 Aug. 1919, and "Story of Tony, La Madre Giovane, I Bambini and a Near Tragedy," 20 Aug. 1920.

51. Jack Woods, "What Chicago Parishes Are Doing for City Young People: Off-the-Street Clubs for Catholic Youth," *New World,* 11 Mar. 1921; *Tenth Annual Announcement,* 21–26; Koenig, *Caritas Christi Urget Nos,* 2:853–54, 981–85; Amberg, *Madonna Center,* 64; David A. Badillo, "The Catholic Church and the Making of the Mexican-American Parish Communities in the Midwest," in Jay P. Dolan and Gilberto M. Hinojosa, eds., *Mexican Americans and the Catholic Church, 1900–1965* (Notre Dame: University of Notre Dame Press, 1994), 277.

Conclusion—Catholic Settlements

1. Constance Elberton, "The 'Torpedo Gang,'" *New World,* 6 Mar. 1925.

2. *New World* articles "Mrs. Mary E. Dunne Norton," 11 Oct. 1918, "Catholic Woman's Clubs," 27 Dec. 1918, "Woman Social Worker of National Prominence Meets Sudden Death," 6 Feb. 1919, "Mrs. Catherine G. Joyce," 19 Mar. 1920, "Miss Minnie H. Kent," 26 Mar. 1920, Jack Woods, "What Chicago Parishes Are Doing for City Young People: Off-the-Street Clubs for Catholic Youth," 11 Mar. 1921, "St. Jarlath's Parish Club," 22 Apr. 1921, "Italian Immigration," 28 June 1921, and "A Social Center for Sacred Heart Parish," 11 Apr. 1924; *Chicago Daily Tribune* articles "League Plans Benefit to Aid Day Nurseries," 12 Nov. 1939, and "Catholic League Women Plan Charity Card Party," 16 Feb. 1954; Piehl, *Breaking Bread.*

3. Gene D. L. Jones, "The Chicago Catholic Charities, the Great Depression, and Public Monies," *Illinois Historical Journal* 83 (Spring 1990): 13–30; Kenneth J. Heineman, *A Catholic New Deal: Religion and Reform in Depression Pittsburgh* (University Park: Pennsylvania State University Press, 1999).

4. Suellen Hoy, *Good Hearts: Catholic Sisters in Chicago's Past* (Urbana: University of Illinois Press, 2006); Deborah A. Skok, "Catholics, the War on Poverty, and the Civil Rights Movement: Marillac House, 1947–1967" (Unpublished seminar paper, University of Chicago, 1992).

Selected Bibliography

Interviews and Correspondence

Diane Durante, interview with author, Chicago, Ill., 16 June 2005.
Noel Horn, correspondence with author, 2004–2005.

Newspapers and Journals

Catholic Charities Review, 1917–1930.
Chicago Record-Herald, 1904–1912, 1914.
Chicago Tribune, 1893–1960.
Monthly Calendar, 1901–1903 (continued as *Vincentian Weekly*).
New World, 1893–1930.
Queen's Work, 1914.
St. Mary's Calendar, 1905–1928.
St. Vincent de Paul Society Quarterly, 1900–1916 (continued as *Catholic Charities Review*).
The Survey, 1914.
Vincentian Weekly, 1910–1925, 1929–1930.

Manuscript Collections

Buck, Robert M., Papers. Chicago Historical Society, Chicago, Illinois.
Daughters of Charity of St. Vincent de Paul Archives (Mater dei Provincialate). De Paul Center Collection, Evansville, Indiana.
Foreign Language Press Survey. Special Collections, Regenstein Library, University of Chicago, Illinois.
Madonna Center Records. Department of Special Collections and University Archives, Marquette University, Milwaukee, Wisconsin.
Missouri Province V Biographical Files. Reverend Paul M. Ponzigione, S.J. Collection. Midwest Jesuit Archives, St. Louis, Missouri.
National Catholic Welfare Conference (NCWC) Collection. Archives Catholic University of America (ACUA), Washington, D.C.
Nestor, Agnes, Papers. Chicago Historical Society, Chicago, Illinois
Parish Annual Reports, 1899–1910. Joseph Cardinal Bernardin Archives, Archdiocese of Chicago, Illinois.
Records of the Society of St. Vincent de Paul. Joseph Cardinal Bernardin Archives, Archdiocese of Chicago, Chicago, Illinois.
St. Vincent's Church Records. De Paul University Archives, Chicago, Illinois.

St. Vincent's Church Records and Biographical Files. DeAndreis-Rosati Memorial Archives of the Congregation of the Mission (Vincentian Fathers), St. Mary's of the Barrens, Perryville, Missouri.
Welfare Council of Metropolitan Chicago Papers. Chicago Historical Society, Chicago, Illinois.

Dissertations and Theses

D'Agostino, Peter. "Missionaries in Babylon: The Adaptation of Italian Priests to Chicago's Church, 1870–1940." 2 vols. Ph.D. diss., University of Chicago, 1993.
Fitzgerald, Maureen. "Irish Catholic Nuns and the Development of New York City's Welfare System, 1840–1900." Ph.D. diss., University of Wisconsin, 1992.
Goodchild, Lester Francis. "The Mission of the Catholic University in the Midwest, 1842–1980." Ph.D. diss., University of Chicago, 1986.
Green, Paul Michael. "The Chicago Democratic Party, 1840–1920: From Factionalism to Political Organization." Ph.D. diss., University of Chicago, 1975.
Hartmann-Ting, Lisa. "Called to Service: The National Catholic School of Social Service and the Development of Catholic Social Work, 1900–1947." Ph.D. diss., Brown University, 2003.
Leazenby, Amy Jane. "Day Nurseries as an Agency for Child Care." Master's thesis, University of Chicago, 1920.
McGuinness, Margaret Mary. "Response to Reform: An Historical Interpretation of the Catholic Settlement Movement, 1897–1915." Ph.D. diss., Union Theological Seminary, 1985.
Nelli, Humbert S. "The Role of the 'Colonial' Press in the Italian-American Community of Chicago, 1886–1921." Ph.D. diss., University of Chicago, 1965.
Pahorezki, M. Sevina. "The Social and Political Activities of William James Onahan." Ph.D. diss., Catholic University of America, 1942.
Walsh, John Patrick. "The Catholic Church in Chicago and Problems of an Urban Society: 1893–1915." Ph.D. diss., University of Chicago, 1948.
Zehren, Maria A. "'The Dangling Scissors': Marriage, Family, and Work among Italian Women in the Clothing Industry in Baltimore, 1890–1920." Ph.D. diss., Georgetown University, 1998.

Published Sources

Abell, Aaron I. *American Catholicism and Social Action: A Search for Social Justice, 1865–1950*. Notre Dame, Ind.: University of Notre Dame Press, 1963.
Addams, Jane. *Spirit of Youth and the City Streets*. Urbana: University of Illinois Press, 1972.
———. *Twenty Years at Hull-House with Autobiographical Notes*. New York: MacMillan, 1910.
Allen, Ann Taylor. "Gardens of Children, Gardens of God: Kindergartens and Day-Care Centers in Nineteenth-Century Germany." *Journal of Social History* 19.3 (1986): 436–49.
———. "Let Us Live with Our Children: Kindergarten Movements in Germany and the United States, 1840–1914." *History of Education Quarterly* 28 (Spring 1988): 23–48.
Amberg, Mary Agnes. *Madonna Center: Pioneer Catholic Social Settlement*. Chicago: Loyola University Press, 1976.
Baker, Paula. "The Domestication of Politics: Women and American Political Society, 1780–1920." *American Historical Review* 89 3 (1984): 620–47.

Bancroft, Hubert Howe. *The Book of the Fair*. Chicago: Bancroft, 1893.

Barrett, James R., and David Roediger. "Inbetween Peoples: Race, Nationality, and the 'New Immigrant' Working Class." *Journal of American Ethnic History* 16.3 (Spring 1997).

Becher, Penny Edgell. "'Rational Amusement and Sound Instruction': Constructing the True Catholic Woman in the *Ave Maria*, 1865–1889." *Religion and American Culture* 8.1 (Winter 1998): 55–90.

Bederman, Gail. *Manliness and Civilization: A Cultural History of Gender and Race in the United States, 1880–1917*. Chicago: University of Chicago Press, 1995.

Bona, Mary Jo. *Claiming a Tradition: Italian American Women Writers*. Carbondale: Southern Illinois University Press, 1999.

Boyer, Paul. *Urban Masses and the Moral Order in America, 1820–1920*. Cambridge: Harvard University Press, 1978.

Broder, Sherri. *Tramps, Unfit Mothers, Neglected Children: Negotiating the Family in Nineteenth-Century Philadelphia*. Philadelphia: University of Pennsylvania Press, 2002.

Brown, Dorothy M., and Elizabeth McKeown. *The Poor Belong to Us: Catholic Charities and American Welfare*. Cambridge, Mass.: Harvard University Press, 1997.

———. "Saving New York's Children." *U.S. Catholic Historian* 13 (Summer 1995): 77–95.

Bukowski, Douglas. *Big Bill Thompson, Chicago, and the Politics of Image*. Urbana: University of Illinois Press, 1998.

Cahan, Emily D. *Past Caring: A History of U.S. Preschool Care and Education for the Poor, 1820–1965*. New York: National Center for Children in Poverty, Columbia University, 1989.

Cannistraro, Philip, and Gerald Meyer, eds. *The Lost World of Italian-American Radicalism*. Westport, Conn.: Praeger, 2003.

Carroll, Michael P. *Veiled Threats: The Logic of Popular Catholicism in Italy*. Baltimore: Johns Hopkins University Press, 1996.

Carson, Mina. *Settlement Folk: Social Thought and the American Settlement Movement, 1885–1930*. Chicago: University of Chicago Press, 1990.

Chauncey, George. *Gay New York: Gender, Urban Culture, and the Making of the Gay Male World, 1890–1940*. New York: Basic Books, 1994.

Chicago Blue Book of Selected Names. Chicago: Chicago Directory Company, 1903.

Chicago Blue Book of Selected Names. Chicago: Chicago Directory Company, 1902.

Chicago Charities Directory, 1906. Chicago: Charities Directory Association, 1905.

Chicago Department of Welfare. Annual Report. 1915.

Chinnici, Joseph P., ed. *Living Stones: The History and Structure of Catholic Spiritual Life in the United States*. New York: MacMillan, 1989.

Clapp, Elizabeth J. *Mothers of All Children: Women Reformers and the Rise of the Juvenile Courts in Progressive America*. University Park: Pennsylvania State University Press, 1998.

Cmiel, Kenneth. *A Home of Another Kind: One Chicago Orphanage and the Tangle of Child Welfare*. Chicago: University of Chicago Press, 1995.

Cohen, Lizabeth. *Making a New Deal: Industrial Workers in Chicago, 1919–1939*. Cambridge: Cambridge University Press, 1990.

Cohen, Miriam. *Workshop to Office: Two Generations of Italian Women in New York City, 1900–1950*. Ithaca: Cornell University Press, 1992.

Connolly, James J. *The Triumph of Ethnic Progressivism: Urban Political Culture in Boston, 1900–1925*. Cambridge: Harvard University Press, 1998.

Coser, Rose Laub, et al. *Women of Courage: Jewish and Italian Immigrant Women in New York*. Westport, Conn.: Greenwood Press, 1999.

Crocker, Ruth Hutchinson. *Social Work and Social Order: The Settlement Movement in Two Industrial Cities, 1881–1930*. Urbana: University of Illinois Press, 1992.

Cummings, Kathleen Sprows. "'Not the New Woman?': Irish American Women and the Creation of a Usable Past, 1890–1900." *U.S. Catholic Historian* 19.1 (Winter 2001): 37–52.

Curtis, Susan. *A Consuming Faith: The Social Gospel and Modern American Culture*. Baltimore: Johns Hopkins University Press, 1991.

Davis, Allen F. *American Heroine: The Life and Legend of Jane Addams*. London: Oxford University Press, 1973.

———. *Spearheads for Reform: The Social Settlements and the Progressive Movement, 1890–1914*. New York: Oxford University Press, 1967.

Deegan, Mary Jo. "'Dear Love, Dear Love': Female Pragmatism and the Chicago Female World of Love and Ritual." *Gender and Society* 10.5 (Oct. 1996): 590–607.

D'Emilio, John, and Estelle Freedman. *Intimate Matters: A History of Sexuality in America*. New York: Harper and Row, 1988.

Diner, Hasia. *Erin's Daughters in America*. Baltimore: Johns Hopkins University Press, 1984.

Dolan, Jay. *The American Catholic Experience: A History from Colonial Times to the Present*. Notre Dame, Ind.: University of Notre Dame Press, 1992.

Dolan, Jay P., and Gilberto M. Hinojosa, eds. *Mexican Americans and the Catholic Church, 1900–1965*. Notre Dame: University of Notre Dame Press, 1994.

DuBois, Ellen Carol, and Vicki L. Ruiz, eds. *Unequal Sisters: A Multi-Cultural Reader in U.S. Women's History*. New York: Routledge, 1990.

Dunne, Edmund M. *Memoirs of Zi Pré*. St Louis: B. Herder, 1914.

Edwards, Rebecca. *Angels in the Machinery: Gender in American Party Politics from the Civil War to the Progressive Era*. New York: Oxford University Press, 1997.

Engh, Michael E.. "Mary Julia Workman: The Catholic Conscience of Los Angeles." *California History* 72.1 (1993): 2–19.

Erie, Stephen P. *Rainbow's End: Irish-Americans and the Dilemmas of Urban Machine Politics, 1840–1985*. Berkeley: University of California Press, 1988.

Ewen, Elizabeth. *Immigrant Women in the Land of Dollars: Life and Culture on the Lower East Side, 1890–1925*. New York: Monthly Review Press, 1985.

Fanning, Charles, Ellen Skerrett, and John Corrigan. *Nineteenth-Century Chicago Irish: A Social and Political Portrait*. Insights Series number 7. Urbana: Center for Urban Policy, Loyola University of Chicago, 1980.

Farina, John, ed. *Essays on the Thought of Isaac Hecker*. New York: Paulist Press, 1983.

Farrell, James T. *Studs Lonigan*. New York: Modern Library, 1932.

Fass, Paula. *The Damned and the Beautiful: American Youth in the 1920s*. New York: Oxford University Press, 1977.

Ffrench, Charles, ed. *Biographical History of the American Irish in Chicago*. Chicago: American Biographical Publishing, 1897.

Fitzgerald, Maureen. "Charity, Poverty, and Child Welfare." *Harvard Divinity Bulletin* 25.4 (1996): 12–17.

———. *Habits of Compassion: Irish Catholic Nuns and the Origins of New York City's Welfare System, 1830–1920*. Urbana: University of Illinois Press, 2006.

Flanagan, Maureen. *Seeing with Their Hearts: Chicago Women and the Vision of the Good City, 1871–1933*. Princeton, N.J.: Princeton University Press, 2002.

Freedman, Estelle B. *Maternal Justice: Miriam Van Waters and the Female Reform Tradition*. Chicago: University of Chicago Press, 1996.

Gabaccia, Donna R. *From Sicily to Elizabeth Street: Housing and Social Change among Italian Immigrants, 1880–1930*. Albany: State University of New York Press, 1984.

Gifford, Carolyn De Swarte, ed. *The American Deaconess Movement in the Early Twentieth Century*. New York: Garland, 1987.

Gilmore, Glenda Elizabeth. *Gender and Jim Crow: Women and the Politics of White Supremacy in North Carolina, 1896–1920*. Chapel Hill: University of North Carolina Press, 1996.

Ginzberg, Lori D. "Pernicious Heresies: Female Citizenship and Sexual Respectability in the Nineteenth Century." In *Women and the Unstable State in Nineteenth-Century America*, eds. Allison M. Parker and Stephanie Cole, 139–61. College Station: Texas A&M University Press, 2000.

————. *Women and the Work of Benevolence: Morality, Politics, and Class in the Nineteenth-Century United States*. New Haven: Yale University Press, 1990.

Gleason, Philip. *The Conservative Reformers: German-American Catholics and the Social Order*. Notre Dame, Ind.: University of Notre Dame Press, 1968.

Glenn, Susan. *Daughters of the Shtetl: Life and Labor in the Immigrant Generation*. Ithaca: Cornell University Press, 1990.

Gordon, Beverly. *Bazaars and Fair Ladies: The History of the American Fundraising Fair*. Knoxville: University of Tennessee Press, 1998.

Gordon, Linda. *Heroes of Their Own Lives: The Politics and History of Family Violence, Boston, 1880–1960*. New York: Viking, 1988.

Gustafson, Melanie. *Women and the Republican Party, 1854–1924*. Urbana: University of Illinois Press, 2001.

Gustafson, Melanie, et al., eds. *We Have Come to Stay: American Women and Political Parties, 1880–1960*. Albuquerque: University of New Mexico Press, 1999.

Halsey, William M. *The Survival of American Innocence: Catholicism in an Era of Disillusionment, 1920–1940*. Notre Dame: University of Notre Dame Press, 1980.

Hapke, Laura. *Tales of the Working Girl: Wage-Earning Women in American Literature, 1890–1925*. New York: Twayne Publishers, 1992.

Harrison, Edith Ogden. *"Strange to Say": Recollections of Persons and Events in New Orleans and Chicago*. Chicago: A. Kroch and Son, 1949.

Herrick, Mary J. *The Chicago Schools: A Social and Political History*. London: Sage, 1971.

Herringshaw, Clark J., ed. *Clark J. Herringshaw's City Blue Book of Current Biography*. Chicago: American Publisher's Association, 1913.

Higginbotham, Evelyn Brooks. *Righteous Discontent: The Women's Movement in the Black Baptist Church*. Cambridge: Harvard University Press, 1993.

Horowitz, Helen Lefkowitz. *Culture and the City: Cultural Philanthropy in Chicago from the 1880s to 1917*. Lexington: University Press of Kentucky, 1976.

Hoy, Suellen. "Caring for Chicago's Women and Girls: The Sisters of the Good Shepherd, 1859–1911." *Journal of Urban History* 23 (Fall 1997): 260–94.

————. *Good Hearts: Catholic Sisters in Chicago's Past*. Urbana: University of Illinois Press, 2006.

Huthmacher, J. Joseph. "Urban Liberalism and the Age of Reform." *Mississippi Valley Historical Review* 49.2 (1962): 231–41.

Ignatiev, Noel. *How the Irish Became White*. New York: Routledge, 1995.

Jones, Gene D. L. "The Chicago Catholic Charities, the Great Depression, and Public Monies." *Illinois Historical Journal* 83 (Spring 1990): 13–30.

Kane, Paula. *Separatism and Subculture: Boston Catholicism, 1900–1920*. Chapel Hill: University of North Carolina Press, 1994.

Kantowicz, Edward R. "Polish Chicago: Survival through Solidarity." In *Ethnic Chicago: A Multicultural Portrait*, ed. Melvin G. Holli and Peter D'A. Jones, 173–98. Grand Rapids, Mich.: William B. Eerdmans, 1995.

Katz, Michael. *In the Shadow of the Poorhouse: A Social History of Welfare in America*. New York: Basic Books, 1986.

Kauffman, Christopher J. *Faith and Fraternalism: The History of the Knights of Columbus, 1882–1982*. New York: Harper and Row, 1982.

Kenneally, James J. *The History of American Catholic Women*. New York: Crossroad, 1990.

Kennelly, Karen. "Ideals of American Catholic Womanhood." In *American Catholic Women: An Historical Exploration*, ed. Karen Kennelly. New York: MacMillan, 1989.

Kirk, Martin J., C.M.F. *The Spirituality of Isaac Thomas Hecker: Reconciling the American Character and the Catholic Faith*. New York: Garland, 1988.

Kitagawa, Evelyn M., and Karl E. Taeuber, eds. *Local Community Fact Book, Chicago Metropolitan Area, 1960*. Chicago: University of Chicago, 1963.

Knobel, Dale T. *Paddy and the Republic: Ethnicity and Nationality in Antebellum America*. Middletown, Conn.: Wesleyan University Press, 1986.

Koenig, Harry C., ed. *Caritas Christi Urget Nos: A History of the Offices, Agencies, and Institutions of the Archdiocese of Chicago.* Vol. 2. Chicago: Archdiocese of Chicago, 1981.

———. *A History of the Parishes of the Archdiocese of Chicago.* 2 vols. Chicago: Archdiocese of Chicago, 1980.

Koven, Seth, and Sonya Michel, eds. *Mothers of a New World: Maternalist Politics and the Origins of Welfare States.* New York: Routledge, 1993.

Ladd-Taylor, Molly. *Mother Work: Women, Child Welfare, and the State, 1890–1930.* Urbana: University of Illinois Press, 1994.

The Lakeside Business Directory of Chicago. Chicago: Chicago Directory Company, 1914–1919.

Lamoureux, Patricia. "Irish Catholic Women and the Labor Movement." *U.S. Catholic Historian* 16.3 (Summer 1998): 24–44.

Leo XIII, *Rerum Novarum.* In *The Papal Encyclicals,* ed. Claudia Carlen, 241–61. Raleigh, N.C.: McGrath, 1981.

Lindley, Susan Hill. "Gender and the Social Gospel Novel." In *Gender and the Social Gospel,* ed. Wendy J. Deichman Edwards and Carolyn De Swarte Gifford, 185–201. Urbana: University of Illinois Press, 2003.

Lissak, Rivka. *Pluralism and Progressives: Hull House and the New Immigrants, 1890–1919.* Chicago: University of Chicago Press, 1989.

Lord, Daniel A., S.J. "A Catholic Social Center." *Queen's Work* 1 (Oct. 1914): 285–90.

Lubove, Roy. *The Professional Altruist: The Emergence of Social Work as a Career, 1880–1930.* Cambridge, Mass.: Harvard University Press, 1965.

Macleod, David. "Act Your Age: Boyhood, Adolescence, and the Rise of the Boy Scouts of America." *Journal of Social History* 16.2 (Winter 1982): 3–20.

May, Martha. "The Historical Problem of the Family Wage: The Ford Motor Company and the Five Dollar Day." In DuBois and Ruiz, *Unequal Sisters,* 275–91. New York: Routledge, 1990.

McCaffrey, Lawrence J. "The Irish-American Dimension." In McCaffrey et al., *Irish in Chicago,* 1–21.

McCaffrey, Lawrence J., et al., eds. *The Irish in Chicago.* Urbana: University of Illinois Press, 1987.

McCarthy, Kathleen D. *Noblesse Oblige: Charity and Cultural Philanthropy in Chicago, 1849–1929.* Chicago: University of Chicago Press, 1982.

McDannell, Colleen. "'The Devil Was the First Protestant': Gender and Intolerance in Irish Catholic Fiction." *U.S. Catholic Historian* 8 (1989): 51–65.

McGovern, James J., ed. *The Life and Letters of Eliza Allen Starr.* Chicago: Lakeside Press, 1905.

McGreevy, John T. *Parish Boundaries: The Catholic Encounter with Race in the Twentieth-Century Urban North.* Chicago: University of Chicago Press, 1996.

McGuinness, Margaret Mary. "Body and Soul: Catholic Social Settlements and Immigration." *U.S. Catholic Historian* 13.3–4 (Summer 1995): 63–75.

McSorley, Joseph. C.S.P. *Father Hecker and His Friends: Studies and Reminiscences.* St. Louis: B. Herder, 1952.

McTighe, Michael. *A Measure of Success: Protestants and the Public Culture in Antebellum Cleveland.* Albany: State University of New York Press, 1994.

Meagher, Timothy J. *Inventing Irish America: Generation, Class, and Ethnic Identity in a New England City, 1880–1928.* Notre Dame, Ind.: University of Notre Dame Press, 2001.

Meagher, Timothy J., and Ronald H. Bayor. *The New York Irish.* Baltimore: Johns Hopkins University Press, 1996.

Meder, Leonora Z. *First Semi-Annual Report of the Department of Public Welfare.* Chicago: Western Newspaper Union, 1915.

———. "The Utilization of Municipal Agencies in Relief Work." In *Third Biennial Meeting of the National Conference of Catholic Charities*, 273–85. Washington, D.C.: Catholic University of America, 1914.

Merriam, Charles. *Chicago: A More Intimate View of Urban Politics.* New York: Macmillan, 1929.

Mersch, S.J., Émile. *The Whole Christ: The Historical Development of the Doctrine of the Mystical Body in Scripture and Tradition.* Translated by John R. Kelly, S.J. Milwaukee: Bruce, 1938.

Meyerowitz, Joanne J. *Women Adrift: Independent Wage Earners in Chicago, 1880–1930.* Chicago: University of Chicago Press, 1988.

Michel, Sonya. *Children's Interests/Mothers' Rights: The Shaping of America's Child-Care Policy.* New Haven: Yale University Press, 1999.

———. "The Limits of Maternalism: Policies toward American Wage-Earning Mothers during the Progressive Era." In Koven and Michel, *Mothers of a New World,* 277–320.

Mills, Edward Laird. *The Advancing Church: Studies in Christianizing America.* New York and Cincinnati: Methodist Book Concern, 1926.

Moloney, Deirdre M. *American Catholic Lay Groups and Transatlantic Social Reform in the Progressive Era.* Chapel Hill: University of North Carolina Press, 2002.

Moran, George E., comp. *Moran's Dictionary of Chicago and Its Vicinity.* Chicago: George E. Moran, 1895.

Moran, Jeffrey P. "'Modernism Gone Mad': Sex Education Comes to Chicago, 1913." *Journal of American History* 82.2 (Sept. 1996): 481–513.

Mulkerins, Thomas M. *Holy Family Parish Chicago: Priests and People.* Chicago: Holy Family Press, 1923.

Muncy, Robyn. *Creating a Female Dominion in American Reform, 1890–1935.* New York: Oxford University Press, 1991.

Murolo, Patricia. *The Common Ground of Womanhood: Class, Gender, and Working Girls' Clubs, 1884–1928.* Urbana: University of Illinois Press, 1997

Nelli, Humbert S. *Italians in Chicago, 1880–1930: A Study in Ethnic Mobility.* New York: Oxford University Press, 1970.

The New Sunday School Companion, Containing the Baltimore Catechism. New York: Benziger Brothers, 1898.

Nolan, Janet. *Servants of the Poor: Teachers and Mobility in Ireland and Irish America.* Notre Dame, Ind.: University of Notre Dame Press, 2004.

Norris, Kathleen. *The Story of Julia Page.* New York: Grosset and Dunlap, 1915.

Oates, Mary J. *The Catholic Philanthropic Tradition in America.* Bloomington: Indiana University Press, 1995.

———. "The Role of Laywomen in American Catholic Philanthropy." *U.S. Catholic Historian* 9.3 (1990): 249–60.

Odem, Mary E. *Delinquent Daughters: Protecting and Policing Adolescent Female Sexuality in the United States, 1885–1920.* Chapel Hill: University of North Carolina Press, 1995.

Odencrantz, Louise. *Italian Women in Industry: A Study of Conditions in New York City.* New York: Russell Sage Foundation, 1919.

O'Grady, John. *Catholic Charities in the United States: History and Problems.* Washington, D.C.: National Conference of Catholic Charities, 1930.

Orsi, Robert. *The Madonna of 115th Street: Faith and Community in Italian Harlem, 1880–1950.* New Haven: Yale University Press, 1985.

Pascoe, Peggy. *Relations of Rescue: The Search for Female Moral Authority in the American West, 1874–1939.* New York: Oxford University Press, 1990.

Pedersen, Susan. "Catholicism, Feminism, and the Politics of the Family during the late Third Republic." In Koven and Michel, *Mothers of a New World,* 246–76

Pegram, Thomas R. *Partisans and Progressives: Private Interest and Public Policy in Illinois, 1870–1922*. Urbana: University of Illinois Press, 1992.

Peiss, Kathy. "'Charity Girls' and City Pleasures: Historical Notes on Working-Class Sexuality, 1880–1920." In DuBois and Ruiz, *Unequal Sisters*, 157–66. New York: Routledge, 1990.

———. *Cheap Amusements: Working Women and Leisure in Turn-of-the-Century New York*. Philadelphia: Temple University Press, 1986.

Perlmann, Joel. *Ethnic Differences: Schooling and Social Structure Among the Irish, Italians, Jews and Blacks in an American City, 1880–1935*. New York: Cambridge University Press, 1998.

Perry, Elizabeth Israels. "From Achievement to Happiness: Girl Scouting in Middle Tennessee, 1910s–1960s." *Journal of Women's History* 5.2 (Fall 1993): 76–77.

Piehl, Mel. *Breaking Bread: The Catholic Worker and the Origins of Catholic Radicalism in America*. Philadelphia: Temple University Press, 1982.

Residents of Hull-House. *Hull-House Maps and Papers*. New York: Thomas Y. Crowell & Co., [1895].

Richards, A. J. *Italian Americans: The Racializing of an Ethnic Identity*. New York: New York University Press, 1999.

Rodgers, Daniel T., "In Search of Progressivism," *Reviews in American History*, Vol. 10, No. 4 (Dec. 1982): 113-32.

Roediger, David. *The Wages of Whiteness: Race and the Making of the American Working Class*. London: Verso, 1991.

———. *Working toward Whiteness: How America's Immigrants Became White*. New York: Basic Books, 2005.

Rose, Anne C. "Some Private Roads to Rome: The Role of Families in American Victorian Conversions to Catholicism." *Catholic Historical Review* (January 1999).

Rose, Elizabeth. "From Sponge Cake to Hamentashen: Jewish Identity in a Jewish Settlement House, 1885–1952." *Journal of American Ethnic History* 13.3 (1994): 3–23.

———. *A Mother's Job: A History of Day Care, 1890–1999*. New York: Oxford University Press, 1999.

Rosen, Ruth. *The Lost Sisterhood: Prostitution in America, 1900–1918*. Baltimore: Johns Hopkins University Press, 1982.

Rosenzweig, Roy. *Eight Hours for What We Will: Workers and Leisure in an Industrial City, 1870–1920*. Cambridge: Cambridge University Press, 1983.

Rousmaniere, John P. "Cultural Hybrid in the Slums: The College Woman and the Settlement House, 1889–1894." *American Quarterly* 22.1 (Spring 1970): 45–66.

Ruffins, Faith Davis. "'Lifting as We Climb': Black Women and the Preservation of African American History and Culture." *Gender and History* 6.3 (1994): 376–96.

Ryan, John A. *A Living Wage*. New York: MacMillan, 1920.

Ryan, Mary. *Cradle of the Middle Class: The Family in Oneida County, New York, 1790–1865*. Cambridge: Cambridge University Press, 1981.

Schiavo, Giovanni E. *The Italians in Chicago: A Study in Americanization*. Chicago: Italian-American, 1928.

Seller, Maxine. "The Education of the Immigrant Woman: 1900–1935." *Journal of Urban History* 4.3 (May 1978): 307–30.

Shanabruch, Charles. *Chicago's Catholics: The Evolution of an American Identity*. Notre Dame, Ind.: Notre Dame University Press, 1981.

Shaw, Stephen J. *The Catholic Parish as a Way-Station of Ethnicity and Americanization: Chicago's Germans and Italians, 1903–1939*. Brooklyn, N.Y.: Carlson, 1991.

Sister Mary Barbara Regan: First Assistant of the Saint Louis Province of the Daughters of Charity of St. Vincent de Paul, 1910–1930. St. Louis: Wellington Printing Company, n.d.

Skerrett, Ellen. "The Catholic Dimension." In McCaffrey et al., *Irish in Chicago*, 22–60.

Sklar, Kathryn Kish. *Florence Kelly and the Nation's Work: The Rise of Women's Political Culture, 1830–1900*. New Haven: Yale University Press, 1995.

———. "Hull House in the 1890s: A Community of Women Reformers." *Signs* 10 (Winter 1985): 658–77.

Skocpol, Theda. *Protecting Soldiers and Mothers: The Political Origins of Social Policy in the United States.* Cambridge, Mass.: Belknap Press of Harvard University Press, 1992.

Skok, Deborah A. "Organized Almsgiving: Scientific Charity and the Society of St. Vincent de Paul in Chicago, 1871–1918." *U.S. Catholic Historian* 16 (Fall 1998): 19–35.

Slawson, Douglas J. *The Foundation and First Decade of the National Catholic Welfare Council.* Washington, D.C.: Catholic University Press, 1992.

Smith, Joan K. *Ella Flagg Young: Portrait of a Leader.* Ames, Iowa: Education Studies Press, 1976.

Smith, Judith E. *Family Connections: A History of Italian and Jewish Immigrant Lives in Providence, Rhode Island, 1900–1940.* Albany: State University of New York Press, 1985.

Smith-Rosenberg, Carroll. "The Female World of Love and Ritual: Relations between Women in Nineteenth-Century America." *Signs* 1.1 (Autumn 1975): 4.

Sollors, Werner, ed. *The Invention of Ethnicity.* New York: Oxford University Press, 1989.

Spain, Daphne. *Gendered Spaces.* Chapel Hill: University of North Carolina Press, 1992.

Stanton, Elizabeth Cady, et al., eds. *History of Woman Suffrage.* Vol. 3. Reprint. Salem, N.H.: Ayer, 1985.

Stead, William T. *If Christ Came to Chicago.* New York: Clarion Books, 1964.

Stebner, Eleanor J. *The Women of Hull House: A Study in Spirituality, Vocation, and Friendship.* New York: State University of New York Press, 1997.

Sturdevant, Lynda M. "Girl Scouting in Stillwater, Oklahoma: A Case Study in Local History." *Chronicles of Oklahoma* 57.1 (Spring 1979): 34–48.

Taves, Ann. *The Household of Faith: Roman Catholic Devotions in Mid-Nineteenth Century America.* Notre Dame, Ind.: Notre Dame University Press, 1985.

Taylor, Graham. *Chicago Commons through Forty Years.* Chicago: Chicago Commons Association, 1936.

Tenth Annual Announcement of the Catholic Woman's League, 1903–1904. Chicago: Catholic Woman's League, 1904.

Tentler, Leslie Woodcock. *Seasons of Grace: A History of the Catholic Archdiocese of Detroit.* Detroit: Wayne State University Press, 1990.

———. *Wage-Earning Women: Industrial Work and Family Life in the United States, 1900–1930.* New York: Oxford University Press, 1979.

Thernstrom, Stephen. *The Other Bostonians: Poverty and Progress in the American Metropolis, 1880–1970.* Cambridge, Mass.: Harvard University Press, 1973.

Third Biennial Meeting of the National Conference of Catholic Charities. Washington, D.C.: Catholic University of America, 1914.

Vecoli, Rudolph J. "Prelates and Peasants: Italian Immigrants and the Catholic Church." In *The Other Catholics,* ed. Keith R. Dyrud, Michael Novak, and Rudolph J. Vecoli, 217–68. New York: Arno Press, 1978.

Warren, Allen. "Popular Manliness: Baden-Powell, Scouting, and the Development of Manly Character." In *Manliness and Morality: Middle-Class Masculinity in Britain and America, 1800–1940,* ed. J. A. Mangan and James Walvin, 199–219. New York: St. Martin's Press, 1987.

Weber, Kate. "Concert Proceeds Will Furnish New De Paul Nursery." *Chicago Tribune,* 8 Apr. 1923.

Welter, Barbara. "The Feminization of American Religion, 1800–1860." In Barbara Welter, *Dimity Convictions,* 83–102. Athens: Ohio University Press, 1976.

Wood, Sharon E. *The Freedom of the Streets: Work, Citizenship, and Sexuality in a Gilded Age City.* Chapel Hill: University of North Carolina Press, 2005.

Yans-McLaughlin, Virginia. *Family and Community: Italian Immigrants in Buffalo, 1880–1930.* Ithaca: Cornell University Press, 1971.

Youcha, Geraldine. *Minding the Children: Child Care in America from Colonial Times to the Present.* Cambridge, Mass.: Da Capo Press, 1995.

Zunz, Olivier. *The Changing Face of Inequality: Urbanization, Industrial Development, and Immigrants in Detroit, 1880–1920.* Chicago: University of Chicago Press, 1982.

Index